IVY LEAGUE
WEALTH SECRETS

Ivy League Wealth Secrets

That the Master Planners Don't Want You to Know!

Keith R. Soltis

Outskirts Press, Inc.
Denver, Colorado

Ivy League Wealth Secrets
That the Master Planners Don't Want You to Know!
All Rights Reserved.
Copyright © 2010 Keith R. Soltis
V1.0 R1.1

Outskirts Press, Inc.
http://www.outskirtspress.com

ISBN: 978-1-4327-4650-6 Paperback
         978-1-4327-5147-0 Hardback

Library of Congress Control Number: 2009940773

Outskirts Press and the "OP" logo are trademarks belonging to Outskirts Press, Inc.

PRINTED IN THE UNITED STATES OF AMERICA

Dedicated to the tireless professionals of
the insurance and financial services industry.
Their efforts make the world a better place.

Author and Publisher Disclaimers

This work contains the opinions and ideas of its author, and is designed to provide useful advice in regards to the subject matter covered. However, this publication is sold with the understanding that neither the author, nor publisher, is engaged in rendering legal, accounting or other professional services. If legal advice or other expert assistance is required, the services of a competent, professional person should be sought. Any discussion of taxes herein or related to this document is for general information purposes only and does not purport to be complete or cover every situation. Tax law is subject to interpretation and legislative change. Tax results and the appropriateness of any product for any specific taxpayer may vary depending on the facts and circumstances. You should consult with and rely on your own independent legal and tax advisers regarding your particular set of facts and circumstances.

The author and publisher specifically disclaim any responsibility for liability, loss or risk personal or otherwise that is incurred as a consequence directly or indirectly of the use and application of any of the contents of this work.

This is an original work of the author. This book is largely a reflection of the author's personal and professional experiences and contains a number of anecdotes to help illustrate his beliefs. Within this book are a number of hypothetical examples. These are used for illustrative purposes only and do not represent the performance of any specific product. Any similarities to any other written work are due to the narrow focus of financial services writing and editing. Any specific repetition in various published works, unless noted, is an unintentional result of the nature of financial services industry terminology in which the author is involved.

The author references certain products generally, including mutual funds, life insurance, and variable contracts, among others. It is important to note that variable products and mutual funds are sold by prospectus and are subject to market risk. Your principal value may decline. Like most annuity contracts, they contain exclusions, limitations, holding periods, surrender charges, and other terms for keeping it in force. Before investing, carefully consider the investment objectives, risks, charges and expenses of the mutual fund and/or variable annuity as well as their investment options. This and other information is contained in the prospectus.

CONTENTS

INTRODUCTION

Why does thinking about money seem to cause so much stress? Financial discussions seem to bring up feelings of anxiety for many people as well. Imagine a life where money doesn't cause you any worry, confusion, or anxiety. Imagine a world where we all understand the science of money. A life where there is no fear surrounding money and personal finance. Imagine a life where you are in control of your money . . . and your money is not in control of you!

The rich do get richer, and you can too. The reason that the rich get richer is often overlooked. Most people would simply like to argue that they aren't rich because they weren't born with a silver spoon in their mouth. While that is a convenient excuse for not reaching your full financial potential, many others were born in worse straits than you and managed to climb their way to the pinnacle of financial success. The rich get richer because they have something saved. Once you can develop the discipline and habits to save something, a new world of opportunities opens up to you. You would be surprised at how the world takes on a new life and a new view with a few dollars in your pocket. New opportunities begin to present themselves to you.

Not everyone gets into an Ivy League School, but anyone can benefit from that type of education. While attending the Wharton school at the University of Pennsylvania, I was lucky enough to have access to some of the greatest financial minds in our nation. I was taught the secret science of money and wealth building. Now I want to share it with you. Once you understand the formula, and you can identify the key players, it is easy to accumulate wealth for yourself.

Most of us are taught by our parents at a young age to work hard and to study hard. The educational system assures that we are taught the basics of reading, writing, arithmetic, history, and science. Many of us get great educations and refine these skill sets to very high specialties. Unfortunately, along the way, very few of us are ever given any basic consumer financial education. I have worked with thousands of clients and very few, if any, have ever had a course that taught them the basics of consumer finance.

Few people have been properly trained on how to select the right mortgage program for themselves, or how to compare and contrast automotive financing options. Is it more advantageous to lease, finance or pay cash for a vehicle? Most people don't know how to properly structure their consumer debts or school loans, how to select the appropriate limits and levels of insurance, how to utilize their 401(k) plans and retirement programs, or how to maximize tax deductions that are legally allowable to them.

Unfortunately, most of us learn the rules of finance by playing the game . . . a basic trial-and-error approach. As we learn, we can end up transferring tens of thousands, if not hundreds of thousands of dollars away unnecessarily. It is one thing not to know this is happening, but it is quite another to ignore these facts once they are pointed out to you.

I have worked with thousands of clients in my career. Most would like to be able to save more. Many say things like: "We just don't know where our money goes." This is by design. Most of us know how to celebrate a 25-cent coupon victory, but we are less likely to identify the major culprits who confiscate our wealth. We accept that we cannot change the rules of the financial services industry, our tax system, corporate America, or the banking system.

Our goal is to facilitate some basic discussions about fiscal literacy and consumer awareness. We want to show you how to highlight areas where you may be transferring away your wealth, and to recapture the wealth that others are taking from you. This occurs at many different levels and many different times throughout your life, and it is critical for you to identify and eliminate these unnecessary financial transfers. This book is designed as a forum for us to do just that.

For the past 15 years, I've spent my life working with individuals, businesses, labor unions, and government entities. We often consult with them about whether it makes sense for them to work with a financial professional. In the end, some of these people and entities chose not to work with a financial professional, but most do. I've found that over time, as the stakes get higher and the account balances grow, many people turn to professionals for advice and guidance.

I've been asked at many points in my career to put some of my thoughts down on paper and to share with you my reasons for using financial professionals. The financial planning industry has been under attack for decades over conflicting advice or unnecessary advice. Part of this book is designed to help you understand whether or not you should consider using a financial professional and how to design a selection process for what you would want your financial professional to do.

Remember, if you don't have your own process and you don't have your own selection criteria, you will most likely fall default to someone else's process. This can often result in you being manipulated by a salesperson or a corporation. Clearly, most individuals do not need a financial advisor to help buy stocks or mutual funds for them. There are plenty of online resources that can provide you similar research to that of a traditional financial planning professional. In the end, I believe the primary reason for hiring a financial professional is for the guidance, counseling, and coaching that comes along with that professional. In short, you should look to partner with a financial coach instead of a salesperson. A salesperson operates on their (or their company's) agenda, while a coach focuses on your agenda.

Most of our clients have come to us at a point in time when their planning needs become complex. Initially it may not be very difficult to select a few mutual funds, stocks, or purchase some cheap term insurance for family protection. If that's your only goal, you probably do not need a financial advisor and might be better off purchasing these products on your own. Most of our clients come to us looking for coordinated and integrated strategies designed to help them solve complex financial issues and to make sure that their strategies are properly aligned to create greater efficiency within their plans.

A good financial advisor is like a financial coach and should operate and work with you to help achieve your personal objectives and goals. If their goals are to sell you products that are in line with their company's stated sales goals, beware, and consider moving on to someone new. Ideally, they should be looking at every aspect of your finances, identifying areas of inefficiency and determining appropriate strategies to help free up and find your money, not only to fund the products they want to sell you, but to improve your cash flow and upgrade your lifestyle along the way.

Some people are of the opinion that they do not need an advisor. There are many "do-it-yourselfers" out there who are managing their own portfolios, selecting their own insurance policies, and creating their own retirement planning strategies. There is nothing wrong with this approach either. Some people are highly organized and efficient, and can manage their finances themselves. Others may not have an interest in the topic, and still others would rather focus their time in another area.

One thing is pretty clear. Most people don't need a financial advisor to help them simply purchase financial products. Many advisors also seem to be confused by their role. They believe that their role is to sell products. Nothing could be further from the truth! The role of a financial advisor should be to serve as your financial coach and your chief financial officer. Their role is to help you compare and contrast the benefits of varying financial strategies. Once this is accomplished, they may work backward to help you select the appropriate products to put you in a position to achieve your financial goals.

Whether or not you choose to use a financial professional, this book aims to provide a clear understanding of money, and strategies to build wealth and protect it more efficiently. We also aim to provide you with a conceptual framework for building your own financial decision-making process.

Not everyone attends business school. This book is designed to give everyone a glimpse of practical, real world business school training. Quite a bit of our training at Wharton was devoted to analyzing case studies that helped us gain insight and knowledge into how countless successful entrepreneurs built their companies and amass their fortunes. These entrepreneurs had a secret for success, the same one my parents learned over time.

Once upon a time, in an era called the 1960s, there was a woman named Mary and a man named August. During that time a higher premium was placed on love than financial gain. My parents met on a blind date and fell in love immediately. They began to picture a life filled with love, happiness, children, and one day, grandchildren.

Reality set in and the Laws of Economics dictated that they needed someplace to live, in order for their dreams to come true. So, they set off on their path to build their own American Dream. Our father, August, graduated from college, and after a brief stint in teaching, acquired two separate Master's degrees in advanced sciences. He ran a hospital lab for nearly a decade before deciding that the financial pressures of having three children and a lovely wife were going to create larger financial burdens than a director at a hospital laboratory could provide. At the age of 35, with three kids ranging in ages from newborn to age nine, he entered law school at night to provide a better future for his family.

Mary graduated from nursing school and became the first person in her family to ever graduate from college. Nursing school in those days was equal to our tougher than traditional college. It would be nearly two decades longer before she received her official college diploma, in addition to her diploma from nursing school. Years later, she would also be the first in her family to obtain her Master's degree as a school administrator. Both August and Mary pursued the American Dream and fought for years to stay ahead of the financial curve . . . and pay off those student loans!

My parents were never major consumers or major spenders in their own right. They lived for their children, and got up every day to work hard as productive members of society. They taught us the value of hard work and discipline. Fortunately, that story has a happy ending, as their home is paid off, they're growing their dollars for retirement, and they were able to send three children to Ivy League schools. I can't help wonder how much easier their life could have been for them, if they had been trained on wealth building strategies.

Our story picks up where theirs leaves off, and tells the tale of a family trying to build a brighter and better future in America. My siblings, Bradley, Kelly, and I each chose our own paths. The three of us never wanted anything growing up, but we were all aware that we did not grow up rich. Our parents spent whatever extra money they had on two major things: education, and making sure that we were involved in every activity available.

Like most suburban kids, we were enrolled in summer school (the voluntary kind), cub/girl scouts, tee ball, soccer, football, wrestling, basketball, track and field, field hockey, karate, ice skating, music, ballet, weightlifting, and gymnastics, We were average at most of these activities, and good at others. As money was tight, we understood that we had to make choices. We could only pick so many options (I skipped ballet), but we were not allowed to quit during the season. We could quit after the season (and we sometimes did), but we could never quit during the season! This was an important lesson that taught us responsibility and a lesson about money at the same time.

The three of us had a natural passion for athletics and sports. While education was always given top priority in our house, our first love was athletics. As the first son, I got to serve as the experiment. Luckily, I was able to use athletics as a spring board to launch our family into a new circle. We would soon move out of the musty gyms and into the world of the socially and financial elite (as outsiders) in the Ivy League.

As a kid, I had dreamed of playing football for Joe Paterno, and the Nittany Lions at Linebacker University. As a slightly undersized linebacker, despite receiving all-state honors, I was largely overlooked. I played at a small school, which forced me to play as a defensive end or outside linebacker position. I stood at a whopping 6'2" tall and slightly under 200 pounds. This was not enough to gain the interest of Joe Paterno and Penn State. However, my parents value-system and my grounding in a strong education background, did give me one advantage. I was able to turn the heads of Ivy League coaches; and therefore, I was able to gain access to one of the greatest (if not the greatest) financial institution in America, thanks largely to my athletic prowess.

I headed to the University of Pennsylvania and the Wharton School of Business to begin a new chapter in my life where I would learn finance, athletics, and a few life lessons. I was granted acceptance into one of the best business schools in the world, and would be able to play football at one of the highest levels, in the Ivy League Conference.

If you know anything about Wharton, you would know that it is a very competitive environment. Most people know Donald Trump went there, but few people know how competitive it really is. Most of the students who graduate are vying for top positions in investment banking, corporate finance, trading, major accounting firms, and consulting positions.

My brother, sister, and I all were lucky enough to be in this position. (Bradley graduated from Harvard and Kelly from Cornell). We definitely benefited from our parents balanced parenting program that provided an equal emphasis on excelling in both athletics and academics. My education opened the doors to a fantastic career in financial services.

I consider it my personal calling and passion to try to make a difference in the world every day. My parents taught me long ago that if I wake up in the morning and try to help everyone else get what they want, that eventually I'll get what I want, and much more. In doing so,

I picked a career that allows me to lead a life of significance and touch people's lives in many different ways.

I'm excited about the fact that I've been able to help families actually use plans that we've created for the purpose of educating their children. I'm proud of the fact that I've delivered life insurance death claims to widows and widowers in their darkest hour, and I've been there to deliver the checks that will allow their incomes to continue when high net-worth executives developed debilitating illnesses such as epilepsy or mental/nervous disorders. The plans we design have also allowed our clients to continue their income via disability insurance and long-term care programs.

I've developed some strong beliefs and convictions about the right ways to plan (and the wrong ways). I'd like to share some of the right ways with you. I believe that in order to be a good financial professional, you need to act with conviction and believe that you are doing the very best that you can for your clients.

Self Assessment Exercise

Please review the follow statements for accuracy. Do you believe the same?

1. Investing: Reinvesting dividends in capital gains is the secret to building long-term wealth.

2. Retirement Plans: Generally speaking, making the maximum contribution to your 401(k) or defined contribution plan is a great way to build wealth for myself and my family.

3. Taxes: Getting money back on my tax return seems to be a great strategy and helps me take care of some unseen bills once a year. Sometimes, I even use it for a vacation.

4. Debt Management: Making extra payments to my mortgage is a great way to quickly eliminate my debt and help me become debt free. A bi-weekly mortgage is a great way for me to cut additional years off the life of my loan. A 15-year mortgage, generally speaking, is always better than 30-year mortgage because it reduces the duration of the loan.

Would it surprise you to learn that all of the above statements are inaccurate? In fact, those strategies can cause you to transfer more of your wealth unnecessarily. We will attempt to explain why in the following chapters.

CHAPTER 1
AMERICAN DREAMS
TWENTY-FIRST CENTURY
AMERICAN DREAMS

The Challenge

Your mission, should you choose to accept it, is to pursue the American Dream. The American Dream often includes the pursuit of owning your home, raising your family, educating your children, driving the cars of your choice, wearing the clothing you want, and ultimately retiring in comfort, while realizing all of your hopes, dreams, and desires. Along the way, you may even get to take a few vacations.

The challenge is that all of these things cost money. Unfortunately, most of us are not born with a substantial amount of available capital. Therefore, in order to fund the American Dream, we are forced to save our money and borrow from others. In doing so, along the way we may end up transferring a lot of our wealth. Many planners tend to focus on an accumulation method only. At some point, it becomes almost impossible to save enough to fund all of these goals. We want you to see that there are many ways to build wealth and many different strategies that can be employed to help get you there (beyond just saving).

Saving and investing are critical aspects to achieving your financial goals, but you can find money in many other places. By focusing on where your money is going, you can often recapture the money that you unnecessarily transfer. These dollars can then be redeployed to help you achieve your goals.

Let's take a look at what a typical American Dream might cost.

Housing

Costs to finance a home are, approximately $350,000.

Automobiles

At an approximate cost of $25,000 per vehicle. Many Americans will finance or lease new cars approximately every five years. Let's take a look at what it will cost for you to enjoy that new car scent every five years. If you purchase new cars every five years from age 25–70 you will have purchased 10 new vehicles per person. That's an average lifetime cost of about $250,000 per individual or $500,000 per couple. (Before the interest expense!)

Educational Funding

Funding education for yourself and/or your children, the average cost for a four-year public school is $15,000 per year for four years ($60,000 total). The average cost for a private educational institution is approximately $30,000 per year for four years. This amounts to a grand total of about $120,000+ over four years for a private college.

Unfortunately, while you will have many years to save for the expense of college, you will also have to account for and overcome the enormous inflation rate associated with an increasing cost of secondary education. The annual increase in college costs continues to outpace the basic inflation rate. Currently, college costs are trending upward at a rate of 5 to 6 percent annual increase. Future cost can equate to about $416,700.

Let's take a look at how much you'll need to save in order to fund these purchases and costs so that you can enjoy the American Dream during your working years.

Financing Your American Dreams

Mortgage Down Payment: 20 percent down: $75,000. Thirty-year fixed rate mortgage in the amount of $280,000 carries a principal and interest payment of 6 percent of $1,678 per month. (Plus property taxes and insurance.)

Automobiles

If you save up the funds to pay for each vehicle, it will take five years to accumulate $25,000 at 6 percent, saving $370 per month (per vehicle).

Costs of Financing Each Vehicle Outlined

If you need to have the vehicle today and you don't have the money saved, you will need to finance or lease the vehicle. In order to finance the vehicle, you will incur a different set of expenses. You will not be earning interest on your savings and you will now be transferring interest to others.

> Auto Loan Amount: $25,000
> Auto Loan Term: 5 Years (60 months)
> Interest Rate: 6%
> Monthly Auto Loan Payments: $438.32

Figure 1.1   Monthly Payments on a $25,000 Vehicle.

Principal Balance $25,000

Interest Expense $3,999 or about $800 per year. It doesn't sound like a lot, but that's 16 percent more expensive than the original sales price.

Total Cost $28,999

What if you could eliminate the $800 of extra annual interest expense and save it for yourself? The same $800 compounding at 8 percent for your 45 year driving lifetime could grow to over $300,000. Multiply that number by two if your spouse also drives. Could $600,000 help fund your retirement? What if we could show you a way to fund your purchases without transferring the interest to the automotive finance company?

Educational Funding*

In order to have college fully funded by the time your child starts college, you would need to either deposit about $110,000 the day your child is born, or save approximately $1,035 per month for 18 years (starting the day your child is born). The investment would need to grow at a rate of return of 8 percent *every year* (not very likely). And the stock market could not correct itself. At a 6 percent rate of return,

---

* Please see the financial disclaimer on page 348 for more information.

you would need to contribute $1,250 per month to reach this goal. Few can afford to do that?

Retiring in Comfort

You can't wait to retire so that someone else can pay these bills! Think again, the days of retiring on the fat, company-paid pension with a gold pocket watch and a rocking chair are long gone. Here again, your quality of retirement will be up to you.

Let's assume you would like to retire with an annual income of $80,000 per year. Where will the income come from? Social Security may account for approximately $20,000 per year of your annual income. Another fixed amount may come from your pension or employer-sponsored retirement plan (if you're lucky enough to get one).

The balance will be up to you. Assuming you would need to cover a shortfall of approximately $50,000 per year from your personal savings. . . . How much will you need in your retirement account in order to make ends meet?

If we assume a 5 percent rate of return during your retirement years (conservative investments), you would need to have approximately $1 million saved in your retirement account. That $1 million account will generate the $50,000 of interest that you can use to offset your living expenses. If you need more than $50,000; simply increase the amount in your capital base. In this example, $2 million would spin off about $100,000 of gross income. If you earn more, you can increase your distributions or build your capital base for a rainy day. We have not assumed 8–10 percent of returns in retirement because it is unlikely that you would have the bulk of your assets subject to the peaks and valleys of the stock market at that time.

How Will You Be Able to Save a Million Dollars?

If you are 30 years old today, you only have 35 years to save. In order to accumulate $1 million dollars by the age of 65, you would need to invest $450 per month for 40 years at 8 percent. (It sounds like a lot but it is really only about $15 per day.) Unfortunately, due to the impact of inflation (covered in a later chapter), by the time you reach age 65, $1 million will not buy what it can purchase today. This is because inflation eats away and erodes our purchasing power each year. You will need to save even more money in order to accumulate $1 million in today's dollars. Realistically, you will need to save more like $13,000 annually to hit the future inflation adjusted goal.

If you do not have enough (less than $1 million) in your account, you may also need to draw down on the principal balance in addition to taking interest distributions each year. This will help you cover the annual shortfall, but you will also slowly deplete your capital base and eventually, may run out of money. What then?

Finally, you may need to pay for some other events in life such as a wedding, or unforeseen medical expenses. You may also want to set some money aside to give to your kids as a head start in life.

How much will all this cost and why would anyone want to pursue this dream? Where should you begin and who can you rely on to help you fund your American Dream? Relax, it's not as scary as you may think. It is serious business but it can be done. Part of it will need to be done by you, and we'll show you how to get a little help along the way from others as well. Success will require a plan, some tracking, and a little discipline . . . but it can be accomplished!

First you will need a roadmap and a guide. Be aware that while there are many paths to success, some paths are less treacherous than others. You must be careful to avoid many of the wealth traps, toll takers, and trolls who live under the proverbial financial bridges along your road to success.

Let's Summarize the Costs of the American Dream in a Quick Example

- ✓ Home Financing Costs: $20,000 plus taxes and homeowners insurance costs of approximately $5,000 for a total of $25,000 per year.
- ✓ Automobile Payments: $5,000 to $6,000 (per vehicle), plus automobile insurance at about $1,000 to 1,500 per vehicle.
- ✓ Educational Saving Costs (per child): $12,000 private school and about half for a state school ($6,000).
- ✓ Retirement Savings Contribution Goal: $13,000
- ✓ Income Taxes: $20,000 (to fund the American Dreams of others).
- ✓ Total Cost of the Basic American Dream: $69,000 to $76,000.
- ✓ Extra Expenses: $6,000 to $12,000 per each additional child for education savings and another $5,000 per vehicle in the home.

A family of four, with two drivers, could easily have a fixed cost of over $90,000 annually.

These are only the costs to have a decent roof over your head, a vehicle to get you to and from work, a brighter future for your kids, and a retirement many years from now. These costs only represent the tip of the iceberg. They don't include things like books for school, cable television, heat, and electric for your home, gas for your car, internet, telephones, and so on. These requirements don't even figure in vacations, personal care, clothing, birthdays, or holidays. Add those costs in and we see that you may need gross earnings of over $150,000 per year to live a solid middle class lifestyle!

Unfortunately, most families don't earn anything close to that figure. Clearly there is something wrong here. There has to be a better way. There is—it starts with a complete understanding of who is driving up these costs and then learning how we can eliminate or reduce them?

What Are My Chances of Success?

The Study of 100 Men

The 100-man story is a widely used historical study that was compiled by the Department of Health and Human Services that found that for every 100 people in the workforce, the following outcomes would exist at age 65:

➤ On average, roughly 16 out of 100 do not live to reach age 65.
➤ Sixty-six who do live to reach age 65 have incomes at or below $20,000 annually. This forces them to become dependent on their children, government, or charity, or requires them to continue working in some capacity beyond age 65.
➤ Fourteen will have income in excess of $30,000, giving them the ability to be financially independent. Unfortunately, $30,000 of annual income does not provide a very substantial quality of life.
➤ Only four people have an income in excess of $50,000 annually, which make them both financially independent and successful. Some would argue that the number would have to be much larger than $50,000 annually in order to maintain the current standard of living of many individuals.

Source: Social Security Administration, Office of Research and Statistics, April 2000.

Why is it that 96 out of 100 people studied with strong middle-class jobs and incomes throughout the course of their working careers failed to achieve any substantial financial security and success in retirement?

How can it be that only 4 percent of Americans will become financially successful in their retirement? Aren't we the world's wealthiest nation?

For many years, the response by the financial services community was simply that people fail to plan. We know that many of these people are planning, but unfortunately, may be working with advisors that don't truly understand all of the moving parts of a successful plan. Why does it seem more difficult than ever to succeed financially, given the advancement in our technology and culture?

What's the Problem?

We seem to have all of the ingredients for success, yet most people never fulfill the American Dream. Why is it that many of us come up shorter than we planned in our financial goals? We seem to have plenty of access to financial information. However, there seems to be little evidence of widespread knowledge in financial matters.

What is the problem and why do we come up short financially? We have the largest middle class in the entire free world. People have jobs that pay well. There are plenty of opportunities in America. Most of us want to succeed financially.

In studying this behavior for nearly 15 years, we found that people's inability to save has two basic components. (1) The smaller part is the lack of personal discipline to save. Most people want to save. They just can't seem to find the money. What's left after the government, banks, automotive finance companies, and credit card companies get paid? (2) The bigger problem facing us is the general lack of fiscal literacy.

Many people have no access to their accounts without paying surrender charges or penalties. They're deferring income into retirement plans, and prepaying mortgages while carrying nondeductible debt. Many people don't even know how much they owe. They need to look it up. They use one credit card to pay for another bill, and postdated checks to pay for others. Many people even resort to gambling or buying lottery tickets as their hope for financial security.

One Foot on the Gas and One on the Brakes?

Let's take a look at how the average American drives down the Financial Road of Life. Picture someone driving down the highway with one foot on the gas and one on the breaks. He can't figure out why the car won't go any faster. He's trying everything he can think of:

buying new tires, adding high-grade motor oil, and putting a high-grade of gasoline into the vehicle in an attempt to get it to move faster down the road. It doesn't make any sense. As an outsider, you probably want to shout, "Just take your foot off of the brake!"

Unless you have properly coordinated and integrated plans, you may be inadvertently doing the exact same thing with your financial plan. This is due to a lack of understanding of how money works.

You won't know until you take stock of your current financial status with a financial checkup. Make sure to examine all the areas that you may be unnecessarily transferring money. You can then recapture that money, and put it to use for yourself. Next, we can identify a more efficient way for you to build and create new wealth. Ultimately, we can begin circulating your capital more efficiently so that it performs more than one task simultaneously.

I hope that after you read this book you will change how you think about money. I want you to understand not only how to purchase financial products, but also how to create efficiency with your money. We will explore simple, yet effective methods of reducing and/or eliminating many of the common transfers of your wealth. The savings from these measures could be substantial.

The application of your new knowledge should create more options and offer additional financial opportunities for you. Most of us lack new ideas. We have become robotic in our routine financial dealings. We end up letting others control our money. We've been slowly and systematically defeated by banks, taxes, and the burdens of our personal consumer debts.

Your chances of substantially increasing your wealth will be based on your skill of *creating* situations, *controlling* your outcomes, and then *profiting* from them. We want to help change your life by teaching you how to establish your own financial decision process. This is not about finding better investments or cheating on your taxes. It is about making informed decisions.

You can live the life you've always dreamed about. You don't need to live a life of clipping coupons, purchasing cheaper products, or adhering to a budget. Systematic wealth building is exactly the opposite. It is an empowered process that allows you to control the outcome.

Knowledge is power. You must use your knowledge to create your financial environment. Consider the cost of not knowing (or not acting) on something. Most people make their financial decisions with incomplete data. They operate somewhere between opinion and fact, between myth and reality. It will be up to you to identify what is opinion and what is fact in your own financial lives.

Old Beliefs

In the area of personal finance there seems to be great confusion between opinion and fact. People seem to happily rely on the advice from friends, newspapers, and even strangers. Misinformation has cost all of us an enormous amount of lost money in the form of unnecessary transfers.

Lack of a defined financial decision process created this confusion. Confusion caused us to put off or avoid making important financial decisions. Ultimately, a lack of a defined process can also cause us to unnecessarily transfer large portions of our wealth. If you stand for nothing, you will fall for anything. If you don't have your own process, the financial institutions will be happy to provide you with one. If others control your thought and decision process, they also control your financial outcomes.

Demographics

Do you understand how demographic trends can impact your financial decisions? The government and the financial institutions understand these trends. You must understand upcoming events and the changing demographics of your country. Changes are necessary and you need a financial thought process that accounts for these variables.

Whose Money Is it?

It seems like financial institutions, corporations, and the government are all standing in line for their share of your money. Where do you and your family stand in this line?

There is another way to increase your wealth without the worry of risk. It's called efficiency. You should have the finer things in life and pursue enjoyment in every area of your life.

Pennies versus Dollars?

Many of us are penny wise and pound foolish. We scrutinize minor purchases and clip coupons each week while thousands of dollars are flying out the window annually. Implement a process. Instead of a $0.50 coupon victory, your savings could be thousands of dollars with no additional risk of loss to your capital.

In order to change your current path, you must expand your thought process through knowledge. Your new knowledge can allow you to make better financial decisions. Without this process, you may suffer unintended financial outcomes. Your thought process must change. Once you master these concepts, you may be able to create an opportunity that you didn't have before. Remember, not too long ago, we believed that the earth was flat! The solution is a thought process, not product purchases. We need strategies based on knowledge to help you make better financial decisions.

Are You Willing to Make a Change?

Americans are some of the most educated people on the planet. Many of us fight and struggle to give our children every advantage possible from the time they are born. We do our best to make sure they gain admittance into the best preschool and kindergarten, and attend the finest grammar schools, high schools, and universities in the nation. But why do we allow them to fail financially over the long run?

Your Personal Accumulation System: Creating Your Financial Environment

In order to begin building wealth, you will need a place to start. The attention you pay to the banking process and your flow of capital is an essential part of the wealth-building process. All money flows through the banking system. They will either work for you with multiplier effects or against you with interest based transfers. You will need to develop a new personal banking and wealth accumulation system over time. This process begins with an understanding of how financial institutions work.

The government sees you as a taxpayer, banks view you as a borrower and source of deposits for *their* use and investment companies see you as a stream of fees. There will be no financial freedom until you can minimize the burdens of dealing with them.

Wealth Erosion

Americans overpay on their income taxes by not taking advantage of legitimate ways to reduce taxes. Interest on automotive finance, consumer loans, and credit card debts are defeating us. Expenses and fees take even more. Meanwhile, people are struggling to pay off their homes with bad mortgage plans designed by banks. These plans often help the bank more than they help you. Additionally, many people have the wrong type of insurance plans. They often overpay on their premiums and rarely achieve a return on their premium payments.

We'll examine why many people fail and explore the factors that are constantly working against us. We've all have to conquer the same financial forces. These wealth-eroding forces include: market corrections, taxes, inflation, accidents, disability risk, lawsuits, loss of employment, premature death, creditor claims, lawsuits, and bankruptcy. If you can learn how to eliminate or minimize these risks, what would prevent you from taking action?

How much time do you spend each year planning your finances relative to how much time you spend planning your family vacations? There is a price to pay for success and a price to pay for failure.

The question is: Which price do you want to pay?

Your personal money supply is only a finite amount, regardless of the income level that you can earn. In order to grow your wealth despite limited resources, you will need new ideas. We want to provide you with strategies and concepts of how you can have your money work for you, in multiple ways so that your system can become more effective and efficient. In doing so, we can help you fulfill all of your consumer wants and desires, while still leaving large amounts of dollars that can be saved to build your own personal wealth.

Millions of people use financial professionals and advisors along with smart tax professionals, attorneys, realtors, and other financial professionals. People save money on an ongoing basis each year to satisfy their future needs and pour plenty of gasoline into their financial vehicles in an effort to keep them on the Road to Wealth. Despite these efforts, many of these people will not achieve their final goals. This is because other factors are eroding their wealth faster than they can build it. If you are not able to defend your money effectively from these forces, you will be drained by them. Many of these money transfers are ignored by the vast majority of financial advisors. The result is a financial plan that is not equipped to work under many different circumstances.

How many times have you asked somebody to show you the financial numbers? Most people don't understand that there are different kinds of money. Figures lie and liars figure. It is easy to get caught up in partial data; but you need to see the big picture, as well as the details.

Many of us only understand the science of math, because that's all that is taught by our educational system. Most people don't understand that money itself is a commodity that is constantly changing in value and wears out over time. This fact makes the use of spreadsheets less important in your planning process. Spreadsheets typically use fixed returns as the basis for their calculations. If you believe that money and math act the same, you may be very disappointed when you reach the end of the rainbow.

Numbers and projections only tell part of the story. You can't drive math, you can't live in math, and you certainly can't educate your children with math. Math is only part of the equation. If you're using that as the method to create your roadmap for financial success, you may be in for a rough ride.

Our strategy is designed to help you grow and protect your wealth at all times. We also want you to understand the concept of lost opportunity cost. I learned about this in my first day of business school and it should be a concept you factor into all of your money decisions.

Why Don't We Save?

Some people believe the problem lies with people consuming and spending first, then saving later. While this is definitely part of the problem, it is not the only culprit. Wealth transfers also need to be examined. The American culture promotes spending, over saving, and as a nation, our savings rate is woefully low compared to other developed, industrialized nations. Take a look at Figure 1.2 to see how our saving rate has fared as a nation.

How can we reverse this trend? Knowledge is the key. Understanding why, how, and where to save is critical. We try to fill this void through promoting fiscal literacy. Let's examine who's responsible for the roadblocks on the road to financial success. These culprits are not new faces. But we need to examine how each of them extracts a pound of flesh from you throughout your lifetime.

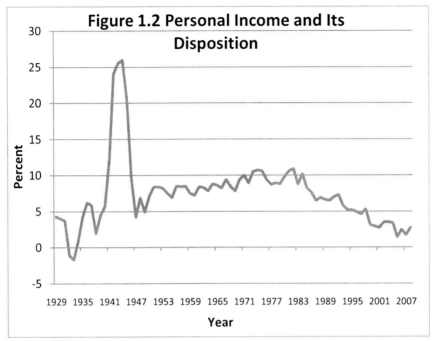

Source: U.S. Bureau of Economic Analysis

Figure 1.2   Savings Rate Chart

Figure 1.3   Factors which impede savings.

Wealth Raiders

The primary culprits are:

Corporations invent new and exciting products each and every year that are designed to make you feel that the current products are no longer sufficient to meet your needs.

Banks and the Federal Reserve System control the entire money supply. Our government is moving us closer and closer to a welfare state by continuing to spend more than it can ever hope to bring in.

Inflation is a culprit that rots away our wealth and keeps the middle-class down. It represents the largest hidden tax that you will ever end up paying.

Market Corrections are the financial markets that seem to create and then eliminate your wealth through booms and bust cycles—leaving everyone wondering why this happens. We can't predict when the next cycle will come. What if the bulk of our money is invested in financial markets at the wrong times? Are we expected to predict the precise day when we should pull our money out of the equity markets?

Government and Taxes control the money supply, and determines the level of taxes that we pay. Why is the science of money such a closely guarded secret?

Most people are not wealthy. Many live month-to-month. It would seem evident enough that the information they received from the traditional sources is not effective. Today, in the greatest country in the world, many people still struggle to meet their financial obligations. Let's explore the secret science of money, and examine the habits and strategies of those who have successfully built their wealth.

Can you name one new financial product that has worked—all the time? Of course not. The only way to win is to develop a coordinated approach. As we compare strategies, we must also compare real dollars (purchasing power), and understand what our dollars will purchase when converted into goods and services in the future.

The wages of the average American have been declining for several decades. This is proven by comparing what we can buy with that money when converted into goods and services. Unless you take yourself out of the system and find ways to maximize wealth and generate multiple values for your money, you don't stand a chance against the system. You must take steps to reduce taxes and wealth transfers in every possible area of your life.

When and where you build your wealth has a lot to do with where you will ultimately end up financially. The most important thing to consider is which financial vehicles will be the most efficient. Which of these vehicles will provide you the most protection along the way and what costs are associated in using each of those vehicles (products)?

The secret to getting ahead is starting. A thousand-mile journey begins with a single step, and the first stride is usually the toughest. We want to help you maximize your quality of life. We want you to live in the best possible home you can, drive the nicest car, and educate your children at the best school available. We want you to wear the type of clothing that you enjoy, and dine at restaurants that you love. In order to fund all of these desires, we first need to identify the money you are transferring and recapture it for your own use.

The driving, underlying theme of this book is centered on the fact that you'll need to find the money to meet your financial goals. Most people think this means cutting back in other areas of their life in order to save more money . . . or clipping coupons. As we've continued to discuss, our primary goal is to first find the money that you're transferring away unnecessarily or reinvesting in other areas without thought. Each financial decision should be made with the complete understanding of how that decision impacts other areas of your financial life. As we examine your tax situation, it becomes critical to step out of the role of mindless reinvestment of non-qualified or non-deferred investment gains. You must examine whether it makes sense to reinvest your gains and earnings back into the same instruments or to simply earmark that capital for another purpose. Before you blindly reinvest your dividends and capital gains, in non-qualified accounts, you should go through a practical exercise. Ask yourself: "Where could these dollars do the most good?" In order to do so, you may need to move that capital into a decision account. Once it's in your decision account, you can go through an annual or a more frequent exercise of reviewing how that capital could be repositioned elsewhere within your financial model to do the most good for you and your financial situation.

Options may include using it to pay down debt and eliminate high interest expenses in your life, funding IRAs or Roth IRAs, taking advantage of company matching dollars on retirement plans, reducing or eliminating expensive insurance contracts, or converting never ending bills, such as term life insurance. These decisions should be carefully reviewed by each individual, with the assistance of their financial professionals. The decision to implement any combination of these strategies should be an individual decision and should be focused on the goal of maximizing your plan.

Here are some of the largest obstacles that prevent you from building wealth:

1. *Not saving enough money.* This problem can usually be fixed by either paying attention to where dollars may be flying out the window unnecessarily or where you may have some automatic reinvestments that could be better suited to help you grow your long-term wealth in other areas of your plan. If that doesn't work you may have to find a way to generate more income to help cover that shortfall.

2. *Investing in the wrong places, or at the wrong times.* Two of the key elements to financial success include:

    a. The right timing (knowing when to buy and when to sell a particular investment) . . . this book will not be centered on that philosophy because most of those so-called systems offer little more than educated guesses.

    b. Time in the market or being able to stay in over long periods of time. We all know that financial markets tend to move upward over long periods of time, however, life often gets in the way. As we age, our health may deteriorate, or we may die before the markets come back to the levels that we hope for. Additionally, accidents, lawsuits, creditors, and helping our children or our parents financially may impact our ability to build wealth. These life issues can often impact our ability to time our market based decisions. Therefore, we want to show you how a layered and structured approach that is properly coordinated can help you stay invested in some areas while leaving capital available to deal with the financial challenges of life in others.

3. Information. There are many financial media programs dedicated to providing financial information. We have news programs and channels that are devoted to financial services industry. Unfortunately, much of the advice is conflicting or outright wrong. There are dozens of periodicals devoted to investing as well. Much of what is written in the mainstream financial media is product based.

Self Assessment Exercise

Planning Questions

✓ Is your cash flow positive or negative each month?

✓ Do you have a written budget?

✓ Do you know how much you should be saving monthly?

✓ How often do you review your financial situation?

Chapter Highlights

➤ Understanding the cost of the American Dream.

➤ Examine your own chances of success.

➤ Gain an understanding of the barriers to building your wealth.

➤ Learn why you need to create an environment for your wealth to flourish.

CHAPTER 2
BUILDING YOUR OWN
WEALTH PYRAMID

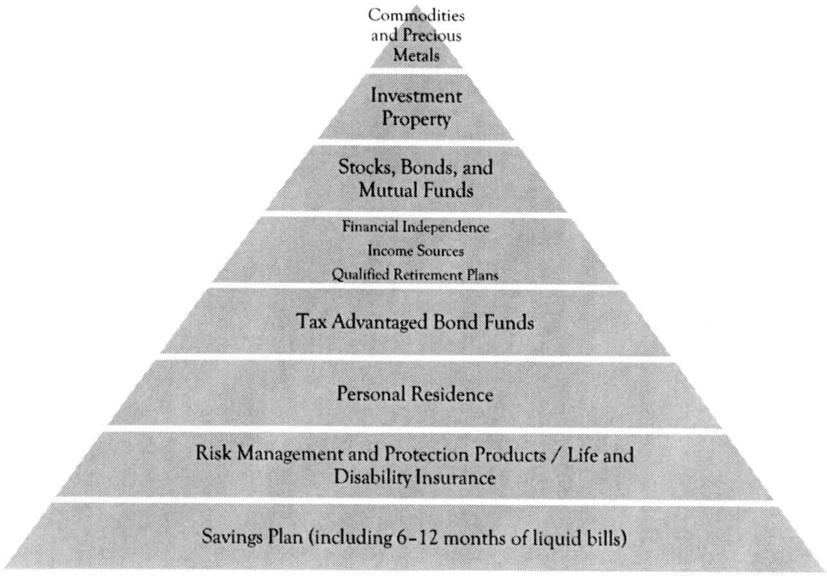

Commodities
and Precious
Metals

Investment
Property

Stocks, Bonds, and
Mutual Funds

Financial Independence
Income Sources
Qualified Retirement Plans

Tax Advantaged Bond Funds

Personal Residence

Risk Management and Protection Products / Life and
Disability Insurance

Savings Plan (including 6-12 months of liquid bills)

Figure 2.1   Building Wealth by the Numbers

Building Wealth by the Numbers

In order to build wealth, you will need to create your environment. The proper environment consists of the right layering and integration of the moving parts of your plans. You'll need to identify assets for use in both short- and long-term plans and objectives. Assets should be identified for immediate consumption, mid-range goals, and long-term consumption needs.

You will also need to create a pool of capital to earmark for use during the inevitable periods of market corrections, so that other assets may remain fully invested. By segmenting your assets accordingly, you will be able to take advantage of any opportunity that comes your way, while still providing yourself with the security and safety you'll need to meet your short-term obligations. Your ideal plan should combine elements of saving, accumulation, and risk management.

Your ideal plan should function if you live longer than you expect so that you won't outlive your assets. It provides you with access to your funds in the event of an emergency or to fund an opportunity. It would also allow you to tap into capital for all your business needs, and it self-completes if you became sick, hurt, or can't work. We also want to make sure that your family will get 100 percent of the value from your plan in the event of death, without paying additional income taxes or other costs.

Additionally, your plan should be able to protect your assets effectively in the event of lawsuits, creditor claims, and even bankruptcy proceedings (based on the local laws). Ideally, some of your assets may accumulate in a tax-deferred or tax-free environment. We would also like to see competitive internal rates of return and guaranteed rates of return wherever possible.

Open Architecture

We need the flexibility to make changes as circumstances arise or change. You should maximize your liquidity, use, and control (or access) of your dollars while you're building them. Once we construct the framework, we can focus on the various strategies for your underlying investments to build your wealth. In order for a truly sound financial package to be created, its components should fit together in an integrated and coordinated format.

Savings Plan
(including 6–12 months liquid bills)

Cash Reserves: First you need to secure a firm foundation for your plan. The foundation of your plan should include a strong cash reserve position (6 to 12 months liquid and accessible cash reserves). The first step is for you to be liquid. We want the equivalent of 50 percent of your gross annual income in liquid asset classes. Make sure that you have access to at least 6 to 12 months of your current monthly bills (obligations) at all times. If you don't have this cushion, you must reconsider your investing plans.

How would you survive, or continue to contribute to your investments if you have an interruption in income? Without adequate cash reserves (cash, money markets, insurance cash values, open access to home equity lines, and so on), you may find yourself locked out of opportunities, or in dire straits in the event of an emergency.

We also need to make sure that you are working toward becoming debt free. It doesn't help much to build wealth on only one side of your ledger (your assets), if you are losing similar or greater interest on the other side (your liabilities). Have a plan to become debt free and work diligently to remove the yoke of that debt.

Ultimately, you should be saving 10 to 15 percent of your gross annual income. We believe that it should be saved in an area that allows you to make confident decisions. It shouldn't go into only one investment.

Risk Management and Protection
Products / Life and Disability Insurance

Protection Strategies: Your plan should be funded no matter what. Your protection component may include elements of saving. Ideally, the plan should be self-completing in the event of any major risk during your life, including a premature death or disability. The plan should be able to provide funding sources when you cannot. We want to make sure we engineer a plan that operates on an open architecture *and* combines the ability to defend against uncertain outcomes. Your plan should perform under as many risks or sets of circumstances as possible.

Personal Residence

Primary Residence Real Estate: Your primary residence can also be an important component of both your long-term wealth building goals, and your use assets. Mortgage interest deductions may help offset taxes in other areas of your plan.

Financial Independence
Income Sources
Qualified Retirement Plans

Financial Independence: Once your protection plans are firmly in place as the foundation of your program, you can begin to develop a retirement strategy designed to recreate your paycheck once you move from a position of person-at-work, to capital-at-work. Will you become financially independent at ages 45, 55, 65, or beyond?

Stocks, Bonds, and Mutual Funds

Retirement Savings: We want you to examine funding qualified plans, ideally only up to the company match, since even a good match can make up for a lot of sins. Then we can determine whether it makes sense to put anything above the match.

Tax Advantaged Bond Funds

Mid-Range Accumulation: Many people focus only on retirement planning. Many things can happen between the time you graduate from school and the day that you retire. Often, plans are not well equipped to provide access to capital between ages 25–59. Where will the money come from to fund these expenses if you need it? We'll also need to consider the advantages of nonqualified (nonretirement accounts), tax-deferred, and tax-free investing.

It's important to also build wealth in areas outside of your home equity and retirement plans, but remember to plan carefully. Some of these investments may be highly overrated since they're subject to very large fluctuations and have limited tax benefits. These are things like listed securities and hard assets. Try to choose areas and products that provide multiple benefits.

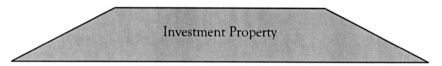

Real Estate Investing: You may desire to invest in a rental property or buy a second home or vacation place. These assets can also provide opportunities to build wealth in non-market correlated asset area. Additionally, they may include other benefits, such as a potential tax deductions, depreciation, or rental income.

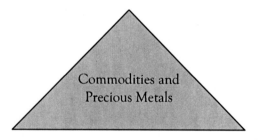

Commodities: Inflation is one of the most dangerous enemies to our wealth. Major increases in inflation can devastate our purchasing power and wipe out fortunes. In the event of inflationary periods or hyper-inflation, most of us would want to possess a certain quantity of goods and materials that others would like to have . . . no matter what. Precious metals such as gold, silver, and copper, and commodities such as salt, sugar, and tobacco have proven to hold their value during periods of instability and uncertain financial times.

Your Money Supply

Imagine if you could keep all of your gross earnings. Where does it all go? Taxes take a huge bite (nearly one-third off the top).

Household expenses and lifestyle expenditures consume most of what is left. In most cases with what remains after an individual income has been taxed at the federal, state, and local level, there is a capital surplus that can be used to provide the necessities, conveniences, and amusements in life. These things may include but are not limited to food, shelter, clothing, recreational activities, travel, educational funding, and other miscellaneous spending habits. Very few people have enough left over at the end of each monthly bill cycle to save.

You need to either find a way to save or find the money that others are stealing from you. Always pay yourself first. Small amounts can add up pretty quickly. Seek to eliminate any unnecessary wealth transfers in your life. This is an important step in building wealth. Once you develop a disciplined habit of building and accumulating wealth, it will become much easier to pay yourself before you spend.

Our next rule for building and accumulating wealth is to prioritize your goals. The risks and uncertainties in life can create financial disasters at any given time and in a moment's notice. Therefore, it is imperative to build on risk management strategies and protection plans into your overall financial picture. These products should serve as a cornerstone for any financial plan and should be developed as the foundation to build your savings, growth, and accumulated assets.

Circulating Capital

Once you have accumulated capital, you will have the ability to circulate your capital to create additional uses for your money. Unless you are fortunate enough to have the funding provided to you by some extraordinary means such as luck or an inheritance, you will have to start at ground zero.

When you attempt to draw funds from a bank, financial services firm or an insurance company—they usually ask you to the same question: How much have you put in? You are likely to need substantial amounts of capital at various points in your lifetime. With that in mind, you need to begin somewhere. You will need a saving strategy in order to plug in our capitalist system. If you do, it can offer you great rewards. If you don't save any capital, you will be locked out of opportunities.

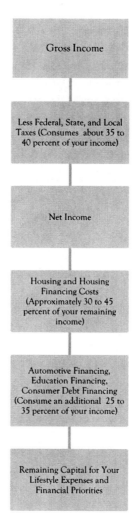

Figure 2.2   Cash-Flow Worksheet

Circulating Capital versus the Accumulation Method

Who are the principal architects of your current financial system? I spent many years studying this, first at Wharton Business and then practicing in the field for nearly 15 years. I can tell you that the principal architects of our current system include the banks, financial services industry, Corporate America, and even our government. They make the rules and control the financial systems.

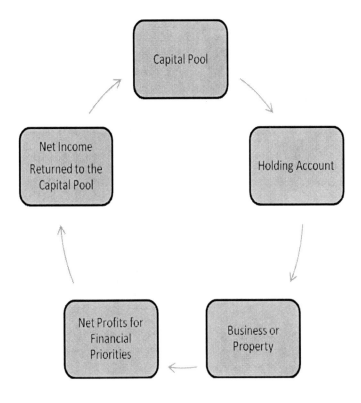

Figure 2.3   Circulating Capital

The key is for you to understand that if you don't have your own system, you will default into their system.

Most people are working with financial professionals who have been taught and believe that if we just hold hands and hang in there, things will get better. What if they don't? We may not be able to wait around and simply hope for the stock market to correct itself and bail us out once again. We can't count on the government bailing us out or waving a magic wand to fix things.

Regardless of your political persuasion, we can all agree that in order for things to get better, we can't wait for someone else to fix the problems for us. We need to step in and take action. The first step toward taking action lies in understanding the concept of circulating capital.

A Restaurant Example

How does a restaurant make money? We know that we hand them our money and they feed us. That part is easy, but where does the food come from? How much does it cost to make a meal? How does the restaurant earn a profit? If it were easy, everyone would do it.

First, a restaurant owner needs to buy a building or lease space to operate the business. He will need to rent or purchase fixtures, lighting, a kitchen, ovens, and so on. He also needs to purchase the food ingredients that they turn into entrées.

Eventually the cooks that prepare these foods will turn them into delicious meals that will be sold to guests of the restaurant. Upon eating the food, the guests will pay their bill and leave. The proceeds from the bill will be aggregated with other bills and provide revenue to their restaurant business.

Not all of that revenue is profit. A portion of that revenue must be used to pay for employee's salaries, pay for food ingredients, and fund the fixed and variable operating costs outlined earlier, such as rent, gas, electric, insurance costs, and other expenses. If the restaurant is successful, the owner will achieve a profit above and beyond the operating costs of the business.

Once they earn a profit, they have the ability to make choices. They can either choose to reinvest into the business and perhaps expand more entrées offering more choices for their patrons. They may elect to use it to advertise, in an effort to drive more people into their business. These efforts may increase the profits even further the second time around. They might choose to invest the profits into another business venture. This option may provide a second use for the same dollar. They could also choose to take the profit from the business as a salary or a cash distribution. In this case it will be taxed and then set aside for future use in another area (to spend or save).

If you understand this basic concept, you now understand the application of circulating capital. Circulating capital is about choices and keeping your money in motion. It is the premise of our capitalist system. Many people seem to be very content to leave their money invested in passive investments where the capital is not really circulating. These would include passive places such as stocks, bonds, mutual funds, and other traditionally exchange listed securities, bonds, CDs, and so on.

By purchasing these instruments, you are technically an owner of these businesses, but have no decision-making authority in the daily operations business or any material decision-making power over whether to reinvest capital into the primary business or take a dividend or profit distribution. Your money is being controlled by someone else.

By creating additional businesses and other entities for you to control, you will essentially create second, third, and fourth uses for your money. A world of opportunity will open up to you. You may also find yourself open to a new world of tax deductions as a business owner.

Smart business owners keep a small portion of capital available for future use (recapitalization), versus using it all for immediate consumption. Ultimately, all money is destined to be spent; the question is how? Once the finished works are sold, the proceeds will replace the capital used to create them, along with a profit. The new profits can also be used to create something of value, either in the form of services or actual consumable goods.

All of us are faced with the choice between present enjoyment that includes immediate expense and expenditures; and future enjoyment that puts a portion of your money (or capital) in a side account to either earn more money passively or actively. Ultimately, these dollars will also be converted back into goods and services, and then spent.

Why Save?

It's tough to start a business venture or fund an investment without any money. You will need to begin somewhere. No one who saves should be considered cheap or a miser; they're simply putting some capital away for a rainy day, such as a squirrel gathering nuts in the forest (you only need so many nuts per day). The smart capitalist also allows for a contingency fund. He realizes that there may be a day when there are not enough nuts readily available, so he puts some in a hiding place, usually inside of another tree. This way he can carry himself through the lean periods where the tree does not provide a plentiful bounty. Imagine if he could find a way to earn interest on his surplus supply of nuts?

The desire or impulse to spend is the same impulse that drives us to consume, eat, or engage in instant gratification. We must learn how to control these impulses in all areas of our lives. Sometimes these impulses are powerfully overwhelming. It usually passes pretty quickly and only occurs from time to time. If you can learn to control these urges you are halfway home.

On the other hand, the impulse that prompts us to save comes from a desire to better our condition or quality of life. This is a desire that although is calm and steady, remains persistent. From the day we are born until the day we die, most of us are constantly seeking ways to improve our quality of life. In the span of time between these two points, there are but a very few moments where any one of us are either perfectly content or completely satisfied to be without any want or wish of improvement of any kind.

Growing our personal wealth is the primary means that most of us strive towards—improvement in this quest to better our condition. The most obvious way that any of us can get in the game is by saving some part of what we earn . . . either regularly, annually, or on some extraordinary occasion. The impulse for spending impacts all of us at some time, and some of us at all times. Most would agree that the need to save as a way to better our condition in life is necessary.

How should we get started? The wealth of an individual or a business can only increase by what is saved. Whatever you save from your revenue sources or cash flow, adds to your wealth. You can then either employ it for yourself by hiring others to work for you (more services), or you can lend it to others *at an interest rate* to allow them to use it for growth in their businesses (earning you passive interest). This can be accomplished by either directly lending to the end user, by purchasing shares (stocks) in a company, or by letting a bank or third party do this for you (for a price).

Wealthy people understand that helping others is the key to real growth from circulating capital. A real capitalist knows that by increasing the amount of money that is saved, to be employed at a later date for the maintenance of productive hands, he will create more opportunities. They can also increase the number of those hands. Ultimately, the additional workers will add to the value of your stock and profits. This is the principle of circulating capital.

The key is balance in life and wealth building. How to enjoy life while saving: Sometimes wealthy people are criticized for spending. In the end, both the rich and poor spend everything they earn. Both groups are actually very similar. In each case, everything saved is spent eventually, but by an entirely different set of people. A rich man spends a portion of his revenue on entertaining guests and buying extravagant services and toys that leave little to nothing behind after their consumption.

The other portion of their revenue is saved for the sake of future profit. It is employed as investment capital that is also immediately consumed just as quickly. This time the funds are consumed by a different set of people. These people are laborers, manufacturers, service providers, and financers who are able to apply their skills to reproduce the revenue with a profit above the value of their annual consumption (returning his investment plus a profit).

By saving a part of these additional profits every year, they are able to replenish their investment capital and increase their investment. He not only perpetuates the maintenance of these other productive hands, but he begins to create a perpetual fund that will serve to fulfill many of his future needs and wants. Therefore, once established, the perpetual funding of this process becomes a sacred formula that must be protected and guarded for the ongoing support and maintenance of all productive hands it supports. Every time we are tempted to use a shortcut by diverting funds from the destination of new productive hands, we diminish the future growth of our enterprise . . . and cut short our real wealth potential!

How to Build Your Banking and Saving System: B.Y.O.B?

The only place where you start out on top is . . . digging a hole! Unfortunately, many of us are all too familiar with this position. How much of the banking functions do you control as it relates to your financial needs? Most of us don't understand that we finance everything we buy. We either pay interest to someone else or give up the interest you could have earned otherwise. We call this *opportunity cost*.

You can use your capital pools to purchase vehicles, fund home improvements, pay for vacations, fund yours or your family's education, and help your children get a head start in life (all of this can be accomplished without transferring interest to others). The key is to build wealth in areas that you can easily access and at favorable rates and terms. However, you must always be an honest banker. Always pay your bank back. If you do, your capital will be there for you when you need it.

The personal savings banks that you will create are pools of money that you own. They're not physical bank buildings; they're buckets of money that you may use strategically for the rest of your life. Some of these pools can offer additional benefits and features. For example, some may offer tax benefits and others may be protected from creditors and bankruptcy proceedings. You can use them to create more access, use, and control over your dollars.

Most of people's money is tied up in retirement plans and home equity. You will also need sources of money to improve your life-style before you reach your golden years. This additional liquidity can be created within your personal savings banks and pools. You can use them to begin eliminating fees and interest you were paying to others and reducing future taxation.

Try to eliminate every unnecessary transfer of your wealth. You can also create more wealth for yourself by reducing the money you transfer to third parties. If you could learn to reduce these transfers and keep the money for yourself, wouldn't you do it? You may need to unlearn some information. You must be willing to approach your situation from different perspectives. Remember, your mind is like a parachute; it only works when it's open!

Chapter Highlights

> Understand the importance of having a game plan. Develop a chronological outline for how and where you build wealth.
> Design a plan with an open architecture. You'll need the flexibility to make changes as life moves.
> Pay close attention to your cash-flow needs, and understand how circulating capital differs from traditional accumulation planning.
> Understand why it's important to save regularly.

CHAPTER 3
HISTORY OF MONEY AND BANKING

To know where you are going, you must explore where you came from. By understanding how and where money comes from, we can begin to break down the walls of secrecy and confusion that cloud our ability to make informed decisions with money. Once we understand money better, it becomes less intimidating. Once we become familiar with the topic, it becomes easier for us to confront our own finances and develop real strategies for accumulating wealth more efficiently.

The sole function of money is to circulate consumable goods and services. By employing money effectively, we can access all of the provisions, materials, and finished goods that we want. Money makes sure these goods and services can be bought, sold, and distributed to others.

Most people believe that money is beyond the understanding of mere mortals. It is generally accepted that as a fact of life, money is beyond our sphere of control. Why is money so mysterious that it can't really be understood or defined properly? What does money represent today? Is it the money we have in our pockets? Is it a coin, paper money, numbers on a piece of paper, statements on a checking or savings account, or is it nothing more than a definition of our purchasing power? How do you view money?

Before we had the money system, we had the barter system. Barter was defined as a direct exchange of things with like value. The exchange was not necessarily monetary in nature because these items were valued for what they represented, rather than being held as a medium or standard of exchange to be used later for something else. Both items have intrinsic value that enables them to be accepted by the other parties and used for a fair and deliberate exchange. It's interesting to note that labor may also be exchanged for barter, when it is perceived to have an intrinsic value. How do you value your time?

If we go back to the dawn of civilization, we see that people were initially roaming the earth either naked or barely clad in animal skins for warmth. They were constantly hungry and trying to survive, seeking any way to try to protect themselves and their families from the elements and other creatures that were looking to harm or eat them, or steal their feeble possessions.

In this basic state of existence, man simply tried to fulfill his needs as they occurred to him. When he was hungry, he would hunt or fish for survival. If he was cold, he covered himself in animal skin. His shelter consisted of caves and simple dwellings made from sticks, branches, and turf. His hunting tools were self-made. He was self-sufficient—this may have also contributed to his short life expectancy.

Almost every other creature that dwells on earth is self-sufficient in the wild. Every other living creature is independent and doesn't have a natural need for assistance from any other living creature in order to survive. On the other hand, man is almost constantly in need of assistance from others and would be foolish to expect it from them in exchange for nothing.

As families emerged, man understood the need to divide tasks among the household, such as hunting and gathering. As families multiplied, some may have had common needs. As necessity is the mother of invention, the best practices were likely to be developed and shared. In time, experts and artisans emerged in each need classification. Some men fashioned better hunting tools, while others were better at actually hunting! In this manner, the two could barter with each other for the needs of the other. If you give me one of those, I will give you one of these.

Ultimately, this system of individual talents prevailed, and served as the backdrop of our modern system of economic exchanges. Some earthly inhabitants became better at producing houses to provide better protection from the elements (primitive builders); others became great planters that evolved into farming. Others had a knack for harnessing the creatures of the earth into a primitive form of farming animals.

Eventually as the talent pool segmented and people began to evolve in their skill sets, they needed a way to focus their time, talents, and efforts on perfecting their god-given abilities. The only way they could spend time building houses for others is if someone else spent their time hunting to put food on the table. Therefore, a barter or exchange of values became necessary.

At the beginning of this process, exchange was simple. A savage man, who was not particularly skilled at hunting needed to appeal to the self-interest of a hunter. Therefore, he focused his time on fashioning the best spears available in his village. The bargain for his survival consisted of exchanging high quality spears for food! You give me an animal to eat, and I'll give you a spear or two. We're sure this method of exchange lasted for at least a while.

It is human nature to want a fair exchange. What if it only took an hour to make two spears, but it took ten hours to hunt and kill dinner? Is that a fair exchange for the hunter? What if the hunter needed only one spear? How does he trade half of a cow! Worse, what if the hunter had all of the spears he needed, how would the spear maker feed himself? A better system for barter needed to be developed.

Then, as it is now, time and labor was the accepted measure for humans to exchange value. In other words, the amount of time it took to build a shelter would roughly be equal to the amount of time that it would take to kill multiplied by the number of animals. Therefore, a house may have been exchanged for five or ten deer depending on the size of the deer and how many hours it took to build their homes.

Eventually, it became difficult to equate fractional numbers in large quantities. Some farmers or planters only had the need for half of a cow and found it inconvenient to trade a whole cow for four bushels of corn. In this manner of trade, either party was likely to end up with more of one quantity than he needed. This was a better strategy, but a lot still went to waste. Therefore, it became critical for our success as a society to develop a standard measure for equating the quantity of needs with the services that were provided. In other words, we needed an exchangeable value of labor.

In any profession, most of our wants and desires cannot be obtained with only our own labor and skills. Instead, we must find a way to trade the surplus portion, which we create (above and beyond our own consumption needs), with others. In this type of society, we survive by exchanging our talents with others within our business community. This is the basis of trade.

Unfortunately, if one party has nothing that the other party wants, no exchange can be made. In order to avoid the inconvenience of this situation, most people wanted to trade the surplus (extra) part of their goods and labor for something or some other commodity that most other people would be unlikely to refuse.

Many forms were used over the centuries. Some societies chose precious metals, others gem stones. Others created swords, spears, hunting bows, fishing boats, and other items. Ultimately, man decided that metals were the most common element to exchange . . . specifically gold.

Money Is Born

Commodity money developed out of the fact that eventually people want to have a few different items that could be readily exchanged in easier forms through barter than by any others. It was required because these items had certain characteristics that made them useful, and in demand by almost everyone.

Eventually, these items were not only acceptable to trade for other items, but for their own intrinsic value. These items or commodities represented a storehouse of value or wealth that could be exchanged in the future for something else. At this point they ceased being a convenient medium for exchange and actually became what we refer to today as money.

Before money, goods and labor were traded in the form of food, weapons, raw materials, livestock, and building materials. As man evolved in his wants, beyond the basic needs of survival, commodities other than food came into general demand. Different artwork, ornaments, and other items of intrinsic value were prized once there was enough food to go around.

Eventually, man learned how to refine crude elements and ores to craft them into either weapons or tools, the metals were valuable themselves. This started the Bronze Age and gave iron, copper, bronze, and other metals intrinsic value. These metals were traded between craftsmen, merchants, and emerging city–states along different trading routes and at major ports and trading locations.

The metal was originally very small in raw form. It was very difficult because it had to be weighed at each trading location. Eventually, it became a standard practice that people would make them in similar size and stamp them with the current weight. Once they were accepted by a standard weight metric system, they could be valued by just counting the number of pieces. They were small enough to be transported relatively easily when compared against weapons, livestock, and food. In this fashion, metals became the primitive version of functional coins or currency.

The main reason why metals became widely used as a commodity is they met all the requirements for convenient trade or exchange. They were not perishable. They could be melted and reused, divided into smaller units, combined into larger units, and were convenient for purchasing smaller items, which wasn't possible with other precious metals or with livestock. You couldn't just trade a cow's head for something else you wanted! You had to trade the entire cow or find someone else who wanted an entire cow.

Metals were much more portable than raw materials such as: wood, timber, swords, spears, and other valuable items, and they could be precisely measured on both sides of the transaction. As a storehouse and a measure of value, it's very difficult to find a better medium than precious metals. Throughout economic history, they served as one of the few commodities that other objects could be compared to easily.

They were constant. They were measurable. They became ideally suited for this purpose. On every continent around the globe, every nation chose metals as the primary storehouse of wealth and the measure of value as a tried-and-true medium of exchange. The number one metal that is still been selected for this purpose is gold. Gold became the universal money supply measure.

The Goldsmiths

The primary metal that has been used over the centuries over any other metal through trial and error is gold; varying dynasties and many different periods of the word as the commodity default currency. The average person instinctively knows that gold, if all else fails, will work well until something better can be established as a medium of exchange, primarily because there seems to be the right amount to keep its value high enough and rare enough that there seems to be a limited supply. This leads us to the goldsmiths, who worked, refined these coins, and stored these coins in a protected warehouse. The goldsmiths would store and protect the gold for a fee, and would provide written receipts to the owners that could be used for purchase.

These receipts were essentially the first form of paper money. Instead of transporting wheel barrows and wagons full of gold coins for large purchases, clients of the goldsmiths could simply get a letter of credit from a goldsmith who would certify that the buyer had a certain number of gold pieces in an account.

These receipts could easily be transferred with a counter signature of the document at the final destination of exchange for goods or services. The goldsmiths acted in the capacity of guaranteeing these receipts—for a fee, of course. These were essentially the first form of our modern checks (or traveler's checks which were not formally created for another few centuries).

The goldsmiths would lend these coins and receive a payment of interest for the privilege of lending money. They were the first versions of modern day bankers and private equity investors. It seemed silly to lend their own money, while other people's gold was just lying around in the vaults. They reasoned that no one was able to use the gold if it was trapped in the vault.

Goldsmiths discovered they could now lend other people's money. They argued that putting it to work instead of merely allowing it to gather dust was the best course of action for everyone. They knew from experience that very few people who deposited their coins ever wanted to remove their money at the same time. Very few withdrawals ever exceeded more than 10 or 20 percent of the stock pile. It seemed like a great idea to lend to the other 70, 80, or 90 percent at any given time to earn interest on this money. With the extra profits, they rationalized that they could hire more guards to protect the public and expand locations (branches) to help new areas.

The warehouse workers began to act as brokers to loan this money on behalf of the depositors, and the concept of banking as we know it today was created out of this idea. It seemed like it was a shame for money to just sit in their vaults, so why not lend it out and earn a profit, which they could split between themselves and their depositors. In time, savings accounts were created and the banks expanded new territories with new locations (money deposit locations) or wealth confiscation centers. To beat the system, you will have to think like a bank.

It was difficult to transport large amounts of coins over long distances. Additionally, there was the inconvenience of being attacked or robbed along the way and losing all the coins. Therefore, goldsmiths opened banking centers along trade routes. They would store wealth for others in exchange for a receipt stating that these funds would become available upon demand. The goldsmiths not only worked with gold but were able to protect it against invaders with hired armies.

Government Steps In

As goods and services became more readily available, different classes of people begin to blend together and commerce seemed to create a bond of union and trade. The government was created primarily to maintain justice and to guarantee that individual properties would not be infringed. Economic progress was stifled in a society that's constantly warring and people are constantly concerned about someone else stealing their property. They're less apt to put their capital and industry to work because they're constantly worried about someone coming along and stealing it from them. In order to protect their capital, they would dig a hole or hide it. Free markets promote prosperity, liberty, and a sense of independence and they are truly the foundation of our economy.

In many ways we can trace the progress of our economic growth to the efforts of the goldsmiths. Ultimately, their model grew into the basis for our modern day banking system. It is important to understand how they were able to use money to their advantage, and the financial model has not changed much today. Financial institutions will usually attempt to capitalize on your money. If you are beginning to build your wealth efficiently, you will learn from the goldsmiths. You must seek to find ways to control your money supply and generate additional uses for your money whenever possible.

Before you can control your destiny, you need a roadmap, guide, and thorough understanding of the hazards that you may face along the way. Once you define these hazards, you can take care to avoid them. We will spend the rest of our time together identifying these hazards, and providing you with a roadmap for financial success.

CHAPTER 4
OPPORTUNITY COST
DEFINED

We live in a country founded on life, liberty, and the pursuit of happiness. Opportunity is made daily. How you choose to capitalize on your opportunities (or not to act) is your choice. Free will is best measured in terms of opportunity cost.

Opportunity cost or economic opportunity loss is the measurement of the value of the next best alternative foregone as the result of making a decision. There is a price to pay for success and failure. They are roughly the same in the long run, although they look much different in the short run. Which price do you want to pay?

Unfortunately, the opponents often make it more difficult for us to see the real costs (see chapter 7). During my training at Wharton Business, particular emphasis was placed on this concept. I was taught to weigh every decision in our life with respect to opportunity cost. Opportunity cost analysis plays an important part of a company's decision-making process . . . but it is not treated as an actual cost in any financial statement.

The practical definition of opportunity cost sounds like this: If you spend a dollar, the opportunity cost represents not only what the dollar bought; but also what you could have earned if you had the opportunity to hold onto it and allow it to grow. If we follow the same logic, the opposite must also be true. If you manage to hold onto a dollar, and do something with it, you gain both the savings of the dollar and the future growth of that dollar.

Transferred money represents the required payments you will make to financial institutions, the government, or other entities. Transferred money can include taxes, interest on debt, insurance premiums, and service fees such as accounting, legal, and tax fees. I want to shine light on understanding this area so you can find resources to help you increase your wealth and minimize your expenses.

Opportunity cost helps us calculate the real cost of our actions. It allows us to measure the roads not taken. It allows us to measure the impact of doing (or not doing) something. It helps us measure the use of our time and the application of our finances. The next best thing that a person can engage in is referred to as the opportunity cost of doing the best thing and ignoring the next best thing to be done. For example, right now, you don't need to read this book. You could be doing something else with your time. Sleeping, working, eating, reading a different book, watching T.V., shopping, and so on. Therefore, the opportunity cost for reading this book is calculated as what you are giving up for the choice to do something else. Every choice has a consequence; some good and some not so good.

To achieve economic success, you will need to understand opportunity cost. You will also need to have a financial model in your mind. This model represents nothing more than a financial decision making process. It will help you to understand (and calculate) the full impact of your financial choices. Once you are able to fully compare your long-term and short-term benefits...you will be able come to the right financial decisions. Making the correct choice is up to you.

Here's a quick example: For every dollar that we spend or transfer annually, we lose a potential future value as well. If you could manage to save $4,000 and allow it to compound at 7 percent . . . over your working lifetime it could potentially be worth over $600,000. The opposite is true for a $4,000 annual expense (this is the amount of wealth that you would potentially transfer to others). It would be worth even more over life expectancy. This figure would grow exponentially larger over longer time periods, or at higher annual rates of return. This simple illustration table is not designed to represent any specific investment. It is simply designed to offer a new perspective on opportunity costs.

Opportunity Cost
Calculated for 'Valued Client'
Age: 25   Annual Expense: $4,000
Number of Years of Payment: 20   Number of Years of Calculation: 40
Opportunity Rate of Return: 7%

(continued)

(continued)

Year	Annual Expense	Cumulated Expense	Opportunity Rate of Return	Cumulative Opportunity Cost	Cumulative Total Cost
2009	$4,000	$4,000	7%	$0	$4,000
2010	$4,000	$8,000	7%	$280	$8,280
2011	$4,000	$12,000	7%	$260	$12,260
2012	$4,000	$16,000	7%	$1,760	$17,760
2013	$4,000	$20,000	7%	$3,003	$23,003
2014	$4,000	$24,000	7%	$4,613	$28,613
2015	$4,000	$28,000	7%	$6,616	$34,616
2016	$4,000	$32,000	7%	$9,039	$41,039
2017	$4,000	$36,000	7%	$11,912	$47,912
2018	$4,000	$40,000	7%	$15,266	$55,266
2019	$4,000	$44,000	7%	$19,134	$63,134
2020	$4,000	$48,000	7%	$23,554	$71,554
2021	$4,000	$52,000	7%	$28,563	$80,563
2022	$4,000	$56,000	7%	$34,202	$90,202
2023	$4,000	$60,000	7%	$40,516	$100,516
2024	$4,000	$64,000	7%	$47,552	$111,552
2025	$4,000	$68,000	7%	$55,316	$123,316
2026	$4,000	$72,000	7%	$63,996	$135,996
2027	$4,000	$76,000	7%	$73,516	$149,516
2028	$4,000	$80,000	7%	$83,912	$163,912
2029		$80,000	7%	$95,461	$175,461
2030		$80,000	7%	$107,734	$187,734
2031		$80,000	7%	$120,885	$200,885
2032		$80,000	7%	$134,947	$214,947
2033		$80,000	7%	$149,993	$229,993

Year	Annual Expense	Cumulated Expense	Opportunity Rate of Return	Cumulative Opportunity Cost	Cumulative Total Cost
2034		$80,000	7%	$166,093	$246,093
2035		$80,000	7%	$183,319	$263,319
2036		$80,000	7%	$201,752	$281,752
2037		$80,000	7%	$221,474	$301,474
2038		$80,000	7%	$242,577	$322,577
2039		$80,000	7%	$265,158	$345,158
2040		$80,000	7%	$289,319	$369,319
2041		$80,000	7%	$315,171	$395,171
2042		$80,000	7%	$342,833	$422,833
2043		$80,000	7%	$372,431	$452,431
2044		$80,000	7%	$404,102	$484,102
2045		$80,000	7%	$437,989	$517,989
2046		$80,000	7%	$474,248	$554,248
2047		$80,000	7%	$513,045	$593,045
2048		$80,000	7%	$554,558	$634,558

Output Summary:

Total Out-of-Pocket Expenses: $80,000

Total Lost Opportunity Cost: $554,558

Final Total Cost: $634,558

Figure 4.1 Opportunity Cost Table

Common Transfers

Taxes

You must pay taxes; however, we are often paying unnecessary (additional) taxes because of the way we manage our finances. We will show you how to eliminate these losses and exercise greater control of your wealth. If your accumulated money grows through the interest it earns, so might your taxes.

What Do Our Purchases Really Cost Us?

Let's take a look at a balance sheet—what happens when we make our decision independently, or one at a time? Many people finance their cars and consumer debt because they're conditioned to use the credit option for their installment purchases, but they're not considering their real opportunity cost that offsets their gains to the other side of their ledger. They overpay on insurance protection, and make consumer purchases without looking at the big picture.

Insurance Premiums

Many of us will transfer hundreds of thousands of dollars by not coordinating our insurance plans properly. Auto insurance costs may average $2,500 per year, Homeowners $1,000, and Term Life Insurance $750. Total protection costs approximately $3,750 per year. These premiums, invested at interest over your adult lifetime (fifty years), would grow to over $1 million at 6 percent or $2.3 million at 8 percent. That's more than most of us will ever manage to save for retirement! Someone is investing these premiums and growing wealth from these dollars. Would you like to learn how to recover some of these costs?

Term Life Insurance

Many people do not calculate the value of money over time on the premiums spent when looking at the true cost of owning term insurance. You must factor in not only the premiums, but also what those premiums would have been worth had you taken the risk and invested the money yourself. We are not suggesting that people take the risk of not owning insurance, but rather that they need to understand the true cost of owning term insurance.

Recovery Strategy: Use Interest Transfers

Maybe you want the permanent insurance, but you feel that you don't have the money to pay the premiums. There are many people who have money tied up in investments and would not move the principal, but would be willing to move the interest earned on those investments to insurance. They must first understand the increasing tax problem that may exist by compounding their money in a taxable account. This strategy can also help you diversify investment risk, while maintaining your principal position.

Consumer Debts

Consumer debts on your credit cards, automotive financing, and other loans eat up thousands of our dollars annually. Find a way to take yourself out of this vicious cycle.

Strategy: Consider Using Your Home Equity Loans to Eliminate Nondeductible Debt

Many people are caught in the trap of owing large sums of money on cars and credit cards without the ability to deduct the interest. If appropriate, using a second mortgage or refinancing might be a way to potentially deduct the interest expense. Another benefit is that the interest rate charged on the home equity loan may be less than the interest rate charged on credit purchases. This can create an improved cash flow position.

Savings Rates

Did you know the average current savings rate in our country is under 4 percent. That means as a nation we spent more than 96 percent of all the money we earn. How do your own savings percentages compare to that? Take a look at the dollars that you are currently spending. What if you could find a way to save or recapture another 3 to 5 percent of your fixed expense costs? Remember, everything that you do is measured with respect to what everything and everyone else is doing.

Most Americans have no idea how much money they needlessly transfer away during their lifetimes. Look for these unnecessary transfers and expenses and find a way to stop them. The measurable value of opportunity cost is the amount this lost money could have earned for you if it had not trickled out of your wealth bucket.

How much would $100 be worth twenty-five years from now, or fifty years from now . . . if you could hang on to and invest it? Each of us is born with a single timeline. The sooner we put our dollars to work, the greater our future rewards. We are pointing out that the greatest potential for wealth is not just a higher rate of return on your investments, but finding places where inefficiency results in opportunity costs that drain your wealth.

Consider your lifetime earnings. During a normal forty-year working lifetime, several million dollars in actual physical dollars may pass through your hands. The wealth potential of these dollars is exponential.

For example, annual earnings of $75,000 for forty working years would amount to $3 million of total earnings. This is the amount that will pass through your wealth model. At a normal 3 to 4 percent savings rate, most people would be lucky to be able to hold on to $90,000 to $120,000 of these earnings for their financial priorities. Taxes, expenses, interest, and spending consume the balance.

Let's examine your own cash flow transfer costs and see if we can recapture any of it. Imagine if only a small portion were recaptured and invested annually over a twenty-year period or longer. This gives you an idea of the costs that you may be overlooking. How much more money would be in your pocket to reinvest or improve your life if you could eliminate or minimize these wealth transfers? This is the measurable impact of your financial decisions. A reduction of only 5 percent would amount to about $3,750 per year. If that amount was able to grow at a hypothetical rate of return of 7 percent for forty years, it could grow to about $800,000! How would that impact your retirement goals or other financial priorities?

In order to build our wealth more efficiently, we must account for and consider all costs associated with our financial choices. We must compare the costs associated with building wealth by investing; just as we must calculate the overhead operating costs of operating a business for a profit.

The following examples are designed to illustrate our points more effectively. It is entirely possible for an average person to transfer over a million dollars in their lifetime with your everyday consumer decisions. Some of these transfers can be avoided and recaptured for your use. The results may surprise you.

Snapshot summary examples of common costs along with their opportunity costs over our lifetime. The full calculations are available in Appendix B.

1. *Auto Insurance Premium Recoveries:* Have you reviewed your own deductibles lately? A small change in your auto, homeowner's

or other insurance policies could allow you to save the difference in a side fund.

Annual Potential Recovery $500
Opportunity Rate of Return 8%
Value in 10 years $7,243
Value in 20 years $22,811
Value in 30 years $56,642

Figure 4.2   Insurance Deductible Opportunity Cost Example

2. *Term Life insurance premiums*: Have you considered how expensive those term life premiums are? The real cost is much higher than the teaser premiums. Seek to convert this coverage to permanent life insurance as soon as you can find the money to make this happen!

Annual Potential Recovery $1,000
Opportunity Rate of Return 8%
Value in 10 years $14,487
Value in 20 years $45,762
Value in 30 years $98,797

Figure 4.3   Term Life Insurance Premium Example

3. *Cost of Smoking Examined*: What if kids invested $7 a day into a monthly investment builder mutual fund. At a hypothetical rate of return of 8 percent they would build a small fortune.

Annual Potential Recovery $2,400
Opportunity Rate of Return 8%
Value in 10 years $34,767
Value in 20 years $109,828
Value in 30 years $271,879

Figure 4.4   Smoking Example: What does $7 per pack add up to?

4. *Consumer Spending Costs*: Think twice before you make those impulse purchases. Take a look at what even $500 per year can end up costing you.

Annual Potential Recovery $500
Opportunity Rate of Return 8%
Value in 10 years $7,243
Value in 20 years $22,811
Value in 30 years $56,642

Figure 4.6   Consumer Spending Example

If you could take steps to reduce or eliminate these expenses, would you? What's stopping you now? Take a few minutes to review the areas in your investment, insurance, and consumer-based financial decisions to see if you can eliminate some of your own opportunity costs.

Chapter Highlights

➤ Understand what opportunity costs are.
➤ Look for potential opportunity costs that can be identified and recaptured in your own life.

Chapter 5
Choosing Your Guide Along the Road to Wealth
The Ideal Financial Professional Relationship

Figure 5.1   Do you have a personal CFO?

Conflicting Advice

Figure 5.2   Your Trusted Advisor

No one likes to be sold, but most people see value in a coach. Have you worked with product peddlers in the past? Do you have an advisor or a team of financial professionals? Who do you turn to when your team of trusted advisors disagrees on a particular topic, and how do you make that decision? Do you automatically default on the advice of your certified public accountant (CPA)? Do you listen to your attorney? Perhaps you side with your financial advisor. What about your mortgage broker or your realtor? Should you consult your insurance agents? What about your banker and stock broker?

What do you do when your CPA, attorney, and financial advisors disagree on a particular topic? Each of them has your best interest in mind, and each has their reasons for why the others are wrong. Sometimes the so-called experts put you in the middle of the argument. It's a shame when professionals behave in this way. Who decides who is right? Do you go with your gut feel? Most people do nothing!

Let's go back to tenth grade science class. We need a model and a decision-making process to help us find the best solution. What are the benefits and drawbacks of each strategy? Every financial decision you make carries benefits and drawbacks. And every financial decision also impacts every other financial decision in some way. It's like throwing pebbles in a lake. The waves are going to ripple out and intersect at some point; they're going to impact each other.

Choosing an Advisor

Figure 5.3   Are there any trusted advisors left?

All "Trusted Advisors" are not created equal.

The financial services industry has been plagued by flavor-of-the-week financial planning techniques. Many of these so-called planners are nothing more than salesmen peddling products and looking for a way to convince you to buy them. Rarely are there product-based solutions that are part of an overall approach to proper wealth building. Product peddlers and manipulative sales practices by many planners have left the public to view the industry with a lack of trust and confidence. The typical cast of characters may include the following: stock brokers, insurance agents, money managers, financial planners, financial consultants, fee-only planners, hedge fund managers, bank employees, credit unions, and so on.

Often, the advice is very similar. The difference lies in how they are compensated for their services (or lack of service). Some are paid hourly, others by fees. Some earn commission and others a salary. How they are compensated should be less important than what they can actually do with your money.

When selecting a financial professional, it is important that you have a clear line of communication both ways. You need communication of mutual expectations with an upfront agreement. We recommend that you meet with your financial professional at least annually to perform a detailed review and to make sure that your plans are complete and up-to-date. If possible, the ideal situation would also include periodic conference calls that help address any planning needs that pop up before your annual review. This increased contact frequency also helps to keep up with outside market-driven factors, tax law changes, government issues, and other major planning considerations.

Most financial professionals use the following time-proven line of questioning. "How much money do you have?" "Where is your money now?" Next they say, "Just give it to us to manage. We can do better than the other guys." Many emphasize the rate of return on investments. They preach: The faster you want your money to grow, the more risks you must take. Risk tolerance and risk management is not the same thing. If you didn't have to take a risk and you could receive positive rates of return, would you want to learn how?

Some people are not working with a financial professional at all. Usually, it stems from the fact that they believe the financial planners will take them through a manipulative sales process. This can be true of some planners. It is easy to shine a spotlight on the deficiencies of someone's plan and then ask how they are going to solve that plan, but it's quite another to show them how to find the money, present options, and give them choices as to whether they want to address the plan or not.

Many financial planning firms, investment houses, and insurance companies train their planners with a generic approach. In an effort to shrink the sales cycle and generate sales and commissions as quickly as possible, many planners have resorted to some variation of what is called a *needs analysis*. This is a quick, down and dirty analysis designed to identify the short falls and make quick recommendations. Unfortunately, this system makes sure that almost everyone will show up with a shortfall. Next the financial professional will often use the report to his advantage in an effort to close the deal, get you to fund a program, or buy a product.

What makes matters worse is that they have been taught to identify a household monthly budget figure and to use the discretionary capital to fund these programs and products. What happens if you don't have a capital surplus? Few of these planners have been taught how they can actually help you find the money in your programs effectively. If you find yourself working with a planner who only offers solutions when you hand them money, it may be time to seek a new professional.

They produce pages of spreadsheets, and multicolor charts that look like they are really comprehensive. The problem is that by the time the ink is dry and reviewed by the victim (the client), the numbers are wrong. There is little substance in that proposal, just assumptions and guesses at future results.

Most planners focus only on the 3 or 4 percent of money they think people can save. The typical discussion is based on creating a new budget. This often also results in reducing your current standard of living in an effort to grow your accumulated dollars. When more money flows out of your lifestyle money, your standard of living is decreased. It would be important to find the money for savings from somewhere other than your lifestyle. Otherwise, pretty soon you won't be able to afford your current lifestyle.

Budgeting is certainly part of the process, but an equally important part is helping you identify areas where you are transferring your dollars to others and then recapturing them for your own use. In this type of arrangement, we have a level playing field. You will not be manipulated, and the planner must add value.

Needs Only Planning

Many of our peers who are only practicing need-based planning, have clients with plans that often come up short of their intended goals, despite their best efforts. It is a function of the type of planning they're performing. Unfortunately, these problems will occur at the worst possible time in their clients' lives. Life doesn't offer too many do-overs on retirement planning. Most of these plans focus on an accumulated-method based on a defined amount that may be needed some point in the future.

These calculations usually begin by analyzing the amount of money the client has already saved and how much they're currently saving. They need to also assume a rate of return for your investments. This is typically done through another set of discussions surrounding risk tolerance or time horizons. They also need to make an assumption for the increasing cost of goods and services from inflation. There are generally a few types of cookie-cutter plan proposals based on goals like: retirement planning, college funding, insurance needs, or other wealth-accumulation strategies.

Show me the numbers. Wrong. Numbers should be used to verify or test a strategy versus selling a product. Unfortunately, most of these numbers are just basic mathematical spreadsheets. Spreadsheets should only be used as a general roadmap, not as a substitute for a long-term planning relationship. Many people will find themselves in a situation where they have purchased a nice set of mathematical equations (guesses) wrapped in a leather binder, filled with multicolored pie and bar charts.

Many financial planners use spreadsheet analysis and average rates of return to depict your chances of financial success. Unfortunately, markets do not move in a straight line. If you look at any historical records of the financial markets, you will see wide movements between their peaks and valleys. There's even more significant movement on a daily basis. Therefore, it is critical that you understand that these spreadsheets and planning instruments, specifically financial planning software, should be used as only a guide or roadmap for your financial success.

They should not be used as a literal interpretation of your expectations. Your money will perform much differently than what has been illustrated. Take a look at the attached example which shows the difference between actual returns and average returns over a thirty-year period. While both achieve the same average rate of return, one client is in a much better position than other!

Average versus Actual Returns

10 percent returns? Sign me up! . . . Not so Fast.

Most people would jump at the chance to earn 10 percent average annual returns in retirement. But, averages can be misleading, especially for retirement portfolios used to generate income. In retirement, it's often the steep rate of return that will cause investment success or failure. Investment losses in early retirement may jeopardize the sustainability of a portfolio and its ability to generate meaningful income that will last a lifetime. Additionally, losses near the end of your time horizon can cause you to lose large amounts of wealth at a time in your life when you cannot afford to replace it.

The example below illustrates two hypothetical retirement portfolios, assuming the following:

Initial portfolio values—$500,000 for each portfolio.

Portfolio I: S&P 500 calendar year returns from 1969 to 1994.

Portfolio II: Simply reverses the order of the S&P 500 returns.

$30,000 annual withdrawals. Withdrawals increase 3 percent per year to account for cost of living inflation increases.

Average annual return—10.1 percent, on each portfolio

Portfolio I total income—$1,156,591.

Portfolio II total income—$1,156,591.

Ending account balance portfolio I—$19,369.

Ending account balance portfolio II—$2,555,498.

How will your plan hold up to random performance returns? Does your current planner offer any guidance on strategies to combat this potential risk, or does he believe in planning based on average returns? No one can predict the variability in investment returns and their impact on a retirement portfolio. It seems like a birth year or retirement lottery. What will the sequence of returns be during your retirement? At best, you can try to minimize volatility by diversifying your portfolio across various asset classes. Even with diversification, there's no guarantee that your portfolio can sustain you to retirement once you begin taking income. To combat this risk, we suggest a layered approach to retirement savings, including assets that offer guaranteed returns and income sources . . . to balance out your variable asset lifecycles.

10 Percent Average Returns

	Portfolio 1				Portfolio 2		
Year	Investment Return	Withdrawal	Account Balance	Year	Investment Return	Withdrawal	Account Balance
1	-8.40%	$30,000	$427,900	1	1.30%	$30,000	$476,600
2	4.00%	$30,900	$414,030	2	10.10%	$30,900	$493,646
3	14.30%	$31,827	$441,410	3	7.60%	$31,827	$499,385
4	19.00%	$32,782	$492,275	4	30.40%	$32,782	$618,417
5	-14.80%	$33,765	$385,752	5	-3.10%	$33,765	$565,419
6	-26.50%	$34,778	$248,942	6	31.50%	$34,778	$708,917
7	37.30%	$35,822	$305,976	7	16.80%	$35,822	$792,335
8	23.70%	$36,896	$341,596	8	5.20%	$36,896	$796,799
9	-7.30%	$38,003	$278,793	9	18.60%	$38,003	$906,602
10	6.60%	$39,143	$257,966	10	32.00%	$39,143	$1,157,844
11	18.60%	$40,317	$265,631	11	6.10%	$40,317	$1,188,270
12	32.10%	$41,527	$309,451	12	22.40%	$41,527	$1,412,559
13	-4.90%	$42,773	$251,484	13	21.10%	$42,773	$1,667,978
14	21.10%	$44,056	$260,516	14	-4.90%	$44,056	$1,542,024
15	22.40%	$45,378	$273,416	15	32.10%	$45,378	$1,992,099
16	6.10%	$46,739	$243,383	16	18.60%	$46,739	$2,315,890
17	32.00%	$48,141	$273,197	17	6.60%	$48,141	$2,419,903
18	18.60%	$49,585	$274,290	18	-7.30%	$49,585	$2,194,633
19	5.20%	$51,073	$237,535	19	23.70%	$51,073	$2,663,688
20	16.80%	$52,605	$224,883	20	37.30%	$52,605	$3,604,638
21	31.50%	$54,183	$241,605	21	-26.50%	$54,183	$2,597,028
22	-3.10%	$55,809	$178,282	22	-14.80%	$55,809	$2,157,378
23	30.40%	$57,483	$174,997	23	19.00%	$57,483	$2,508,718
24	7.60%	$59,208	$129,107	24	14.30%	$59,208	$2,808,257
25	10.10%	$60,984	$81,111	25	4.00%	$60,984	$2,859,042
26	1.30%	$62,813	$19,369	26	-8.40%	$62,813	$2,555,498

*The hypothetical example is for illustrative purposes, and is not representative of any particular financial product. Past performance is no guarantee of future results.

Today, many people are finding that the traditional means of funding a comfortable retirement can no longer be relied upon. The caps, which are placed on qualified retirement plans, the minimum income replacement percentage of Social Security, and the dwindling number of employer provided pension plans, meaning that a much greater portion of your retirement savings must come from other sources. Where will your retirement income come from? What makes this even more of a challenge is the fact that the more you earn, the more you will need to save.

The more income you make, the lower the percentage of pre-retirement income that will be replaced by Social Security becomes. The income benefit decreases proportionately as your income level rises. This means you will have to save the difference yourself! To see the estimated Social Security retirement income benefit for yourself, use the Social Security quick calculator at www.ssa.gov.

Individuals with the necessary risk tolerance of long-term investments can take advantage of the upside potential of equity investments to accumulate assets for retirement. However, equity markets may be subject to periods of volatility. This raises the question, what would happen if you retire at a time when the stock market and bond prices are both declining (or it may happen a few years into retirement). What effect will this have on your retirement accounts and what can you do to minimize impact on your retirement income streams? Taking the income from an equity based retirement account during a period of negative returns can have a significant adverse effect on the future value of the account. This may ultimately impact the amount of income you have available during retirement, as well as the amount of legacy left to your family.

It's important to include a conservative element in your retirement income strategy now that will give you the future financial flexibility to more effectively manage your retirement income during changing and challenging economic conditions. This is different from having a well diversified asset allocation (or diversification), we are talking about assets that would be held separately and used for this specific purpose. Do you have assets earmarked specifically for the down years in the financial markets? If not, where will your income come from during these negative market performance years? How will your investment portfolio be able to heal?

In order to implement this type of strategy, you would need an alternate source of income that's not significantly impacted by short-term market volatility. Some options might include certificates of deposit, and other conservative savings vehicles. These conservative assets may offer lower overall investment returns over the long run when compared with equities. However, they representative the stable source of income that is essential to your retirement income distribution strategy. If an insurance needs analysis indicates that you should consider the purchase of additional life insurance, and death benefit protection, a whole life insurance policy with a limited premium payment could provide the pre-retirement income protection that you may need (from policy cash values), along with the accumulation of cash values that will build up inside the contract to be used to provide supplemental income.

Assumptions are usually wrong the day they're printed! There are at least four or five variables in every plan, each may constantly change, sometimes the day after it's written. Every day after it's printed, it is going further and further off course from the original coordinates.

By ignoring these wealth eroding forces, they may have a devastating impact on your ability to build wealth. As income taxes change, more of your wealth may also be confiscated. If the market corrects itself, it may take years or decades to recover. Many planners just tell their clients to hang in there and wait for it to get better. But, who can afford a decade of losses if they're age fifty or over?

Traditional planners and other insurance professionals will tell you that you either need to: save more, earn more, get a higher return on your investments, hope that prices do not increase in the future, or put more money into the plan. None of those strategies sound very attractive.

Financial Planning Software

Financial planning software is also easy to manipulate. If they use an assumption of an inflation rate that's on the high side, the proposal may show you that you are running out of money in retirement. Since they don't usually want to come back with a poor scenario that causes them to have a difficult discussion about your financial future, some planners simply opt to lower the future inflation assumption. No one really knows where inflation will be, so just decrease the assumption by a point or two. *Presto chango*, you're set for life (as long as the inflation assumptions are accurate).

What happens if the actual inflation rate is higher than assumed? How will it impact your financial future? We think you need to understand how these variables (planning assumptions) are derived, and that you need to be a part of a process in determining your own variables through a joint exercise with your planners. This is a time-consuming process. This process requires a buy in from both the client and the planner. Ultimately, you need to know how and why the assumptions in your plan were derived (and how they will change over time).

We believe the inflation calculation factor is one of the most important variables in your financial planning assumptions, and many plans have been predicated on false hopes and pretenses because the planner just hasn't been properly trained in the science of wealth building.

What type of answers does your planner have to explain all of these events? Many advisors, set out with the best intentions, and are trained to provide financial advice and help their clients reach their financial goals through a needs analysis. Unfortunately, most of the training and education they have received is not as strong as it could be; and most of their plans will not work under varying circumstances, but only work in their math-based laboratory.

One of my best college economics professors explained that math and money are definitely not the same thing. Unfortunately, most financial planning strategies are clearly focused on mathematical equations. They focus too much on offense and not enough on defensive strategies that emphasize protection. As a result, these plans are vulnerable to all types of changes in the growing world economy and the policies of our government.

The recent changes have redefined the term *trusted advisors*. Clients have just received a huge wakeup call. There are only a *few* trusted advisors that have earned the title and trust. The financial professionals that understand coordinated planning live off the failures of others. The real professionals have the knowledge and skill to do it right!

Your Private CFO

Plug the holes in your Wealth Bucket!

While in management classes at Wharton, I learned about the corporate hierarchy structure. Most substantial corporations have many layers of management. At the very top are the Chief Executive Officers (CEOs) and second in command, the Chief Financial Officer (CFO). You are the CEO of your life and the buck stops with you. You will need complete information in order to make well-informed decisions. Your planner should serve as your CFO.

Figure 5.4   Who is plugging the holes in your Wealth Bucket?

As you build wealth, life gets more complicated. Achieving affluence generally increases the complexity of your decision-making process. The greater your wealth, the more time, knowledge, and energy must be invested into maintaining the growth, protection, and the ultimate distribution of those assets. Hire a personal CFO to help you make decisions.

There are dozens of factors to consider and thousands of financial products to choose from. No one advisor has all of the answers. Most billionaires have teams managing their financial affairs through a coordinated approach to wealth building and protection. You should have the same advantages. The best advisors are usually part of a high-performing wealth management team.

Accountants, insurance professionals, financial planners, attorneys, property and casualty agents, mortgage brokers, and others can offer advice, but because most offer services independent of each other, it's often up to you to sort through the individual recommendations and evaluate each decision on the basis of how it impacts your overall plan.

Every financial decision you make impacts every other financial decision. If you take a look at your aggregate wealth as a bucket of water, you can't drink out of one side without impacting the other side in some way. The ideal solution is to create a wealth management partnership with a planner or firm that can help define and create unique long- and short-term goals through a comprehensive program of investments, savings, insurance planning, tax planning, asset allocation, risk management, retirement, and estate planning strategies.

Partner with a firm that can provide solutions and options in an objective and professional fashion. This firm or planner should provide solutions for many different types of clients. Clients would typically retain this type of firm or planning professional as their personal chief financial officer (CFO).

This approach is in great contrast with the industry model based on encouraging new financial representatives to sell to their friends and family almost immediately after becoming licensed . . . by themselves! Most of these new representatives have little or no training and sell the product of the week. Without a strong team surrounding them, many of these advisors may offer incomplete planning recommendations.

Your chosen professional or team of professionals should coordinate many aspects of your financial life including retirement planning, risk management and insurance, asset management, debt management and cash flow analysis, estate planning, and children's educational needs. Ideally, the firm would contain specialists that can listen closely to their clients and learn about their individual values, goals, and needs. Only then can they craft the strategies and financial engineering necessary to help ensure their continued financial success.

Through the chief financial officer model, you can have the ability to organize all of your advisors and assets accordingly and consolidate them in the same place at the same time. Many firms have substantially invested in the power of technology. Imagine having a single platform where all of your financial matters could be managed.

Your assets, insurance, family's private documents, financial and estate plans, and retirement and cash flow documents. The ideal model provides a single source financial advocate working with you and your advisors to develop integrated financial strategies.

A financial model allows you to effectively organize your assets, investments, and risk management plans. It can help simplify, coordinate, and integrate every aspect of your financial future. Plans are not static. They are constantly evolving. The platform should allow an easy way to review, keep track of, and update your plans. Your model must be able to accommodate your financial goals and plans, provide balance sheet accounting, net worth statements, account aggregation, reviews of important documents including: wills, trusts, prior tax returns, and gift tax returns.

Your private CFO should be simplifying the demands of managing your wealth, in order to enable you to devote more time to your personal life, business, and family. The basis of your planning should be build around a pilot and copilot relationship between an advisor and client.

The benefits you can expect to enjoy in this type of model include instant access to all of your financial-related matters in a single source location. Your accounts and assets should be complete and up-to-date. Balance sheets and cash flow statements should also be updated on a regular periodic basis. You should also have access to top tiered analysis and financial simulators that you and your financial advisor or CFO can collaborate on regularly.

Consider hypothetical situations and actual situations. By using the power of harnessing technology, you are able to have access to updated financial statements, automatically and fully integrated into your comprehensive estate plan, thereby continuously providing you with a meaningful up-to-date snapshot of your financial health. Building wealth is a matter of creating new assets and preserving your existing wealth.

Your financial needs and goals are unique. Your personal CFO should work with you to customize a plan based on the full range of financial and estate planning issues that you are likely to face now and over the course of your lifetime.

Risk Management

Your personal CFO should coordinate with all of your various insurance specialists to analyze your potential financial perils, determine potential risk factors, and provide critical insurance solutions to minimize exposure to those potential perils for you and your family. Your coordinator and the specialist should work together to use their intimate knowledge of your finances and asset structures to provide you with an advantage in identifying and understanding all of your insurance and estate planning needs.

Life, disability income, and long-term care insurance portfolios need to be specifically designed to offer you the best solutions possible. Help protect your loved ones in case of death or disability and offer as many cost recapture provisions as possible.

Selecting the right insurance is the first step, but as things change, you may need to review your insurance portfolio, much like your investment portfolio, the ownership structure of your policies, and whether or not they should be owned by trusts or individuals. You should also review your levels of coverage and types of coverage as your needs may change over time.

Testing: What-If Scenarios

One of the benefits of partnering with a financial professional or an advisor is that you can have the ability to access their knowledge and skills to take a look at many different possible scenarios. Since few of us know what the future holds, it's nice to have the ability to run various what-if scenarios and see the impact of your current strategies.

For example, what if we want to sell our home in the near future? What if my job is relocated? What if my child gets into an Ivy League school? What if I become sick, hurt, or can't work? What if we want to retire earlier?

Most firms have financial calculation software that allows these what-if scenarios to be created. Remember, math and money are not the same thing. It is important for you to use these what-if scenarios strictly as guideline figures only. Trying to plan for more than five to ten years at a time can be a very slippery slope. Ideally, you want to have a general outline and understanding of where you're headed financially, but whether we succeed or not will depend largely upon how often we review our plans and how effective we are at adjusting accordingly at stated, periodic intervals. If you can partner with a planner that will help guide you along the way, stay focused on the plan and continue to service you even when they're not selling you new products, then you will have found a financial professional who is likely to add substantial value to your plans.

If we're going to test for the maximum output, we can only change one variable at a time. This is the only way to conduct a science experiment. Then we conduct the second experiment. We can then determine how the revised outputs would change. If we change two or three variables at once, it is difficult to understand which variable affected the outcome.

My father has a master's degree in science, and explained to me long ago that in a laboratory setting, you need a sterile environment and can only change one variable at a time to account for variable change.

Sometimes, you have to perform multiple tests on that variable to determine the output and how it would impact the baseline sample. A model allows you to first take a look at how each variable impacts the overall output of the model, and then, ultimately, how coordinated or integrated strategies within the model can apply a second or third benefit to your overall outcomes.

A good planner will make sure that you also have built-in cost recovery mechanisms. You should attempt to find and recover any additional money that may be eluding you or siphoned out of your (financial) gas tank. Next, you'll need to coordinate all those different assets and protection classes.

Performance Monitoring, Reporting, and Tracking

Follow-ups: The devil is in the details. Plans succeed or fail based on your ability to monitor and make changes at regular intervals. Many people work with financial professionals who are happy to sell you products, but seem to vanish into thin air when it comes time to review these same programs.

We recommend that you have at least two face-to-face meetings per year with your planner. Many top firms will also provide access to a team of practitioners throughout the year. Some firms will also construct your own personal wealth management site. This may provide you with account aggregation software that can provide automatic daily updates to your financial planning roadmap. Some firms even provide web-based encrypted vaults for many of your personal documents.

Your CFO should also provide ongoing due diligence and monitoring of your insurance carriers and their financial strength as individual companies. Private placement may also need to be explored as an alternative to traditional policies.

Self Assessment Exercise

Do I need to hire a professional? Consider the following questions. Are any of these issues keeping you up at night?

Financial Organization

✓ What do I have? What do I owe?

✓ Is there a way to aggregate all of my financial assets and track the performance and overall asset allocation?

✓ How should I allocate my year-end bonus, tax refund, and any found money that comes my way throughout the year?

✓ How much of my income should I defer, if any, or what amount should I save regularly?

Insurance Planning

✓ Do I have the appropriate property and liability insurance, such as auto and home insurance coverage?

✓ How do I determine the proper deductibles?

✓ Do I need to consider long-term care insurance?

✓ In the event I have a large lawsuit, how much umbrella liability coverage should someone with my level of assets own?

Asset Management

✓ How can I reduce the risk level in my overall portfolio?

✓ Are my various investments performing well relative to their respective benchmarks?

✓ Should I allocate my IRAs, retirement savings plans, 401(k)s, and other accounts differently than that of my taxable accounts?

✓ Should I diversify using hedge funds, real estate investment trusts, commodities, or other nonmarket-correlated asset classes?

✓ How should our assets be owned, should they be owned in individual names as a joint account, tenants in common, or in a trust?

Retirement Issues

✓ What is the overall health of my retirement plan?

✓ Do I have enough money to retire?

✓ What type of retirement am I looking at?

✓ In which bucket of assets should I spend down first, second, and last?

Tax Planning

✓ Are your tax planning strategies looking toward the future?

✓ Do you typically have a written plan of action for managing your tax-based decisions each year, or are you trying to clean up the mess from the following year?

✓ Should I actively manage my capital gains and losses throughout the year? If so, how?

✓ Is it a good idea to get a tax refund? If not, why?

✓ Can I reduce my overall tax bill with regards to my investments?

These are not easy questions. They are not answered by using an internet site or a financial calculator. These are complex issues that will most likely require the collaborative efforts of multiple advisors. Ideally, your personal CFO can assist you in coordinating and integrating the design of these strategies into your ideal master financial plan.

No Shortcuts Here

Avoid the Con Men: Get rich quick with late night marketing . . .
no way!

There are no shortages of get-rich-quick scams out there, all seeking your money. Most of these guys get rich by selling you systems, and tapes designed to teach you how to get rich quick. Their strategies may work for one out of a million people. We usually see them on late night TV, along with the fast food commercials that attack us when we are tired and our minds are at their weakest.

They tell us to call and buy their systems so we can purchase real estate properties with little or no money down. They promote strategies designed to teach us how we can use other people's money instead of working hard and saving our own. How we can place tiny classified ads and become millionaires. Or how we can clear out the junk in our attics and basements to sell them online to make untold fortunes. I'm sure a few people who bought these books and systems have become wealthy, but very few have become as wealthy as people selling you their *systems* for three *easy* installments of $29.95.

The real winners are those that are selling you these systems. Why else would they spend millions of dollars to produce their systems, and then promote it only after midnight on local cable access channels? There are no shortcuts. A disciplined mindset is your best ally.

If I Hire a Professional, What Should I Pay?

You may look to a professional, or maybe you'll do it yourself. Either way, you need to be mindful of fees and expenses. Different firms compensate their professionals in various ways. Some firms charge fees only for their planning, others earn commissions and service fees, and others still earn salaries or a combination of bonuses and salaries. Ultimately, how your financial professional is paid has little consequence, as long as it is fair and mutually agreed upon between you and your planner.

There are also many firms that will not even pay commission if your household account value is under a certain threshold. I find this very interesting, given that many Americans have household portfolios that are substantially below $500,000. Do these firms believe that these people are not entitled to quality financial advice? I can understand that these accounts might not be as profitable as the larger accounts, but you should seek to work with a professional in a firm that values your business, no matter how many zeroes are attached to the statement.

The twenty-first-century planner will have to earn their money differently than they have in the past. It is no longer acceptable for them to earn an income or generate commission simply by adding a little bit of performance value to the portfolio. They must also be able to help you eliminate unnecessary transfers and cut out redundant fees. In short, they must be able to help you find the money to fund your financial programs.

You should seek to partner with planners who will add value many times over by their ability to find money for you, opposed to those who would have you believe that they can outsmart the market, and that their advice is worth renting their brain at above market prices.

There are thousands of advisors to choose from. Not all of them charge the same. I'm not saying you should go to a bargain-basement, do-it-yourself shop if you don't have those skill sets. A good planner deserves to earn a living, and the pricing should be fair. Management fees may vary depending on the level of services offered, number of contacts per year, and the complexity of your needs.

Review and Update Periodically

Even the best laid plans can fail if allowed to run their course without corrections and regular reviews. When I was in the army, we studied the science of ballistic velocity. We learned that if our aim was slightly off, that the bullet would continue off course as it flies through the air. Once it reaches the distance of the target, which may be very far away, the bullet may miss the center mass of the target or entirely. The same is true of our financial projections. Above all, make sure that you and your planner or planning team are keeping up-to-date with regular reviews.

During the course of each year, you should set aside some time to review your finances with your advisor. How do you know whether you have a garden variety financial professional or a personal CFO? Here are a few questions that they should be able to answer. Your review may consist of a telephone conference or a face-to-face interview. Either is fine and is largely based upon the relationship that you and your advisor share.

1. If you have non-qualified or (non-retirement accounts), ask your advisor what they plan to do about the compound tax issue that may begin to impact your investments over time. Do

they have a strategy to help you continue to grow your account while flattening or eliminating your additional taxes over time?

2. What is their backup plan in case diversification doesn't work? While many financial advisors have bet their careers on the concept of asset allocation, there are a few people that feel that asset allocation is nothing more than a myth. At least in the year 2008, asset allocation did appear to be nothing more than a myth, as stocks went down, bonds went down, and even money markets threatened to break the buck. The best approach to combat this risk is generally a layered approach geared toward the utilization of different pools of capital at different points of time. This way, you can weather any financial storm and allow your other remaining assets to remain fully invested during periods of market volatility. Is your advisor currently helping you plan this way?

3. What is your game plan to help me get back the interest that I'm spending on my consumer purchases, the interest on my automotive financing costs, and the interest that I'm paying on my mortgage and other debts? A personal CFO can show you strategies designed to help recover or recapture some or all of these costs.

4. What plans and programs do you have in place to help me recover some of my insurance premium costs?

Chapter Highlights

➤ Should you consider hiring a financial professional?
➤ Design your own selection criteria.
➤ Understand the difference between needs-based planning vs. economic driven strategies.
➤ Do you want to do it yourself, hire a salesman, or a personal financial CFO?

CHAPTER 6
FINANCIAL LAND MINES

SILENT PARTNERS, TOLL TAKERS, AND WEALTH TRAPS IDENTIFIED THE ENEMIES: AVOID THE WEALTH LEAKS IN YOUR PLAN

Figure 6.1   Beware of the Wealth Raiders.

My goal is to help you learn how and why your money may be eroded, confiscated, or transferred without you even knowing it. We want to help you clarify the misinformation from the media, financial books, magazines, newspapers, television, and various other sources. This includes financial advisors who may mean well but who often hurt more than they help. You only have one opportunity to reach your full potential; let's do it the right way.

Let's examine some of the major obstacles that may stand in your way. These factors will affect your life and may impact every financial decision you make. These guys are your silent partners from the minute that you enter the world, until the day you leave.

They are:

1. Government (and Taxes)
2. Corporate America
3. Financial Institutions (Banks, Insurance Companies, Credit Unions, Money Management Firms, and other Investment Service Providers)
4. Media and Information
5. Inflation

Know Thy Opponents: Toll Takers

Figure 6.2   It's tough to fill a leaky bucket.

Your Wealth Bucket Is Leaking!

Who is causing these transfers? In order to prosper financially, you must identify and then create an environment that will allow you to deal with them more effectively. These institutions create situations, control the outcomes, and profit from them. Now you can too. In the past, we may have obtained financial advice from these sources and the outcome wasn't quite what we thought it would be.

You may discover that the financial solutions provided may profit the toll takers more than they will you. Their process often results in higher taxes, more fees, and higher borrowing costs. Owing to a lack of financial understanding, most people are scared to make major financial decisions. Fear paralyzes us and causes us to hesitate when we need to make a crucial decision. In any war, battle, or argument, you will need to know everything about your opponent in order to have a chance of winning.

You versus the Big Boys: Your Silent Partners on the Road to Wealth

Pay no attention to that man behind the curtain. Most of us remember seeing the image of *The Wizard of Oz* being unveiled as no more than an ordinary man operating from behind a great curtain. However, few of us see the mirage that is painted before us by Madison Avenue, New York City and the banking system.

Our goal is to highlight and identify the areas where you may be receiving inaccurate information. This often appears in the media, financial services sales campaigns, magazines, textbooks, and other popular financial mediums. In striving to achieve a better financial life, you need to incorporate the principals laid out in this book into your everyday thinking and actions. Many suggestions may seem to run against the grain of conventional financial teaching.

Cast of Characters

So you graduated from school and got a new job. Welcome to the system! It's time for us to celebrate and everyone wants to come to the party. Banks celebrate when you receive your first paycheck. You'll soon be lending it to them each week using direct deposit. When you go to ask for it back, in the form of a loan, they'll hand it over (plus interest).

The government shows up too. It congratulates you on your new position by taking about 33 percent of your paycheck. The state also crashes the party, takes its cut, along with the city where you live. They make the rules. Don't forget the consumer financing companies and corporate America. They might just bring a few products along for you to check out.

Government

The primary function of the government is to protect its people. Protection from both foreign and domestic enemies includes the personal protection of property and the protection of the sacred American values of life, liberty (freedom), and the pursuit of happiness.

There are some other areas where government is typically involved. Typically, one of those areas is basic education of its habitants and citizens, providing for the poor and indigent of the population, and providing a police force to protect us from domestic problems or violence. A justice system of laws, courts, and jails is an extension of this platform. The government generally provides for national defense, social services, and financial support for ongoing programs to provide for anyone in need, like unemployment programs, disability, and so on.

Infrastructure is often the charge of government. Some projects are funded at the state level, while others at the federal level. Typically, these projects create or enhance roads, waterways, and basic sanitation systems. These projects facilitate trade and transportation for its citizens to move freely within its borders. All of this costs money. Beyond those basic issues, the relevance of government can be widely debated. This book is not a political book, so we will only examine the financial consequences of larger government.

Governments exist at the federal, state, and local levels. They also regulate money supplies, make or pass various financial laws, rules, and regulations that impact and complicate your ability to build wealth. It seems that these rules are often changing. We believe that income taxes are among some of the greatest areas that you are transferring wealth unknowingly or unnecessarily throughout your lifetime.

Once you take into consideration all the different types of taxes, most people are surprised to see how high of a tax bracket they're actually in. This is defined as a percentage of your total income. We want to show you different strategies to lower your taxes without adding any additional costs to what you're currently doing.

Wherever wealth is accumulated, someone will try to take it. Theft has been around since the beginning of time. The concept of theft is very simple. Don't create anything of value; just steal the production of others. The biggest thief in the world is the Internal Revenue Service (IRS). Federal income taxes are one of the most serious financial roadblocks in accumulating wealth. The effects of taxation often affect your financial well-being.

Many people have this feeling but lack the ability to explain how it happens. Here's a quick example: What if you went out for a day of boating in the Caribbean, and were suddenly overtaken by pirates who pulled out guns and cannons and instructed you to give them your money and valuables? Most people would agree that their actions constitute theft.

What if pirates met with the public before the robbery to explain how they were going to divide the contents of your possessions and distribute it among all of them? They feel that since you earn more than them, your wealth should be divided more fairly among the crowd. Sounds like someone in the government likes the concept of Robin Hood. . . . Only, we're not rich villains. Our tax law seems to take money from some people and gives it to other people who didn't earn it. The law benefits one citizen at the expense of another by doing what the citizen himself cannot do without committing a crime.

If you succeed financially, you'll find yourself paying more taxes. You can count on this. Politicians carry out these perversions of law under the concept of taxation. We are dealing with a parasite–host relationship. The government is not capable of producing any revenue, therefore gets all of its sustenance from the productive element of society. Government in general is a parasite and lives off the productive taxpayers (hosts). If the parasite takes all the produce from the host, then both parties die.

Governments have traditionally paid for expenses in three main ways: taxes, printing money, and war (accomplished from plundering their neighboring countries).

Government Spending

Government spending is out of control. It took us 198 years for the government to borrow $1 trillion. By 2007, it rose to 59 trillion. . . . Once we include all of the government liabilities (entitlements, such as Medicare, Social Security, and Medicaid). This represents our national debt. If something is not done soon, we are all doomed.

By 2006, the interest payments alone on our national debt were running over $400 billion per year. Interest payments consume approximately 17 percent of all federal revenue. It now represents the largest, single expense of our nation. This is greater than our budget for our national defense, larger than the combined costs of the Department of Education, Department of Housing and Urban Development, the Justice System, Department of Energy, Department of Agriculture, Department of Labor, Department of State, Department of Transportation, and the Department of Veterans Affairs, combined. The charges are not paid by government; they are paid by American citizens. This money is provided through taxes and inflation. The cost of the interest expenses alone is currently about $5,000 for each family of four. All families pay through inflation, but not all pay taxes. When we examine further we see that the cost to each taxpaying family is higher.

On average, much more than $5,000 is extracted from your family each year, which provides no real benefits and doesn't retire any old debt, it simply goes to interest. Nothing is produced by it. No roads, no government buildings, no welfare benefits, no medical benefits, no salaries, and our standard of living does not increase at all. It does nothing except pay interest (and the interest compounds)! If the government were to completely stop its deficit spending, the total would still continue to grow as a result of the interest on the portion that already exists.

Today interest on the national debt is consuming almost 40 percent of the revenue collected by income tax. The problem is Congress does not live within its income, but it tells its citizens to do it. Other expenses are not only paid from taxes, but by selling government bonds, which causes us to go deeper in debt every year. If we could reduce the size of the bureaucracy of the American government, then personal and corporate income taxes could be potentially eliminated and the government might even have an annual surplus.

Unfortunately, the size of the government continues to grow larger. Today, welfare benefits in almost half of our states are higher than the average wages of many clerical workers. In a handful of states, welfare pays more than entry-level wages for other skilled workers.

Where it is possible for people to vote on issues involving the transfer of wealth, our ballot boxes become weapons where the majority plunders the minority. Eventually when this happens, those who are tired of having the wealth confiscated and carrying the load eventually join those that are stealing wealth, and the productive part of the economy continues to shrink until only the state remains and we reach a state of total socialism.

Today, half of our entitlements, such as Medicare, Social Security, Medicaid, and government retirement programs are all based on the promise of future payments. Many of these are contractual obligations and millions of people already depend on them. That does not mean they can't be eliminated. Even though entitlements represent a huge portion of our budget, we spend over $20 billion per year for food stamps. However, there's no contractual obligation to continue those payments, only the promise of political gain.

We've all seen people pay with food stamps and then leave with luxury handbags. This program has rarely helped the hungry, but simply helps buy votes. Elimination of programs like these may help us operate more efficiently and help pay higher benefits for those who need it.

Unfortunately, the federal government does not abide by the natural laws of paying on a cash basis. Therefore, the money that comes in for future obligations is usually spent immediately and replaced by government IOUs. In the future, when those payments are due, the money must come from revenues collected under current revenue streams.

Take into account the fact that entitlements currently represent about half of all federal outlays (or 50 percent). Now add just the 15 percent that is being spent on interest payments on our national debt. We reach the scary conclusion that nearly two-thirds of all federal expenses are on autopilot, and that percentage is continuing to grow each month.

The only solution is for Congress to stop the spending programs and live within its means. Today, even if we dismantle the military, shut down every agency and bureau, and board up all the government buildings including the White House, we would still only be able to reduce our current spending nationally by about one-third . . . and more of that discretionary spending continues to be eroded by the entitlement programs. The reality is that congress is not decelerating, but accelerating its spending and printing money at a very alarming rate.

Federal Bankruptcy? Is this Possible?

When we use the term *federal bankruptcy*, we don't necessarily mean that the federal government will stop being able to spend money and write checks. The federal government is not likely to stop collecting revenue from taxes any time in the near future. Instead, we mean that at the rate the government is spending money, the checks and money won't buy anything of importance. As our dollar weakens in the world economy, we suffer both at home and abroad.

Government Spending and National Debt Ramifications

The really bad news for us is that the government obtains every cent of the dollars that it will use to pay back the interest on its debts by confiscating it in the first place with taxes and inflation.

During freshman macroeconomics class, I studied the money supply. We learned that the federal government prints and controls our money supply (with the nation's banks). As we examined the money supply further, we also learned that much of our money comes out of one pocket and into another, minus a substantial handling fee from the banking system. Many people look at our national debt figures with a detached fascination. As we read our financial periodicals, we may even remark about the interesting numbers and facts, and sort of chuckle before moving on with our lives. Few of us understand what, if any, difference these numbers make to us personally. You need to understand how it impacts your wealth.

With the prospect of national bankruptcy looming on the horizon, our government continues to make multi-billion or even multi-trillion dollar promises of goods and services from the government. This government seems to grow more parasitically on the produce and energy of the productive part of the American people; yet politicians don't seem to want to do anything about it. Why should one-third (or more) of our income be taken away by income taxes and sales taxes?

When a government gets too big, it runs the risk of collapsing on itself. We have seen this play out many times in world history. Whenever taxes become too onerous on the people, industry and progress is stifled. Unless the politicians learn to live within their means, it will be up to you to learn how to protect yourself from further confiscation of your wealth.

Corporations: Marketing 101 Class

Understand the difference between needs and wants; man is the only living creature that seems to care about the difference of things which in no way affects their use or functionality. Nature has given man the ability to reason, think, and engineer everything that he needs to improve his life better than any of the other animals. He is also the only living creature that does not find his food in the state that he desires. Virtually everything that man needs must be fitted or adapted to his needs.

He cooks his food to the desired temperature. He looks for ways to make his life easier, softer, warmer, and works hard to create a more comfortable environment. He surrounds his body with clothes because he does not like the temperature that surrounds him. He even builds and extends his environment by creating a home that can facilitate a new environment—a better environment than what nature can provide.

He is constantly adapting nature to his needs. As this happened, his tastes became refined and demanding. Mere survival was no longer an acceptable means of living for him. He has developed taste and preference. He has preference in objects of different colors and different forms. He values things for their variety, rarity, shape, and even texture. Man likes the difference of things, and corporations have been created to manufacture, create, and produce an endless supply of products and services to fulfill man's every desire. This is the difference between needs and wants.

Marketing

We're taught how to consume from an early age. We are driven to shopping malls by advertising, public relations, and product promotion specialists.

The comedian George Carlin referenced in one of his final televised performances that America has become nothing more than a coast-to-coast shopping mall, where there are huge mega-malls; and in between each mega-mall lies the mini-malls; and in between the mini-malls are the shopping centers, strip malls, and stand-alone retail centers.

George Carlin left out that on almost every other buildable acre in America, banks were erected to hold our money for us. These banks earn a profit while financing the merry-go-round of constructing a never-ending supply of retail space to serve an unending appetite of consumer purchases. How ridiculous!

Corporate America and Madison Avenue Advertisers

Corporations make consumer products and design various services and other offerings in an effort to enhance and improve both the necessary and convenient items in our lives. With a never-ending supply of gizmos, gadgets, and products, corporations have developed a methodical formula of how to create, build, and sustain a constant consumer base. This is evidenced by the consumer spending component of our gross national product (GNP). It continues to increase decade over decade to the point that now consumers account for nearly 70 percent of all the goods and services consumed in our great nation.

Many of these products have finite lifetimes and need to constantly be replaced over a definite and defined lifecycle. Vehicles wear out, rust out, and break down. They need to be replaced. Colors, design elements, styles, and other enhancements that do not materially affect the products functionality are used to persuade us to replace our existing products. Corporate America is constantly convincing us to purchase unnecessary replacement items.

Caveat Emptor . . . or *buyer beware*. I learned this phrase in one of my first Wharton lecture halls during a freshman-year marketing class. *Marketing* is the science of convincing consumers of the need for a new product or service. We learned all about the four Ps of marketing: product, placement, price, and performance. We learned that Corporate America and Madison Avenue in New York City is not necessarily the friend of the consumer. They are the instrument of the manufacturers and owners of America.

This is why we are more likely to see a luxury car (or two) in the driveway than a healthy retirement account. We have been conditioned to value the perception of wealth above actual wealth, and the true freedom that it offers. Instead, we have become slaves to our possessions. From the time we're born, we're bombarded on a daily basis with a constant and steady supply of advertisements from television, radio, billboards, bumper stickers, and other mass media. Today, we even have buses and subway cars wrapped in advertisements. We see advertisements in taxicabs, elevators, and even attached to the doors in restrooms. Some companies have even paid professional athletes to tattoo their bodies with their logos. It is absolutely ridiculous and it is no wonder why very few of us have a chance of succeeding against corporate America.

The ultimate goal is to get you to spend your money. The deck is stacked against us from the minute we enter the world. Almost as soon as we're brought home from the hospital, our family begins to introduce us to our national pastime: shopping! Function is subordinated to form, feel, color, and texture. Parents purchase items for their children that are not based on practical use but rather on the cosmetic appeal of these items.

By default, we seem to train our young children to become consumers. They're taught to purchase things; to appreciate things for their superficial value.

From the time we're young, we're exposed to toys, fast food, and all types of other manipulative commercials. It's very rare that the hamburger we get at the fast food restaurant looks anything like the one in the commercial. The toys we purchase don't quite seem to have the same allure as they did on the TV commercial.

They make the cars look so attractive in the showrooms, but are never quite as beautiful a few weeks after we purchase them. A year or two after we've had the new vehicle, it has a few cigarette burns in the seats and a few dents on the body paneling from the occasional trip to the grocery store. Once the children have spilled baby formula, cookies, soda, and other sticky substances on our leather seats, a $50,000 vehicle quickly looks like everything else on the road.

You quickly start to realize that Corporate America is not our friend and they're out to get every dollar we have. Unfortunately, we buy into the need to replace and purchase new products well before the original product has outlived its useful lifetime. We have become a consumer culture where people are spending most of their free time buying things they don't need with money they don't have on products that they can't remember why they bought when they get home.

From the time we're children playing with each other, how often have we coveted someone else's toy or personal possession? How quickly do we discard it or toss it away once we possess it? . . . Only to repeat the cycle over and over until we find ourselves buried under the yolk of revolving consumer debt. Remember our discussion on the calculation of opportunity costs.

Financial Institutions

The banking process is arguably one of the most important businesses in the world. Without it, all other businesses come to a stop. Whenever a business transaction takes place, money must flow from one party to another in a short period of time. The flow of money must come from a supply (the banking system). The banking system is a massive network of banks and central banks that span the entire globe. Their capital fuels the world's economies.

The banking industry controls the money supply. There is only a pool of money in the world. This pool is managed by many different institutions such as: banks, insurance companies, corporations, and individuals throughout the world.

It is similar to our own natural ecosystem. The earth surface is covered by water. As the sun heats the water, it evaporates into the atmosphere. The water travels around the earth and returns in the form of rain and other precipitation. In the end, it ends up back in the oceans.

The banking business is similar to that where the money flows from the pool to our hands to meet our financial needs and somewhere along the process it ends up back in the banking system (and the tax system). It is important to pay attention to the banking process. If you don't, you may end up transferring your wealth.

Financial institutions play by different rules than individuals. Specifically, most pension plans, retirement programs, even the Social Security system are designed in a very similar fashion. Typically, they are designed so that capital contributions and payments are made at regular intervals. Next, they are placed in a central account where they can be managed and invested for long periods of time that also offer the added benefit of charging fees and expenses over this time. They are held for as long as possible, and the goal is to pay back as little as possible, typically in the form of interest from the capital base, as opposed to distributing the capital base itself.

There are several advantages to financial institutions by structuring the program in this fashion. First, they're able to charge fees. Typically, these fees are based on a capital base, which is the larger of the two numbers, as opposed to the interest that is paid. Second, they can control the assets, and in some instances, use them for other purposes, thereby obtaining a second or third use of the capital. Finally, they are sometimes able to use them as an asset on their balance sheet in order to acquire other loans or access to other lines of capital. It is important that you understand how this system works so that you can leverage and use it to your benefit.

Banks

How do the banks impact our ability to build wealth? Consider this example: Let's assume that your bank pays you 3 percent interest and charges other customers who want to borrow your money 7 percent interest. That 4 percent difference is called a spread. This is the first way that banks make money. Of course, they are not only lending your money; they are lending parts of every customer's money at various times to many other customers (or borrowers). Sometimes customers may even borrow their own money. Some people have loan balances that are lower than the corresponding amounts saved in CDs with the same institution.

Figure 6.3   Your money will be *safe* with us!

Imagine the same $50,000 that they borrow at 6 percent from their own bank. . . . It is only earning 2 percent in a savings account at the same bank. Talk about driving down the financial highway with one foot on the gas and one on the brakes. . . . *So that's how the bank paid for all of those free toasters and china sets. You always pay . . . Are you beginning to get it? If not reread this chapter over and over again!*

However, you must remember that they are profit-making businesses. They make their money by lending, investing, and accumulating their customers' money, charging fees, commissions, or interest.

The financial institutions also employ very smart people who are creative and skilled in ways to improve their profits.

On the other hand, consumers are generally not experts in most financial matters. Many don't even know how to balance a checkbook. Many have not had any specific or technical training in the art of building wealth or the science of making money. Most consumers are too busy running their lives to notice what these opponents are doing to them.

The banks plundering of the people does not end there. If that were all the banks made, they would not be very profitable and some might even go out of business. Banks have many expenses to pay and could not pay their overhead and earn a profit on only a 4 percent spread. In reality, banks earn interest many times over by using the flow of money concepts.

Banking Example: Additions versus Multiplication

One of my first finance courses explained how banks actually make money. Prior to attending that course, we were of the opinion that banks made money on the spread, which is the difference between the amount they lend and the amount they credit to the depositors.

For example, if you deposited a $1,000 from your paycheck at the end of the week, the bank may credit your $1,000 savings account deposit by 2 percent. Conversely, if you wanted to borrow money for an automotive purchase or a mortgage, the bank may lend you the money at a rate somewhere around 5 or 6 percent interest (maybe higher). The difference between the 2 percent that they are crediting you (depositors) on their money and then lending at 6 percent is about 4 percent. This would mean that for every $1 million the bank has in deposits, they would earn 4 percent annually on that money, or approximately $40,000.

As we begin to take a look at the operating expenses of running a bank branch that includes construction and building costs, leasing costs, employee salaries, advertising, insurance costs, and other fixed operating expenses, we learned that banks need to earn money in other areas.

We also learned the secret science of banking. Banks have mastered the science of multiplying their dollars in order to create many uses on the same dollar. Normally when we borrow money from a bank, we are given a repayment schedule. That payment schedule breaks down the terms, conditions, and timelines for the repayment of my loan.

When we make our mortgage payment, our payment is aggregated with thousands, if not millions of other mortgage payments to the bank. As those dollars return to the banks with the payment schedule, they are not allowed to sit idle in the bank vault. The loan officers at the bank immediately lend them out again, but this time perhaps on an automotive finance loan.

The new payments from the automotive finance loans are again aggregated and returned to the bank where it can be sent out for more loans on credit cards, consumer loans, boat loans, small business loans, equipment financing loans, and so on. Remember, these are the same dollars that were originally lent to you for a mortgage loan!

Most of my clients would be happy with an annual return of 8 to 10 percent. If we could offer that type of return regularly, most people would say: "Sign me up." Not the banks.

We learned that banks generally try to earn anywhere from ten to as many as twenty turns on each dollar that is lent. Therefore, the bank is not only making a 4 percent spread on your deposits, it is also making all of the interest charges on loans 2–20! It is not uncommon for a bank to earn more than 50 percent on each dollar loaned. Remember, this is in addition to the initial spread, and separate from all of their add-on convenience charges, costs, and ATM fees. Keep in mind that all of this is accomplished by lending your paycheck. Without your deposits, the bank would have less to lend.

Some people actually walk into the bank and deposit their paycheck. The teller hands them a deposit slip and a lollipop. They will be earning a very low rate of return for lending the bank their paycheck. Then if they proceed to walk over to the bank's lending department (marked by a small desk, two chairs, and a plant), ten feet away from the teller window . . . they can apply for a loan.

Sometimes the loan is for a lower amount than they have in their bank account! I don't understand this. Why would someone borrow money from a bank at 6 percent when they have the same money in an account that is earning less than 6 percent? We see this all the time. Sometimes it's in a savings account earning 3 percent, or a CD earning 4 percent. Don't they understand that the bank is giving them back their own money? (And charging them interest!) I can understand if they are earning a higher rate of return than the interest rate on the loan.

We ask our clients this question often. Unfortunately, most people like to see that they have money available to them in a savings or checking account. It makes them feel secure. Apparently, people are still willing to pay money as long as someone else will hold their money for them, provide a monthly statement, and pay them a little interest for their deposits (just like the goldsmiths). They don't mind paying the bank a little interest. Few see how this adds up over time.

It's that simple. When you begin to understand how a bank operates, it becomes apparent that you must also conduct your affairs in a similar manner. How many turns are you getting on your money? I can help you begin to think and act like a bank.

Banks are notorious for helping themselves to your wallet. They even have their own process to accomplish this goal. They create plenty of fees. Banks have many financial products such as credit cards, home loans, auto loans, checking accounts, savings accounts, CDs, and ATMs that all create fees; late fees, early withdrawal fees, minimum balance fees, debit fees, and sometimes even fees to talk to a live person. Late fees are a huge business.

Even our billing cycles have been purposefully shortened. Financial firms used to send out the bill fourteen days before, now it's closer to ten days before the due date . . . and due date may even be on a weekend! Wouldn't it be terrific if we could be the bank? If something you thought to be true wasn't true, when would you want to know? Examine things differently and view them from new and different perspectives.

Once your emergency account is funded with 6 to 12 months of expenses saved, you can start to say goodbye to the banks. You can eventually use them simply to handle your checking account. Your savings and investments can start to explore greener pastures and higher potential rates of return.

Inflation

The next hurdle is inflation. When you replace goods in the future, they will most likely cost more. If your money is not earning a rate of return equal to or greater than the rate at which goods and services are increasing, it's a problem. I used to work on garbage trucks when I was in college. It paid really well. Some of the guys used to cash their paychecks and literally stick it under the mattress. And I used to try to educate them and teach them that if you do that long enough, not only will you sleep poorly for the next thirty years, but when you go to pull the money out, it's purchasing power will be rotted away. The purchasing power has been eroded because of the costs of goods and services are ever rising and ever increasing. You need to make sure that you're earning a rate of return equal to or greater than the rising cost of inflation net of taxes. That can become a big number!

Inflation is one of the greatest culprits that will eliminate and erode our wealth over time. It literally causes our money to rot away (in terms of its purchasing power). By taking a look at the following table, you can see that inflation actually eats away and destroys the purchasing power of our dollar on a more consistent and vigorous basis than just about any other factor, aside from an occasional stock market crash.

It is for this reason that you must work diligently to make sure that your investments are earning a rate of return equal to or greater than the inflation rate and net of taxes, at all times. In fact, this margin, the after tax inflation adjusted return is the most critical measurement of your real wealth growth.

Consider it this way. If you cashed your paycheck every week, walked home with $100 bills and stuffed them under the mattress, not only will you have slept poorly for the next 30 years, but when you go to pull that money out and use it, it will literally have been rotted away in terms of its purchasing power. Think about it another way. If you go back to Chapter Four and take a stroll through the history of money, remember that we once used commodities as money. If instead of $1 million under your mattress you had a million ears of corn or a million dollars worth of cows, how much of that corn or how many of those cows would be alive in 30 years. Remember, at one time you had to actually trade those items for something else of value.

We must understand that money is actually a commodity. It is simply used in a paper form or represented as numbers on a computer screen in order to make life easier for us. Never lose sight of the fact that money is a commodity and is just as precious as if you had a million ears of corn in a silo in your backyard! If you don't get that corn moving and generating a second or third use, it will surely rot away and evaporate over time, and your wealth will evaporate along with it.

This is why it continues to amaze me that billions of dollars are invested in certificates of deposit at banks across the nation. There are actually armies of individuals who scan the newspapers religiously each week, looking for the banks who offer the highest rates of return for CDs. These rates are almost always equal to or less than the long-term inflation rate (once adjusted for after-tax yields). It's comical when people brag about the fact that they earned wonderful rates of return through the Carter administration on their CDs and checking accounts. I know that CDs did hit double digit returns. Some people earned 15 percent on CDs. Those people quickly forget, on a relative basis, that inflation was going up at 17 or 18 percent. Therefore, their real rate of return was still flat . . . or negative!

It is for this reason that you must view your money as a commodity, and understand that it must fully be working for you at all times. Ideally, earning two or three rates of return at the same time, and generating additional purposes for you and you alone. This is the same principal that casinos have used for years. By giving you chips to play with instead of actual dollars, it becomes easier for you to make larger bets. There is a detached fascination surrounding the different colored chips that are placed on various gaming tables. In the heat of the moment, anyone can get caught up in the excitement and emotion, and fail to equate those chips with actual dollars. If we were placing $20 bills every roll on the craps tables, we might think twice about each and every roll.

Banks and the casinos both understand that by creating the rules, and forcing people to conform to their rules, they stand a greater probability of financial success over long periods of time. In the end, the law of large numbers and averages, always wins. It is for this reason that you must work hard and diligently with your personal CFO to create a system that helps you slowly take back control of your money, and become your own bank the rest of your financial life.

Example: See the table below to view how your wealth may be eroded to even a 3 percent annual inflation rate. Just follow the last column on the right to see your purchasing power per $1,000 disappear right before your eyes!

Age	Year #	Annual Savings	Cumulative Amount Saved	Potential Return	Wealth Erosion	Account Value
20	1	1,000	1,000	-3.00%	0	$1,000
21	2		1,000	-3.00%	-30	$970

(continued)

(*continued*)

Age	Year #	Annual Savings	Cumulative Amount Saved	Potential Return	Wealth Erosion	Account Value
22	3		1,000	-3.00%	-59	$941
23	4		1,000	-3.00%	-87	$913
24	5		1,000	-3.00%	-115	$885
25	6		1,000	-3.00%	-141	$859
26	7		1,000	-3.00%	-167	$833
27	8		1,000	-3.00%	-192	$808
28	9		1,000	-3.00%	-216	$784
29	10		1,000	-3.00%	-240	$760
30	11		1,000	-3.00%	-263	$737
31	12		1,000	-3.00%	-285	$715
32	13		1,000	-3.00%	-306	$694
33	14		1,000	-3.00%	-327	$673
34	15		1,000	-3.00%	-347	$653
35	16		1,000	-3.00%	-367	$633
36	17		1,000	-3.00%	-386	$614
37	18		1,000	-3.00%	-404	$596
38	19		1,000	-3.00%	-422	$578
39	20		1,000	-3.00%	-439	$561
40	21		1,000	-3.00%	-456	$544
41	22		1,000	-3.00%	-473	$527
42	23		1,000	-3.00%	-488	$512
43	24		1,000	-3.00%	-504	$496
44	25		1,000	-3.00%	-519	$481
45	26		1,000	-3.00%	-533	$467
46	27		1,000	-3.00%	-547	$453
47	28		1,000	-3.00%	-561	$439
48	29		1,000	-3.00%	-574	$426
49	30		1,000	-3.00%	-587	$413
50	31		1,000	-3.00%	-599	$401
51	32		1,000	-3.00%	-611	$389

Age	Year #	Annual Savings	Cumulative Amount Saved	Potential Return	Wealth Erosion	Account Value
52	33		1,000	-3.00%	-623	$377
53	34		1,000	-3.00%	-634	$366
54	35		1,000	-3.00%	-645	$355
55	36		1,000	-3.00%	-656	$344
56	37		1,000	-3.00%	-666	$334
57	38		1,000	-3.00%	-676	$324
58	39		1,000	-3.00%	-686	$314
59	40		1,000	-3.00%	-695	$305
60	41		1,000	-3.00%	-704	$296
61	42		1,000	-3.00%	-713	$287
62	43		1,000	-3.00%	-722	$278
63	44		1,000	-3.00%	-730	$270
64	45		1,000	-3.00%	-738	$262
65	46		1,000	-3.00%	-746	$254

Media

People are sometimes financially manipulated by the media and financial institutions to serve their agendas. The media often gives us misinformation or conflicting messages. Sometimes the people who provide this information are not doing so for any particular financial gain or to harm you, they simply believe they are experts and have some knowledge in a particular area.

This is often done in an effort to promote a strategy or product that they believe will help more people than it will hurt. However, many products that are sold in a vacuum do very little to help any consumers. You would be hard pressed to find even a single product that has solved the financial problems of the masses.

Our formal educational system does very little to train us in the science of money. Financial education is virtually nonexistent. There are courses in art, woodshop, auto shop, dance, and home economics at most high schools. Unfortunately, there are few courses on money. The system fails us in almost every regard with respect to learning how to make wise consumer decisions and instilling the values necessary to prevent us from falling prey to Corporate America.

In fact, most of the educational institutions don't even teach us how to balance a checkbook. In my small family, we have college degrees from Wharton School of the University of Pennsylvania, Harvard University, Cornell University, Fordham University, law schools, graduate school diplomas, and Nursing degrees. Not one of those schools gave us any specific training in how to balance a consumer checkbook! It may have been buried in a textbook, but no classes were offered on basic consumer decision-making skills. We had to learn it from other family members.

What if your family members never learned those skills? Worse, what if they learned the wrong things? Where does that leave you? It is amazing that the country is not in worse financial shape. What a sad state of affairs.

From the time we graduate school, we are bombarded with advertisements. Most of us will have concluded our formal education at around ages 18 to 25. We will continue our informal education for the rest of our lives. This informal education will typically come from traditional media sources such as television programs, newspapers, magazines, radio, billboards, the internet, and so on.

During this time, we will also be subject to the advertising and manipulation of Madison Avenue, American corporations, financial institutions, banks, automotive finance companies, credit card companies, and other special interest groups who are looking to confiscate our wealth.

With life expectancies approaching the century mark, it's impossible to think we can be impervious to this constant advertising bombardment for the next 75 years! You'll be barraged by a never-ending stream of advertisements seeking to confiscate your wealth. The only way to protect yourself is to develop a strategy and system to create a force field around your wealth and mind.

You'll need a game plan and it needs to be grounded in core values, beliefs, and a singular purpose to succeed financially. What do you want to achieve?

Advice: Old Myths and Wives Tales

Where does your advice come from? It's time for you to confront your mistakes. Where do you get your information? It may be learned from our parents who learned it from their parents. It may come from friends, neighbors, coworkers, or financial periodicals. As a result of individual financial experiences, fear has often worked its way into our financial thought process. Stock market crashes, bank failures and closings, unemployment rates, recessions and depressions, foreclosures, and wars have shaped our history. As a result, survival, not success, has become the goal for many. This fear has worked its way into our financial decisions.

The only proven way for getting ahead is creating a coordinated and integrated strategy formed from many different complex moving parts working together in concert with one another to perform the task. Unfortunately, many people want to believe that they're all set because they own some fragmented financial or insurance products.

It's a lot easier to think you're all set. This creates a false sense of security that leaves many people very unhappy when they reach the end of their rainbow and find that their pot of gold is little more than a cup full of tin. Unfortunately, there are many people trying to capture our money while we are trying to hang on to it. Most consumers will fall prey to the never-ending stream of advertisements and commercials. Our goal is to enlighten you a little bit and help you see that there are many corporations and businesses that are trying to convince you that you need the newest, latest, greatest, most improved product available.

It seems that we can't walk into a major appliance or electronics business without them trying to convincing us that the television we're watching the football game on needs to be replaced. How can you possibly enjoy the Super Bowl with only a 42-inch plasma flat screen, when we have 60-inch plasma flat screens in high definition? Are you cheap or something? How can you possibly enjoy the food you brought home unless it's being kept cold in a stainless steel refrigerator! This is madness!

Those who are really in control understand that core values are the most important thing and only by starving the short-term impulse to purchase and satisfying short-term wants are we able to stay on course with our financial goals.

Armed with our new knowledge, the intellectual side of our brain is able to overcome the emotional side and gives us the strength to remain steadfast in our efforts to save capital, which can be used to create real security and real freedom.

Chapter Highlights

Financial institutions have a clear advantage over consumers by knowing the secret science of making money and building wealth. However, learning how to interact with these financial institutions improves your chances of learning the science and building your own wealth.

➤ Understand the default environment for your money.

➤ Examine how financial institutions, Corporate America, and taxes are impacting your wealth.

➤ Take steps to eliminate these costs whenever possible.

CHAPTER 7
TAXES

"No taxation without representation!"

"Taxation *with* representation isn't so great either!"

Figure 7.1   Don't forget your Uncle Sam.

You make a dollar and it's taxed. It's taxed at the federal, state, and local levels. You pay into the Federal Insurance Contributions Act (FICA); you pay into Medicare. When you do have a couple bucks left, you get to go home and pay taxes for the privilege of living in your house . . . (if you're lucky enough to own a home). When you pay your cable, gas, electric, and telephone bill, there are more state taxes to pay. There are more taxes every time you turn around.

When you finally get to keep a couple dollars that you have the ability to make a decision on (spend or save), those dollars are taxed again. Go out to dinner, you pay a tax. Buy groceries, you pay a tax. Buy clothes for the kids, you pay a tax. It's amazing how many taxes we pay, and why there's not a tea party every weekend in Boston. It's crazy. The 16th amendment of the United States allowed taxation and became the first step in a long journey of dependency.

The shell game of lowering tax rates while eliminating deductions has been very profitable for the government. Over the years, the tax laws have become twisted and turned into a Gordian knot of exemptions, deductions, depreciations, shelters, and credits. All of us are expected to comply . . . or else. Who can understand it? Quite a bit of the code seems to contradict itself. Therefore, we need to hire professionals to assist us because ignorance of the law is no excuse.

Why Do We Have Taxes?

Most people believe that taxes are essential to the funding our government budgets for social services. Raising revenue for the government is not the primary purpose of the income tax. The federal government could operate today, even at its present astronomical level of spending, without collecting any taxes whatsoever.

In fact, most of the money now spent is attained that way. This is accomplished by a process of monetizing the debt, and it's done by the Federal Reserve System. The Federal Reserve System creates money out of nothing for the government and the banking industry by issuing government bonds. This causes inflation and the loss of purchasing power. That loss becomes a hidden tax (inflation) that is paid to the government and their banking partners.

When we consider all of the taxes that bombard us on a regular basis, we see that most people are in a much higher tax bracket than they actually believe (or that their accountant is aware or concerned with).

Today, there are also many hidden taxes in our lives as well. These are called *effective taxes*, or the taxes that are hidden inside the products we purchase. For example, in a dozen eggs, there are over 80 imbedded taxes that are all built into the price. These include things like business permits, transportation taxes, excise taxes, licensing fees, inventory taxes, inspection fees, property taxes, and telephone taxes.

In the construction of a new home, there are hundreds of taxes paid. Ultimately, these are passed on to the consumer and hidden in the cost of the final item. When you consider all of the taxes that we must pay in order to live in this country, we see that the government is taking roughly half of everything we earn as productive citizens.

Here's a partial list of many common taxes:

Types of Common Taxes

Accounts Receivable Tax
Building Permit Tax
Commercial Driver's License (CDL) Tax
Cigarette Tax
Corporate Income Tax
Dog License Tax
Federal Income Tax
Federal Unemployment Tax Act (FUTA)
Fishing License Tax
Food License Tax
Fuel Permit Tax
Gasoline Tax
Hunting License Tax
Recreational Vehicle Tax
Sales Tax
School Tax
State Income Tax
State Unemployment Tax Act (SUTA)
Telephone Federal Excise Tax
Telephone Federal Universal Service Fee Tax

(continued)

(continued)
Telephone Federal, State, and Local Surcharge Tax
Telephone Minimum Usage Surcharge Tax
Telephone Recurring and Non-Recurring Charges Tax
Telephone State and Local Tax
Telephone Usage Charge Tax
Utility Tax
Vehicle License Registration Tax
Vehicle Sales Tax
Watercraft Registration Tax
Well Permit Tax
Workers Compensation Tax

And so on . . .

Not one of these taxes existed 100 years ago—and our nation was the most prosperous in the world. We had absolutely no national debt. . . . We had the largest middle-class society in the world . . . and moms stayed home to raise the kids by choice. What happened?

Most of us agree that the American government could use some drastic changes in terms of how it creates and adheres to its budget. This applies to the federal, state, and local budgets. Imagine if governments were held to realistic budgets as opposed to their limitless supply of revenue with levying taxes and the federal government being able to obtain further access to money through the Federal Reserve System and monetizing the debt.

What Is Our Tax Bite?

Tax Freedom Day: The Tax Foundation estimates that the average American works nearly 130 days just to pay for their taxes. This means nearly five months of our annual earnings is confiscated with income taxes each year. It doesn't feel so bad when they extract it in smaller, smooth increments each paycheck, but the net result is the same. When we add on the effect of inflation, add on another eight days. The cost of preparation and reporting your taxes costs us another 10 days. This brings our total close to 150 days or five months out of each year spent working just to pay our taxes. This does not even include Social Security tax, which is twice as large as it appears since your employer pays the same amount that you pay.

The Tax Foundation estimates that the average person spends over $8,000 per year on taxes. This is an individual figure. The number is much higher per household.

The Current System

One of my Tax Department professors argued that taxes and the tax system is complex because they are designed to be complex; and they are unfair because the system is designed to be unfair. Not too many people are happy with taxes. Many government officials talk about tax change and tax reform. At the same time, the laws seem to get more complicated, and they often lead to higher taxes.

Most of us would prefer a tax that is easier to compute, collect, and track. But it doesn't seem that the government's goal is to really raise revenue with higher income taxes, but rather to promote a social agenda designed to redistribute the wealth accordingly.

This is done in accordance with the guidelines of the master planners. The master planners wish for more equality of wealth among the middle- and lower-class. Our current progressive tax system creates more equality of wealth and income among the masses than would result from economic forces alone. There is the perception that we are all paying our fair share. But we forget about the silent tax of inflation. Those at the lower income brackets may feel like they're getting a break, but the master planners know better. Inflation levels the playing field. They allow them to earn an income, and then take it back with inflation.

Most of the reform programs promise simplicity and efficiency and don't deliver. It's up to those who understand the rules to determine who gets to steal what from the others. We hear about alternative proposals for taxation such as a national sales tax or a flat income tax. These plans argue that everyone would pay about the same. This concept punishes everyone accordingly. On the other hand, the current progressive income tax punishes citizens for their economic success. Most of these proposals still offer exemptions for special interest cases plus a whole line of other people with their hands out. These proposals would not do much of anything to cut deficit spending by the politicians.

Demographics

The government understands the demographics of our nation. The changing population will affect social programs. They may want to shift the blame for less retirement income on you. That may help them get re-elected. Maybe they're interested in financing their future, not yours.

The government spends more than they collect. They raise revenue through taxes in order to continue their increased spending. More than the average family spends on food, clothing, and housing goes to some form of tax. Most financial planners mention only a couple of taxes that affect our clients. They are usually income taxes and estate taxes. These are two important foes of wealth, yet they represent only the tip of the iceberg to your overall taxation.

Tax History Lessons

Our founding fathers wanted to create a system that would limit the size and reach of our government. At the constitutional convention, they created a tax system that would not become burdensome on the population, and would work equally on the majority and minority at the same time.

Farmers and cities were supposed to be on a level playing field without shifting burdens from state to state or from those states with large populations to those with smaller populations. The initial framework for our nation's tax laws was to make sure it was equal and fair to the majority and the minority. They came up with an apportioned tax that was spread out equally among the states. That was our first tax system.

Taxes were passed out to the people in two basic ways: direct and indirect taxes. A *direct tax* is a tax paid directly by the citizens. This would be in the form of things such as property, income, or estate taxes. Direct taxes were viewed as dangerous by our founding fathers because they determine that the calculation of these taxes would be a serious invasion of personal property. They did not want the government invading the financial lives of its citizens. They had just fought a war over this exact issue. Direct taxes were initially to be administered by the states.

Indirect taxes are taxes that are passed on at a higher price of the product or service purchased such as an exercise tax or an import tax of some goods or service. This is built into part of the price for these products. You can simply avoid these taxes by not purchasing items that contain these taxes. Initially, during our nation's infancy, these taxes were placed on luxury items only, such as tobacco and liquor products.

Direct taxes were to be levied only in the event of war or a serious government emergency. These taxes would be proportional to the number of representatives that each state had in congress. For example, if New Jersey sends five out of a hundred delegates to the congress, then New Jersey would bare 5 percent of the direct tax.

The idea was to limit the power of the central government. It was treated as an extreme measure only, and direct taxes were not designed for the day-to-day operational funding needed for our government. Indirect taxes were the only means to fund our government.

Procedure needed to be followed in order to levy direct taxes. First, congress needs to justify a particular tax from a written revenue act. The act had to be made a public record, define a specific purpose, and then the purpose needed to be debated openly in public forms. It would then need to be voted on and passed. Once passed, it was assigned an expiration date, and once the expiration date ended, the tax could no longer be collected. Compare this to the concept of general taxation of today.

For over 70 years (1789–1861), direct taxes were levied only four times.

1. Debt repayment from the Revolutionary War.
2. Debt repayments from the War of 1812.
3. Debt repayments from the War of 1812.
4. Debt repayment from the Civil War.

Each time, congress followed the procedures, the system worked, and the direct taxes ended abruptly. During this time, our nation enjoyed a great period of growth and prosperity. In terms of internal affairs, our founding fathers wanted a purposely weak central government. They wanted to make sure that the bureaucracy did not interfere with business affairs.

The politicians became inpatient with this system and in 1913, they convinced the voters to pass the 16th Amendment . . . as a temporary measure. This Constitutional Amendment allowed them to pass general taxation into law, and it's been with us ever since. The public was tricked into voting for a tax that was designed to redistribute the wealth away from the highest levels of society. Instead, they only hurt themselves.

It's funny how people start to believe that some things will never change. How many times have we heard someone say: "The only certain things in life are death and taxes!"

Remember, taxes haven't always been with us. Let's take a brief stroll through the history of American taxes. It's more than just the history of the 16th Amendment. The following summary of historical tax information is pulled directly from the U.S. Treasury web site. Send it to a friend. . . . Here is the web address: http://www.treas.gov/edu cation/factsheets/taxes/ustax.shtml.

History of the U.S. Tax System

The federal, state, and local tax systems in the United States have been marked by significant changes over the years in response to changing circumstances and in the role of government. The types of tax collected, their relative proportions, and the magnitude of the revenue collected are all far different than they were 50 or 100 years ago. Some of these changes are traceable to specific historical events, such as a war or the passage of the 16th Amendment to the Constitution that granted Congress the power to levy a tax on personal income.

Colonial Times

For most of our nation's history, individual taxpayers rarely had any significant contact with federal tax authorities as most of the Federal Government's tax revenues were derived from excise taxes, tariffs, and customs duties. Before the Revolutionary War, the colonial government had only a limited need for revenue, while each of the colonies had greater responsibilities and thus greater revenue needs, which they met with different types of taxes. For example, the southern colonies primarily taxed imports and exports; the middle colonies at times imposed a property tax and a head or poll tax levied on each adult male; and the New England colonies raised revenue primarily through general real estate taxes, excises taxes, and taxes based on occupation.

England's need for revenues to pay for the wars against France led it to impose a series of taxes on the American colonies. In 1765, the English Parliament passed the Stamp Act, which was the first tax imposed directly on the American colonies, and then Parliament imposed a tax on tea. Even though colonists were forced to pay these taxes, they lacked representation in the English Parliament. This led to the rallying cry of the American Revolution that "taxation without representation is tyranny," and established a persistent wariness regarding taxation as part of the American culture.

The Post Revolutionary Era

The Articles of Confederation and Perpetual Union, adopted in 1781, reflected the American fear of a strong central government and retained a lot of the political power in the states. The national government had few responsibilities and no nationwide tax system, relying on donations from the States for its revenue. Under the Articles of Confederation, each state was a sovereign entity and could levy tax as it pleased.

When the Constitution was adopted in 1787, the founding fathers recognized that no government could function if it relied entirely on other governments for its resources, thus the federal government was granted the authority to raise taxes. The Constitution endowed Congress with the power to ". . . lay and collect taxes, duties, imposts, and excises, pay the debts, and provide for the common defense and general welfare of the United States." Ever on guard against the power of the central government to eclipse, the collection of the taxes was left as the responsibility of the state governments.

To pay the debts of the Revolutionary War, Congress levied excise taxes on distilled spirits, tobacco and snuff, refined sugar, carriages, properties sold at auctions, and various legal documents. However, even in the early days of the republic, social purposes influenced what was taxed. For example, Pennsylvania imposed an excise tax on liquor sales partly "to restrain persons in low circumstances from an immoderate use thereof." Additional support for such a targeted tax came from property owners, who hoped to keep their property tax rates low, thereby providing an early example of the political tensions often underlying tax policy decisions.

Though social policies sometimes governed the course of tax policy even in the early days of the republic, the nature of these policies did not extend to the collection of taxes as to equalize incomes and wealth, or for the purpose of redistributing income or wealth. As Thomas Jefferson once wrote regarding the general welfare clause:

"To take from one, because it is thought his own industry and that of his father has acquired too much in order to spare to others who (or whose fathers) have not exercised equal industry and skill to violate arbitrarily the first principle of association, [and] to guarantee to everyone a free exercise of his industry and the fruits acquired by it."

With the establishment of the new nation, the citizens of the various colonies now had proper democratic representation, yet many Americans still opposed and resisted taxes that they deemed unfair or improper. In 1794, a group of farmers in southwestern Pennsylvania physically opposed the tax on whiskey, forcing President George Washington to send federal troops to suppress the Whiskey Rebellion, establishing the important precedent that the federal government was determined to enforce its revenue laws. However, the Whiskey Rebellion also confirmed the resistance to unfair or high taxes that led to the Declaration of Independence did not evaporate with the forming of a new, representative government.

During the confrontation with France in the late 1790s, the federal government imposed the first direct taxes on the owners of houses, land, slaves, and estates. These taxes are called direct taxes because they are a recurring tax paid directly by the taxpayer to the government based on the value of that item. The issue of direct taxes versus indirect taxes played a crucial role in the evolution of the federal tax policy in the following years. When Thomas Jefferson was elected president in 1801, direct taxes were abolished and for the next ten years there were no internal revenue taxes other than excises.

To raise money for the War of 1812, Congress imposed additional excise taxes, raised certain customs duties, and raised money by issuing Treasury notes (T-Notes). In 1817, Congress repealed these taxes and for the next 44 years the federal government didn't collect internal revenue. Instead, the Government received most of its revenue from high customs duties and through the sale of public land.

The Civil War

When the Civil War erupted, the Congress passed the Revenue Act of 1861, which restored earlier excises taxes and imposed a tax on personal incomes. The income tax was levied at 3 percent on all incomes higher than $800 a year. This tax on personal income was a new direction for a federal tax system based mainly on excise taxes and customs duties. Certain inadequacies of the income tax were quickly acknowledged by Congress and thus none was collected until the following year.

By the spring of 1862, it was clear the war would not end quickly and with the Union's debt growing at the rate of $2 million daily, it was equally clear the Federal government would need additional revenues. On July 1, 1862, the Congress passed new excise taxes on such items as playing cards, gunpowder, feathers, telegrams, iron, leather, pianos, yachts, billiard tables, drugs, patent medicines, and whiskey. Many legal documents were also taxed and license fees were collected for almost all professions and trades.

The 1862 law also made important reforms to the federal income tax that presaged important features of the current tax. For example, a two-tiered rate structure was enacted, with taxable incomes up to $10,000 taxed at a 3 percent and higher incomes taxed at 5 percent. A standard deduction of $600 was enacted and a variety of deductions were permitted for such things as rental housing, repairs, losses, and other taxes paid. In addition, to assure timely collection, taxes were withheld at the source by employers.

The need for federal revenue declined sharply after the war and most taxes were repealed. By 1868, the main source of Government revenue was derived from liquor and tobacco taxes. The income tax was abolished in 1872. From 1868 to 1913, almost 90 percent of all revenue was collected from the remaining excises.

The 16th Amendment

Under the Constitution, Congress could impose direct taxes only if they were levied in proportion to each state's population. Thus, when a flat rate federal income tax was enacted in 1894, it was quickly challenged. In 1895, the U.S. Supreme Court ruled it unconstitutional because it was a direct tax not apportioned according to the population of each state.

From 1896 to 1910, the federal government relied heavily on high tariffs for its revenues, lacking the revenue from an income tax and with all other forms of internal taxes facing stiff resistance. The War Revenue Act of 1899, sought to raise funds for the Spanish-American War through the sale of bonds, taxes on recreational facilities used by workers, and doubled taxes on beer and tobacco. A tax was even imposed on chewing gum. The Act expired in 1902, so that federal receipts fell from 1.7 percent of Gross Domestic Product (GDP) to 1.3 percent.

By 1913, 36 states had ratified the 16th Amendment to the Constitution. In October, Congress passed a new income tax law with rates beginning at 1 percent and rising to 7 percent for taxpayers with income in excess of $500,000. Less than 1 percent of the population paid income tax at the time. Tax Form 1040 was introduced as the standard tax reporting form and, though changed in many ways over the years, remains in use today.

One of the problems with the new income tax law was how to define lawful income. Congress addressed this problem by amending the law in 1916 by deleting the word 'lawful' from the definition of income. As a result, all income became subject to tax, even if it was earned by illegal means. Several years later, the Supreme Court declared the 5th Amendment could not be used by bootleggers and others who earn income through illegal activities to avoid paying taxes. Consequently, many who broke various laws associated with illegal activities and were able to escape justice for these crimes were incarcerated on tax evasion charges.

Prior to the enactment of the income tax, most citizens were able to pursue their private economic affairs without the direct knowledge of the government. Individuals earned their wages, businesses earned their profits, and wealth was accumulated and dispensed with little or no interaction with government entities. The income tax fundamentally changed this relationship, giving the government the right and need to know about all manners of an individuals' or business" economic life. Congress recognized the inherent invasiveness of the income tax into the taxpayer's personal affairs. So in 1916, it provided citizens with some degree of protection by requiring that information from tax returns be kept confidential.

The Social Security Tax

The state of the economy during the Great Depression led to the passage of the Social Security Act in 1935. This law provided payments known as unemployment compensation to workers who lost their jobs. Other sections of the Act gave public aid to the aged, needy, handicapped, and certain minors. These programs were financed by a 2 percent tax, one-half of which was subtracted directly from an employee's paycheck and the other half collected from employers on the employee's behalf. The tax was levied on the first $3,000 of the employee's salary or wage.

In 1953, the Bureau of Internal Revenue was renamed the Internal Revenue Service (IRS), following a reorganization of its function. The new name was chosen to stress the service aspect of its work. By 1959, the IRS had become the world's largest accounting, collection, and forms processing organization. Computers were introduced to automate and streamline its work and to improve service to taxpayers. In

1961, Congress passed a law requiring individual taxpayers to use their Social Security number as a means of tax form identification. By 1967, all business and personal tax returns were handled by computer systems, and by the late 1960s, the IRS had developed a computerized method for selecting tax returns to be examined. This made the selection of returns for audit fairer for the taxpayer and allowed the IRS to focus its audit resources on those returns most likely to require an audit.

Figure 7.2   Tax Refunds? . . . Why do this with your paycheck?

What Will Your Tax Bite Be?

There may be little that any of us, as individuals, can do about the current state of taxation in America. However, we must understand that federal income taxes, including Social Security, may end up consuming more than 50 percent of our private income, which means we spend nearly half of each year working to fund government programs.

What can you do? How can you fight back?

The die may have been cast on the first round of taxes (income taxes), but why continue to have your money taxed over and over again?

Choose to take yourself out of the second round of taxes. You can't avoid income taxes entirely. Don't cheat on your income taxes. Many have tried and failed in that endeavor.

It's not just what you earn that counts . . . it's what you keep! Create a new environment for your money to grow. Build your wealth on your terms and eliminate the impact of your silent partners once and for all. Learn the strategies of the game, and allow your new wealth to grow in an environment where it will not be subject to additional taxes.

Identify the least tax-efficient investment of your overall portfolio and optimally attempt to own them in some sort of tax-advantaged account for your retirement plan. This may entail reallocating your 401(k), Individual Retirement Account (IRA), profit-sharing plans, or other defined contribution accounts. Small changes like this can help yield far more in returns than timing the market or trying to pick the right funds.

The Capital Gains Tax

I cannot think of a more unjust tax than the Capital Gains Tax. In this scenario, you take all the risk of investment selections making prudent investment choices, and hanging in there for the long haul. Eventually, when you do make money, the government steps in and confiscates a portion of it for the privilege of living in this country. In years when the market is down, you are capped at a $3,000 annual tax write off on your losses. Something is wrong with this picture. Once you understand how capital gains work, why would you want to continue to make your life more difficult by reinvesting dividends and capital gains in the same exact instruments in your nonqualified, nonretirement accounts?

How Can You Defer or Minimize Your Taxes and Control When and How You Pay?

In all likelihood, you will probably need to design a plan that uses many different financial products. Remember, a single product solution will not usually offer you the maximum tax benefits and access to your money that you strive for. Here are a few highlights.

Qualified Retirement Plans

Qualified retirement plans allow us to defer our taxes and the calculation of the taxes due. If you believe that taxes will be lower at the time when you withdraw your funds, then you may benefit from funding a qualified plan. Unfortunately, the opposite is also true. What if taxes or your income increase in the future? How will that impact your wealth?

529 College Savings Plans

529 college savings plans are state-sponsored investment programs. They can offer tax-free growth on assets designed to be used for qualified educational purposes.

There is no guarantee by the issuing with a municipality or any government agency. With very few exceptions, if withdrawals are made from a 529 plan for purposes other than education, they are considered non-qualified withdrawals, and they are subject to federal—and possibly state—tax penalties. Specifically, the earnings portion of the non-qualified withdrawal will be included in the recipient's gross income for federal tax purposes, the earnings will be subject to a 10 percent federal tax penalty.

There may be tax benefits and other advantages to plans offered by a resident investor's state. Investors should consider the potential benefits offered (if any) to residents by their own state's plan (if available) prior to considering another state's plan. The availability of tax or other benefits may be conditioned on meeting certain requirements such as residency, purpose for or timing of distributions, or other factors; and in some states, additional state tax penalties may apply to the earnings.

It is also important to note that assets in a 529 Plan could impact the beneficiary's ability to qualify for grants and student loans and that annual asset charges for a 529 plan may be higher than corresponding share classes of underlying mutual funds.

Permanent Life Insurance

Permanent Life Insurance plans can offer many different tax advantages and uses over your lifetime. You must be able to overcome the initial liquidity limitations of these products, in order to fully realize the benefits of these products over a longer period of time. When designed properly, these contracts can provide substantial tax benefits.

Municipal Bonds

Depending on your tax bracket and time horizons, municipal bonds may also provide an attractive alternative to taxable accounts.

Roth IRAs

Roth IRAs can offer tax-free growth on assets designed to be used for a specific purpose. The downside is that in order for them to work, they will lock up your funds after only one use for a long period of time, and you'll only derive one use for this money.

Tax Refunds

Do you get one? If so, why? Let's examine the real cost of a refund. I can never understand the excitement and satisfaction people feel when they get a tax refund. The figure should not be a mystery. They spend a lot of time trying to justify getting the money back, only to find out it was theirs all along. They act as if they won something, when in reality, they lost.

What's the rate of return that the government gives you on your overpayment of taxes? Otherwise known as a refund? *Zero!* Sometimes you have to hire an accountant or another tax professional to help you get your overpayment back. Did you ever get a thank you letter? You gave them too much money, earned a 0 percent rate of return, had to pay someone else to help get it back, and they didn't even thank you.

The average refund is almost enough to make a car payment every month for the whole year. A $3,000 refund could create an improvement of $250 a month for your standard of living. You would also have the opportunity to invest it and potentially earn some interest of your own. What if you invested the money in a short term CD each year and then spent it? How much interest could you earn over your working lifetime?

You might want to consider using your tax refund in a more effective manner by changing your withholding election in an effort to get even more in your paycheck, which can be deferred into other areas such as funding your Roth IRA or a college savings account. How about paying for your consumer purchases instead of financing them or funding qualified plans with a potential match?

The most important result of adjusting your withholding on your paycheck is that you would have liquidity, use, and control over your dollars. We would rather owe the government a few hundred on April 15 than have them owe us something.

Age	Year #	Annual Savings	Cumulative Amount Saved	Potential Return	Wealth Erosion	Account Value
22	1	$200	$200	7.00%	$0	$200
23	2	$200	$400	7.00%	$14	$414
24	3	$200	$600	7.00%	$43	$643
25	4	$200	$800	7.00%	$88	$888
26	5	$200	$1,000	7.00%	$150	$1,150
27	6	$200	$1,200	7.00%	$231	$1,431
28	7	$200	$1,400	7.00%	$331	$1,731
29	8	$200	$1,600	7.00%	$452	$2,052
30	9	$200	$1,800	7.00%	$596	$2,396
31	10	$200	$2,000	7.00%	$763	$2,763
32	11	$200	$2,200	7.00%	$957	$3,157
33	12	$200	$2,400	7.00%	$1,178	$3,578
34	13	$200	$2,600	7.00%	$1,428	$4,028
35	14	$200	$2,800	7.00%	$1,710	$4,510
36	15	$200	$3,000	7.00%	$2,026	$5,026
37	16	$200	$3,200	7.00%	$2,378	$5,578
38	17	$200	$3,400	7.00%	$2,768	$6,168
39	18	$200	$3,600	7.00%	$3,200	$6,800
40	19	$200	3,800	7.00%	3,676	$7,476
41	20	$200	4,000	7.00%	4,199	$8,199
42	21	$200	4,200	7.00%	4,773	$8,973
43	22	$200	4,400	7.00%	5,401	$9,801
44	23	$200	4,600	7.00%	6,087	$10,687
45	24	$200	4,800	7.00%	6,835	$11,635
46	25	$200	5,000	7.00%	7,650	$12,650
47	26	$200	5,200	7.00%	8,535	$13,735
48	27	$200	5,400	7.00%	9,497	$14,897
49	28	$200	5,600	7.00%	10,540	$16,140
50	29	$200	5,800	7.00%	11,669	$17,469
51	30	$200	6,000	7.00%	12,892	$18,892

(continued)

(continued)

Age	Year #	Annual Savings	Cumulative Amount Saved	Potential Return	Wealth Erosion	Account Value
52	31	$200	6,200	7.00%	14,215	$20,415
53	32	$200	6,400	7.00%	15,644	$22,044
54	33	$200	6,600	7.00%	17,187	$23,787
55	34	$200	6,800	7.00%	18,852	$25,652
56	35	$200	7,000	7.00%	20,647	$27,647
57	36	$200	7,200	7.00%	22,583	$29,783
58	37	$200	7,400	7.00%	24,667	$32,067
59	38	$200	7,600	7.00%	26,912	$34,512
60	39	$200	7,800	7.00%	29,328	$37,128
61	40	$200	8,000	7.00%	31,927	$39,927
62	41	$200	8,200	7.00%	34,722	$42,922
63	42	$200	8,400	7.00%	37,726	$46,126
64	43	$200	8,600	7.00%	40,955	$49,555
65	44	$200	8,800	7.00%	44,424	$53,224

Figure 7.3   The Cost of Getting a Tax Refund Illustrated

Compound Taxes: Reinvesting Dividends and Capital Gains

Compound Interest Exposed: To reinvest or not to reinvest? Auto-pilot to mediocrity and failure? How much of your wealth will be transferred along the way? What if everything you believed to be true about this strategy turned out not to be true? Have you ever paused to consider the fact that reinvesting dividends and capital gains can actually create a compound tax along with compound growth potential?

It seems that most people are familiar with the potential rewards of compounding the interest in their accounts, but few people are familiar with the tax ramifications that are associated with the same potential growth on these accounts. As the interest is earned, taxes can pile up pretty quickly.

Tax compounding is the most common problem with taxes that impact our nonqualified investments. Compound growth makes your money look like it grows on paper. It typically begins with a lump sum investment and includes regular amounts added to the account each year. Your account may also grow as the interest is earned or paid.

Many people continue to roll the interest earned right back into the principal balance of the investment account that continues to add to this compounding effect. The result is an ever increasing 1099 form and a corresponding increased tax that often goes unnoticed. Here's a Quick Example:

Compound Gains					
Calculated for 'Valued Client'					
Present Value: $100,000 Number of Years: 30					
Annual Payment: 0 Tax Bracket: 30 percent					
Annual Interest: 6 percent Opportunity Rate of Return: 6 percent					
Year	Account Balance Beginning of Year	Annual 1099 Reported	Annual Tax Due	Cumulative Tax Paid	Cumulative Lost Opportunity Cost	Total Tax plus Lost Opportunity Cost
1	$100,000	$6,000.00	$1,800.00	$1,800	$108	$1,908
2	$106,000	$6,360.00	$1,908.00	$3,708	$337	$4,045
3	$112,360	$6,741.60	$2,022.48	$5,730	$701	$6,431
4	$119,102	$7,146.10	$2,143.83	$7,874	$1,216	$9,090
5	$126,248	$7,574.86	$2,272.46	$10,147	$1,897	$12,044
6	$133,823	$8,029.35	$2,408.81	$12,556	$2,764	$15,320
7	$141,852	$8,511.11	$2,553.33	$15,109	$3,837	$18,946
8	$150,363	$9,021.78	$2,706.53	$17,815	$5,136	$22,951
9	$159,385	$9,563.09	$2,868.93	$20,684	$6,685	$27,369
10	$168,948	$10,136.87	$3,041.06	$23,725	$8,510	$32,235
11	$179,085	$10,745.09	$3,223.53	$26,949	$10,637	$37,586
12	$189,830	$11,389.79	$3,416.94	$30,366	$13,098	$43,464
13	$201,220	$12,073.18	$3,621.95	$33,988	$15,923	$49,911
14	$213,293	$12,979.57	$3,839.27	$37,827	$19,148	$56,975
15	$226,090	$13,565.42	$4,069.63	$41,897	$22,810	$64,707
16	$239,656	$14,379.35	$4,313.80	$46,211	$26,952	$73,163
17	$254,035	$15,252.11	$4,572.63	$50,783	$31,616	$82,399
18	$269,277	$16,156.64	$4,846.99	$55,630	$36,850	$92,480
19	$285,434	$17,126.03	$5,137.81	$60,768	$42,708	$103,476
20	$302,560	$18,153.60	$5,446.08	$66,214	$49,243	$115,457
21	$320,714	$19,242.81	$5,772.84	$71,987	$56,517	$128,504

(continued)

(*continued*)

Year	Account Balance Beginning of Year	Annual 1099 Reported	Annual Tax Due	Cumulative Tax Paid	Cumulative Lost Opportunity Cost	Total Tax plus Lost Opportunity Cost
22	$339,956	$20,397.38	$6,119.21	$78,106	$64,594	$142,700
23	$360,354	$21,621.22	$6,486.37	$84,592	$73,545	$158,137
24	$381,975	$22,918.50	$6,875.55	$91,468	$83,446	$174,914
25	$404,893	$24,293.61	$7,288.08	$98,756	$94,378	$193,134
26	$429,187	$25,751.22	$7,725.37	$106,481	$106,430	$212,911
27	$454,938	$27,296.30	$8,188.89	$114,670	$119,696	$234,366
28	$482,235	$28,934.08	$8,680.22	$123,351	$134,278	$257,629
29	$511,169	$30,670.12	$9,201.04	$132,552	$150,288	$282,840
30	$541,839	$32,510.33	$9,753.10	$142,305	$167,844	$310,149

Account Summary:
Final Balance: $541,839
Total Cost Paid to Achieve Final Value: $410,149
Final Look: It took $410,149 to grow the account to $541,839.

The government is a silent partner in this account. While they don't take any risk in the actual account, they do participate in all of your gains. They throw a party every year and celebrate your wise investment decisions by confiscating a portion of your gains.

While you spend your time focusing on finding the right rates of return and the best places to put your money, they're counting on the taxes due on their end. It is true that your interest is compounding, but at the same time, so is the tax due in the future. What happens when you go to distribute that money? You will likely face a huge tax bill. Sometimes compounding can even increase your risk. The longer you compound your account, the more likely it becomes that future market corrections may impact your nest egg. Compounding works best in an environment that works in connection with other separate accounts that are growing in tax-free (or tax-favored) instruments.

It is widely accepted that compound interest is the eighth wonder of the world. Not to reinvest dividends in capital gains has been viewed as insanity. Unfortunately, much of what is popular and promoted by the investment community is the exact opposite of what most people should do. While reinvesting dividends in capital gains can give you the opportunity to accumulate wealth, it is also true that it causes some new taxes. It's taxed while it's growing and as it continues to grow to a larger figure. As this occurs, your incremental taxes will grow along with it.

If we follow this line of logic then it must also stand to reason the ninth wonder of the world would be compound taxes. We can help you uncover some of these hidden costs so that you may make more informed decisions about where and how to grow your money. It's important to understand that an investment with compounding taxable interest also has a defined cost. The taxes on the gains represent a cost to maintain your investment regardless of where that tax comes from.

Many people reinvest their investment earnings into their investment accounts. As they do this, they end up paying additional taxes each year out of their personal cash flow. At some point in the future, taxes due can actually exceed their annual income.

Very few people pay the taxes due on their investment interest gains from the principal balance. It often comes from another source, which we call *cash flow*. The taxes due from these investments are hidden in the details of their overall tax picture, and therefore often go unnoticed each year unless someone else, such as a professional, points it out.

It is easy to focus on the amount we have in our accounts. Some of these gains are real, but others are only apparent. What if in order for you to accumulate that amount in your left pocket, you had to reach into your right pocket for the taxes due on your gains? You would have to account for these taxes in your net profit calculation. Most people end up paying more taxes than they have to.

In order to draw a fair comparison between investment strategies, we must account for the costs associated with growing our capital. These include both taxes and opportunity costs. When you take the money from your investment account to pay a tax that could have been avoided, it includes both the tax and what the tax money would have earned for you had you been able to hold onto them and continue to invest them.

Most people don't want to pay more taxes. Generally, people prefer to avoid the taxes if they knew how. Whenever you end up paying a tax that could have avoided, you give up the tax, as well as the opportunity cost on that money. These taxes must be viewed as a maintenance fee or cost for your investment. The investment gain creates taxable income that is reported to the government in Form 1099.

How Do We Solve This Problem?

A simple concept called *netting* comes into play. Take a look at the Alternate Strategy example. Instead of blindly reinvesting dividends and capital gains, or the interest from our CDs and other fixed accounts, what if we had that interest deposited into an accumulation account where we could make decisions with it at the end of the year? We might be in a much better position. Then we would have the power of choice. Depending on where our incomes come from and how the financial markets are performing, you may have more options for successfully avoiding future tax traps.

This is a simple concept. Interest gains will be reported on a 1099 tax form. Initially, the appropriate tax amount should be set aside for the IRS. However, the balance should not be blindly reinvested, but should be given consideration to whether it should be directed to a different investment that may have additional tax benefits . . . or to pay down debt if your debts carry a higher rate.

There are a few options that usually make sense to consider. There are benefits and drawbacks to each of these options, but a great place to start might be looking into Roth IRAs, real estate investments, municipal bonds, and dividend paying permanent life insurance. Consider the following example:

Alternate Strategy									
Calculated for 'Valued Client'									
Present Value: $100,000 Number of Years: 30									
Annual Payment: $0.00 Tax Bracket: 30 percent									
Annual Interest: 6 percent Opportunity Rate of Return: 6 percent									
Year	Account Balance Beginning of Year	Annual 1099 Report	Annual Tax Due	Cumulative Tax Paid	Cumulative Lost Opportunity Cost	Total Tax and Opportunity Cost	After Tax Available Capital	Cumulative Gains on Repositioned Capital	Original Amount plus New Account Gains
1	$100,000	$6,000	$1,800	$1,800	$108	$1,908	$4,200	$4,452	$104,452
2	$100,000	$6,000	$1,800	$3,600	$330	$3,930	$4,200	$9,171	$109,171
3	$100,000	$6,000	$1,800	$5,400	$674	$6,074	$4,200	$14,173	$114,173
4	$100,000	$6,000	$1,800	$7,200	$1,147	$8,347	$4,200	$19,476	$119,476
5	$100,000	$6,000	$1,800	$9,000	$1,756	$10,756	$4,200	$25,096	$125,096
6	$100,000	$6,000	$1,800	$10,800	$2,509	$13,309	$4,200	$31,054	$131,054
7	$100,000	$6,000	$1,800	$12,600	$3,415	$16,015	$4,200	$37,369	$137,369

Year	Account Balance Beginning of Year	Annual 1099 Report	Annual Tax Due	Cumulative Tax Paid	Cumulative Lost Opportunity Cost	Total Tax and Opportunity Cost	After Tax Available Capital	Cumulative Gains on Repositioned Capital	Original Amount plus New Account Gains
8	$100,000	$6,000	$1,800	$14,400	$4,484	$18,884	$4,200	$44,064	$144,064
9	$100,000	$6,000	$1,800	$16,200	$5,725	$21,925	$4,200	$51,159	$151,159
10	$100,000	$6,000	$1,800	$18,000	$7,149	$25,149	$4,200	$58,681	$158,681
11	$100,000	$6,000	$1,800	$19,800	$8,766	$28,566	$4,200	$66,654	$166,654
12	$100,000	$6,000	$1,800	$21,600	$10,588	$32,188	$4,200	$75,105	$175,105
13	$100,000	$6,000	$1,800	$23,400	$12,627	$36,027	$4,200	$84,063	$184,063
14	$100,000	$6,000	$1,800	$25,200	$14,897	$40,097	$4,200	$93,559	$193,559
15	$100,000	$6,000	$1,800	$27,000	$17,411	$44,411	$4,200	$103,625	$203,625
16	$100,000	$6,000	$1,800	$28,800	$20,183	$48,983	$4,200	$114,294	$214,294
17	$100,000	$6,000	$1,800	$30,600	$23,230	$53,830	$4,200	$125,604	$225,604
18	$100,000	$6,000	$1,800	$32,400	$26,568	$58,968	$4,200	$137,592	$237,592
19	$100,000	$6,000	$1,800	$34,200	$30,214	$64,414	$4,200	$150,299	$250,299
20	$100,000	$6,000	$1,800	$36,000	$34,187	$70,187	$4,200	$163,769	$263,769
21	$100,000	$6,000	$1,800	$37,800	$38,506	$76,306	$4,200	$178,048	$278,048
22	$100,000	$6,000	$1,800	$39,600	$43,192	$82,792	$4,200	$193,182	$293,182
23	$100,000	$6,000	$1,800	$41,400	$48,268	$89,668	$4,200	$209,225	$309,225
24	$100,000	$6,000	$1,800	$43,200	$53,756	$96,956	$4,200	$226,231	$326,231
25	$100,000	$6,000	$1,800	$45,000	$59,756	$104,756	$4,200	$244,257	$344,257
26	$100,000	$6,000	$1,800	$46,800	$66,070	$112,870	$4,200	$263,364	$363,364
27	$100,000	$6,000	$1,800	$48,600	$72,951	$121,551	$4,200	$283,618	$383,618
28	$100,000	$6,000	$1,800	$50,400	$80,352	$130,752	$4,200	$305,087	$405,087
29	$100,000	$6,000	$1,800	$52,200	$88,305	$140,505	$4,200	$327,844	$427,844
30	$100,000	$6,000	$1,800	$54,000	$96,843	$150,843	$4,200	$351,967	$451,967

Account Summary:

Final Balance: $451,976

Total Cost Paid to Achieve Final Value: $250,843

Final Look: It took $250,843 to grow the account to $451,967

Flattening the tax is the first step. The second step it reducing or eliminating the taxes due over a period of time. By slowly distributing the capital base over a period of time, we are able to reduce the amount of taxable interest earned. What if we drew our accounts down at the rate of 5 percent of the principal per year and repositioned those assets into a tax-free environment? In this example, it would take us about 20 years to drain the capital (taxable) base and migrate those assets into a tax-free environment. Our liquidity would not change much as the transfer would be very gradual in nature. This strategy would likely eliminate more of the future taxes due on our accounts.

Basically, we would move 5 percent of the taxable left pocket asset, to the tax-free right pocket. Over a period of 20 years, you would effectively move all of this account out of the tax picture without impacting much liquidity. If liquidity is not a big concern, this can be accomplished in a much shorter period of time. If 5 percent is too much to move, consider moving the interest gains only at first.

Sometimes the full effect of the savings from this strategy is confusing. Let me help clarify. The real benefit here is the differential in annual taxes paid. By netting the account out, and paying the taxes annually each year out of your gain, you have essentially flattened the tax. It will no remain at the same level for the life of the contract.

In doing so, you've taken your cumulative tax from the sum on the first screen, to the new sum. This saves you approximately $90,000 over a 30-year period. This differential in savings of taxes also needs to be accounted for and added into your final figures. Now you are about even. This is the second turn (or use) of your same dollars.

As you now understand the concept of opportunity cost, you also understand the concept of opportunity rewards. Like taking some, or all, of that additional savings, perhaps saving it in a side fund. You now have created the potential to grow these funds for a second time. If you do so in a tax favored environment, you may pick up the new compound growth in a new tax free, environment. When you do that, you see that you come out ahead. This represents the third turn (or use) of the same dollars.

You also may have term life insurance that can be converted into a product that has an actual rate of return. Term life insurance is a cost (an expense), with no internal rate of return. Zero percent . . . unless you die. Remember, it still has a death benefit, but the insurance companies know this math too. They only pay out on about 2 to 3 percent of those term life policies. Mist of the people live beyond the expiration term (usually 20 or 30 years), and simply drops the coverage. Remember, at this point the insurance company keeps all of the premiums paid along with all of the interest paid to date . . . and beyond!

By converting the term life insurance into a permanent product, you could pick up additional recoveries of the term-life premiums, along with the lost opportunity cost associated with those term-life premiums . . . since they would be recovered over time by using a permanent insurance platform. This is the fourth turn (or use) on the same dollars!

Imagine if all of your interest and future gains could accumulate tax-free? What would prevent you from incorporating this strategy into your plans?

Practical Exercise: Consider alternate options for your compounding interest. Say no to autopilot strategies.

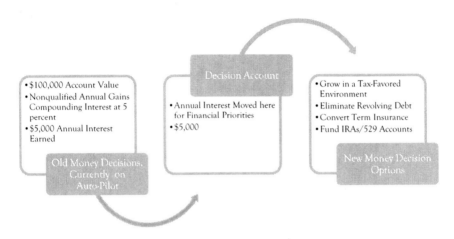

Decision Account

• $100,000 Account Value
• Nonqualified Annual Gains Compounding Interest at 5 percent
• $5,000 Annual Interest Earned

• Annual Interest Moved here for Financial Priorities
• $5,000

• Grow in a Tax-Favored Environment
• Eliminate Revolving Debt
• Convert Term Insurance
• Fund IRAs/529 Accounts

Old Money Decisions, Currently on Auto-Pilot

New Money Decision Options

Figure 7.4   How to Potentially Flatten Your Taxes: Step By Step

Retirement Taxes

It's interesting to note that most people, who have a statement balance of $100,000 in their retirement account, believe that they actually have $100,000 in that account. The reality is they probably have more like 60 or 70 percent ownership in that account, with the government (comprised of state, local, and other entities), owning the other 30 to 40 percent. The government always gets its pound of flesh. Where will taxes be in the future? What rates will you pay when you withdraw your money? Take a look at where taxes have been in the Table 7.3? Are you still comfortable only deferring your taxes?

Some people are happy to pay their taxes without itemizing their deductions. If you are happy with the standard deduction, you can skip this section. If you are not content with the crumbs of the standard deduction, you may want to try this next exercise. This exercise is a practical application designed to help you take a look back at where you've paid taxes in the past and how you may be able to reduce your income tax exposure in the years ahead. The first thing that you should do is dust off your past few year's tax returns.

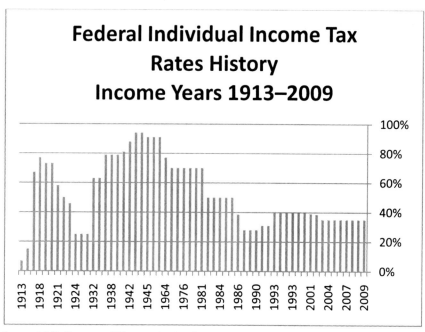

Source: U.S. Bureau of Economic Analysis

Figure 7.5   A History of the Highest Annual Marginal Income Tax Rates from 1913 to 2009

Try to locate Form 1040 which is the actual tax return and look at the first page where the line items are numbered. You can then begin to use some of the following suggestions to take a look at your own tax returns, and identify areas where you may be currently overpaying taxes currently or where you may be likely to continue paying higher taxes in the future.

Tax review exercise: Here's a quick exercise to help you take control of your taxes. Discover ways to help turn your long-term goals and retirement dreams into a reality. There are many potential ways to reduce your current taxation. Take a look at your own prior year's tax return(s) and pay specific attention to specific lines. Look at each of these areas and then identify places that you can reposition capital in years to come in an effort to minimize your future taxation.

Our goal is to help you build a foundation for building a comprehensive long-term tax reduction game plan that also helps you meet your financial goals. Talk to your tax and financial professionals for details on your specific financial strategies. For many individuals, the first step toward creating your long-term financial plan is to review Tax Form 1040. This form contains a broad picture of your overall financial situation and may provide clues about other opportunities to reduce taxes hidden just beneath the surface. Here are some ideas for you and your financial professional(s) to look for in your Form 1040 listed section by section starting from the top.

Lines 8A and 9A. These lines identify interest and dividend income that may affect your tax situation. How can you continue to receive an interest and dividend income without increasing your tax burden? Answer: Tax-deferred products such as annuities and IRAs offer the potential to grow your assets without paying taxes on these earnings until money is withdrawn. Money withdrawn, earnings are subject to ordinary income tax. Withdrawals may be subject to a surrender charge, taxed as ordinary income, and prior to age 59½ may be subject to a 10 percent federal tax penalty. You may also want to consider a more strategic approach to include tax-favored products, as these investments may be eligible for reduced tax rates, or to utilize products that can allow your dollars to grow tax free, like a Roth IRA. Certain individuals may also be subject to the alternative minimum tax.

Line 9A, Line 9B. Dividends. Consider dividends that may be eligible for a 15 percent capital gains rate. These are reported in box 1B of Form 1099-DIV.

Line 12. Certain retirement plan contributions can help business owners save more. You may also want to speak with your lending institution about interest rates on loans that you may have. Currently, the maximum long term capital gains rate is 15 percent. Whenever possible, offset gains with losses that occurred within the same year. You may also have losses that can be carried over from year to year, so it's important to keep accurate records of your investment transactions.

Line 13. Capital Gains. Why pay taxes on money you're not using. Answer: Short-term capital gains are taxed as ordinary income tax rates. Long-term capital gains are currently taxed at a rate of approximately 15 percent, if you're in a tax bracket of 25 percent or higher. Try to find products providing tax deferral on your money until you need it. Put yourself in control of your tax decisions!

Line 15. Consider converting to a Roth IRA if you are using your traditional IRA as a source of income. The converted amount will be taxable, but all future distributions will be tax-free. Coordinate this strategy with your CPA and your personal CFO.

Line 15A, 15B. Total IRA distributions taxable amounts.

Line 16A, 16B. Total pensions and annuities taxable amounts. Question: Are you nearing age 70½ and interested in reducing your tax liability. Are you currently taking periodic 72T or 72Q payments that are greater than your need? Answer: Consider other ways to take your IRA distributions, pensions, and annuities that may help minimize your current tax liability. You may be able to reduce the amount of your periodic 72T payments by making a one-time change to your calculation method. If you're over age 70½, make sure that you aren't overlooking a long forgotten IRA when determining your required minimum distribution amount. Failure to take a required minimum distribution may result in a penalty tax of 50 percent based on the amount you should have taken.

Line 17. Review your older mortgages. Since very little interest paid is tax deductible, check with your lending institution regarding refinancing opportunities for your mortgages. This can be important if you are planning on distributing qualified money that has not yet been taxed, as it can offset some of the taxes due.

Line 25. Contributions to a qualified to a health savings account (HAS) may be deductible depending upon your health insurance plan. Use tax Form 8889 to calculate your allowable deductions.

Line 28. Self-employed, SEP, SIMPLE, and qualified plans. If you own your own business you are taking advantage of the contribution limits for these plans? Would an individual 401(k) or SIMPLE allow you contribute more? The SEP and individual 401(k) contribution limits can provide significant opportunity for contributions. To make an even larger tax deductible contribution, consider a one-person defined benefit plan.

Line 32. IRA deductions. Are you making the most of your IRA and other 401(k) plans? When saving for retirement, consider making regular contributions to an IRA. Depending upon your situation and the type of IRA, contributions may be tax deductible. Question: How can I reduce capital gains on highly appreciated assets? Answer: Consider gifts to your favorite charities. Instead of gifting cash to a charity, consider gifting appreciated stock or mutual fund, which otherwise would have triggered capital gains. Upon the sale of your assets to a charitable remainder trust (CRT), you may qualify for an income tax deduction or help to reduce capital gains taxes on highly appreciated assets. Work with your tax and legal professionals before implementing any of these strategies as they may unintentionally impact other areas of your plan.

Line 60: Additional tax on IRAs and other qualified retirement plans. Are you currently taking or are planning on taking withdrawals from your IRA, qualified plan, or annuity prior to age 59½? If so, these early withdrawals could result in a 10 percent federal tax penalty. Ask your financial professional about alternative ways to take early withdrawals that allow you to avoid this additional tax.

Line 63: Your total tax. Question: How can you reduce your total tax bill overall? Answer: To reduce your overall tax bill, by maximizing your contributions to your company through retirement plans. Once you've reached your ideal contribution limits to these plans, consider contributions to other types of tax deferred retirement tools, such as annuities and permanent life insurance plans. Annuity products can provide guaranteed income for life, as well as death benefits for beneficiaries during your asset accumulation phase.

Work with your tax and legal professionals before implementing any of these strategies as they may unintentionally impact other areas of your plan.

If your deductions barely exceed the standard deduction on a regular basis, you may want to consider bunching deductions. This strategy consists of timing your itemized deductions to any extent possible, such as charitable contributions, so that you alternate between itemizing deductions and taking the standard deduction in alternate years. This may be advantageous in years where your income is higher.

Chapter Highlights

> Are you coordinating strategies with your professionals each year? If not, why not? It's possible that some of the things that you're trying to accomplish may be causing a negative impact in other areas of your plan. It is for this reason that you should make sure that all of your advisors meet (or speak) annually to coordinate your strategies whenever possible. Your personal CFO can help coordinate your strategies accordingly.

> Understand what taxes are and where they came from.

> Have you explored the impact of compound taxes in your own financial life?

> Examine the real costs of a refund.

> Have you taken steps to reduce or eliminate additional taxes in your financial life?

CHAPTER 8
CONSUMER DEBTS

Figure 8.1   The Debt Wagon

Managing Your Debt

Our parents' and grandparents' generations may have followed a cash-only spending philosophy, but today, most Americans cannot imagine living without at least some debt. Very few of us are able to pay cash for a home or a car and there may not be any reason to purchase that way. The ability to borrow money when it's needed on favorable terms is a privilege, earned only by carefully managing your debt obligations.

Many financial professionals regard borrowing money as a double-edged sword. For example, it could be used to finance long-term goals, such as home ownership, starting a business, or funding an education. Over time, these programs tend to increase in value and return far more than the cost to purchase them. Used in excess to constantly save for short-term consumer items, such as electronics, clothing, vacations, and so on, debt can become an overwhelming burden.

Manage your credit record. Most lending decisions are made on the basis of your credit record, also known as your credit report. Lenders size you up to determine how much credit, if any, to grant you. They take into account the following: your character; how responsibly will you handle your credit obligations; how you have repaid previous debts; and what financial assets are at your disposal to pay off your debts.

When credit is used properly, in can serve as a catalyst to our overall economy. It helps families deal with emergency situations. It can help ease the burden of large, financial consumer purchases and can make payments more convenient and secure. It can also be used to your advantage to enlarge your opportunities and accomplish your long-term priorities.

Credit becomes debt if you don't have the money to pay for your current purchases. There's a difference between a debtor and a creditor. A *debtor* owes money with the intention to pay, while a *creditor* can repay right now. There's a price to pay for buying now and paying later, and that price is called interest.

By using other people's money, you pay interest but you are also spending your future, because you don't have the funds to pay for it now. The interest you pay to rent someone else's money can put your family into a very difficult financial situation. It isn't often worth the temporary joy that accompanies many of these frivolous purchases.

How Much Debt Can You Afford?

What is your financial ability to assume a certain amount of debt?

Do you have enough money coming in the door each month to pay all your bills? Examine your cash flow situation and make sure that the sum of your total debt payments is less than 30 to 50 percent of your gross annual income.

Choices

Today, consumers have many choices in terms of how to borrow money. For example, you could use your credit cards to finance major purchases or even a college education. However, there might be a better choice such as government subsidized student loans, or financial aid directly from the educational institution. These typically carry a lower interest rate and defer payments until after you finish school. In contrast, you may use part of your home equity line of credit to pay for a car, but you must consider whether you want to make the car payments over a long period of time. Whether you do this homework yourself or seek the help of an advisor, understanding your options and then appropriately matching the type of loan for your need is a key part to affective debt management.

The Cost of Your Debt

Interest rates constantly move up and down. As a result, the loan you took out several years ago at what was then a great interest rate, may not be such a great rate today. Lower interest rates may also allow you to refinance an existing loan and lower your monthly payments or combine multiple outstanding consumer debts into one easy payment. If you keep the same monthly payment at the lower rate, it may allow you to repay the loan on a more rapid basis.

We are a nation that works hard and plays hard. From the time we are young, we are taught to work hard for what we want. We are told to chase down our dreams and make them a reality. Get into a good college, get a solid job, and build your own American Dream. Unfortunately, many of us have skipped a few lessons about hard work and sacrifice along the way. Many recent college graduates feel that they are entitled to the finer things in life simply because they graduated from school. It is not uncommon for them to run out and buy a car as a reward for their years of sacrifice.

We don't blame them for this ritual; the automotive advertising firms have trained them to believe that they are entitled. In fact, according to the guys selling cars: "Everyone is entitled to reward themselves." The problem here is that the young college graduate is tricked into carrying the yoke of consumer debt before he ever has a chance to save anything for himself. He is building wealth . . . for the automotive finance company!

Now that he has his shiny new automobile, he can more easily turn the heads of the young ladies. Once he falls in love, he will need a better place to live than his parent's basement. He is likely to rent an apartment (until he can save enough to buy a house). Now he is also building wealth for his landlord. At some point, the couple chooses to get married (time to pay for a wedding), and have children (kids are great, but are also expensive to raise). P.S. His shiny new car is now an old beater with stains on the seats and dents all over the doors.

Next he and his family may need more space to live in. He may need to raid (borrow from) his 401(k) plan to provide a down payment for his first home purchase. Since he wants to pay off the home as quickly as possible, he selects a short mortgage duration. This causes him to make huge mortgage payments to the bank. The effects of this obligation lessen his ability to save for himself even further.

Now he really needs his job. His spending is virtually on auto-pilot. He cannot afford to miss a single payment or his credit will suffer. Unfortunately, life moved pretty quickly and he never really had time to save up an emergency fund.

He now sleeps on a mattress that he bought on a credit card. He eats food from his financed stainless-steel refrigerator, he puts on his financed clothing, and he hops into his leased vehicle to commute to work. He then works all week to save a few dollars in his company sponsored retirement plan. He can't touch those dollars till age 59 ½ years old. He thinks that's great!

At the end of his 6-day work week, he commutes home in his financed vehicle, pays for gas along the way with a credit card. If he has any extra money, he sends them to the bank so that his mortgage will be paid off early. This way when he retires, he can take out the money from his retirement plan (which hasn't been taxed yet) at higher tax rates, because he will no longer have his mortgage interest deduction available to minimize his tax burden.

He is building wealth for everyone else, paying himself last, and wondering what happened. I want you to be in control of your financial decisions. Imagine if he didn't have to pay any interest to these financing companies?

Age	Year #	Annual Savings	Cumulative Amount Saved	Opportunity Rate of Return	Cumulative Opportunity Cost	Cumulative Account Value
22	1	$2,000	$2,000	7.00%	0	$2,000
23	2	$2,000	$4,000	7.00%	$140	$4,140
24	3	$2,000	$6,000	7.00%	$430	$6,430
25	4	$2,000	$8,000	7.00%	$880	$8,880

Age	Year #	Annual Savings	Cumulative Amount Saved	Opportunity Rate of Return	Cumulative Opportunity Cost	Cumulative Account Value
26	5	$2,000	$10,000	7.00%	$1,501	$11,501
27	6	$2,000	$12,000	7.00%	$2,307	$14,307
28	7	$2,000	$14,000	7.00%	$3,308	$17,308
29	8	$2,000	$16,000	7.00%	$4,520	$20,520
30	9	$2,000	$18,000	7.00%	$5,956	$23,956
31	10	$2,000	$20,000	7.00%	$7,633	$27,633
32	11	$2,000	$22,000	7.00%	$9,567	$31,567
33	12	$2,000	$24,000	7.00%	$11,777	$35,777
34	13	$2,000	$26,000	7.00%	$14,281	$40,281
35	14	$2,000	$28,000	7.00%	$17,101	$45,101
36	15	$2,000	$30,000	7.00%	$20,258	$50,258
37	16	$2,000	$32,000	7.00%	$23,776	$55,776
38	17	$2,000	$34,000	7.00%	$27,680	$61,680
39	18	$2,000	$36,000	7.00%	$31,998	$67,998
40	19	$2,000	$38,000	7.00%	$36,758	$74,758
41	20	$2,000	$40,000	7.00%	$41,991	$81,991
42	21	$2,000	$42,000	7.00%	$47,730	$89,730
43	22	$2,000	$44,000	7.00%	$54,011	$98,011
44	23	$2,000	$46,000	7.00%	$60,872	$106,872
45	24	$2,000	$48,000	7.00%	$68,353	$116,353
46	25	$2,000	$50,000	7.00%	$76,498	$126,498
47	26	$2,000	$52,000	7.00%	$85,353	$137,353
48	27	$2,000	$54,000	7.00%	$94,968	$148,968
49	28	$2,000	$56,000	7.00%	$105,395	$161,395
50	29	$2,000	$58,000	7.00%	$116,693	$174,693
51	30	$2,000	$60,000	7.00%	$128,922	$188,922
52	31	$2,000	$62,000	7.00%	$142,146	$204,146
53	32	$2,000	$64,000	7.00%	$156,436	$220,436
54	33	$2,000	$66,000	7.00%	$171,867	$237,867
55	34	$2,000	$68,000	7.00%	$188,518	$256,518

(continued)

(continued)

Age	Year #	Annual Savings	Cumulative Amount Saved	Opportunity Rate of Return	Cumulative Opportunity Cost	Cumulative Account Value
56	35	$2,000	$70,000	7.00%	$206,474	$276,474
57	36	$2,000	$72,000	7.00%	$225,827	$297,827
58	37	$2,000	$74,000	7.00%	$246,675	$320,675
59	38	$2,000	$76,000	7.00%	$269,122	$345,122
60	39	$2,000	$78,000	7.00%	$293,281	$371,281
61	40	$2,000	$80,000	7.00%	$319,270	$399,270
62	41	$2,000	$82,000	7.00%	$347,219	$429,219
63	42	$2,000	$84,000	7.00%	$377,264	$461,264
64	43	$2,000	$86,000	7.00%	$409,553	$495,553
65	44	$2,000	$88,000	7.00%	$444,242	$532,242

Figure 8.2   Consumer Debt Example

Each $2,000 saved equated to roughly $500,000 by age 65 in the above example. Do you want to recapture this wealth for yourself? If so, you'll need to commit to becoming debt free. You should carry as little debt as possible. I want you to have zero balances on your credit cards. I don't want you to have to finance any of your automobiles. I've illustrated what that cost is and how much of your wealth is confiscated by automobile financing companies and other consumer financing companies.

Self Assessment Exercise

Warning Signs

These are some basic warning signs to help you determine whether you're actually on the road to wealth or on the road to financial ruin. I'm in this business because I believe I can have a dramatic impact on people and their ability to build wealth, and I'd like to share with you some of the common problems or traps we see on a regular basis. Here are some signs that you may be on the road to financial failure.

Debt Management Quick Quiz

✓ Are you juggling bills with your own bill paying lottery?

✓ Do you have any debts that don't have any payments due for one to three years from now? This could be on a home electronics credit card, furniture card, or specialty retail credit cards.

✓ Are you using your home equity to pay off old bills while you're still charging up your credit cards?

✓ Are you in a position where you must finance your next major purchase (new automobile or home), or do you have a choice to pay for it in other ways?

✓ Do you fund holiday purchases or vacations as they come due or are you spending next year's money?

Automotive Financing

The Challenge

Automobiles: If you save up the funds to pay for each vehicle, it will take five years to accumulate $25,000 at 6 percent savings of $370 per month (per vehicle).

Outlined Costs of Financing Each Vehicle

If you need the vehicle today and you don't have the money saved, you will need to finance or lease the vehicle. In order to finance the vehicle, you will incur a different set of expenses. You will not be earning interest on your savings; you will now be transferring interest to others.

Monthly Payment on a $25,000 Vehicle

Principal of $25,000

Interest Expense: $3,999 or about $800 per year. It doesn't sound like a lot, but that's 16 percent more expensive than the original sales price.

Total Cost $28,999.

Auto Loan Amount: $25,000
Auto Loan Term: 5 Years (60 months)
Interest Rate: 6 percent
Monthly Auto Loan Payments: $438.32

What if you could eliminate the $800 of extra interest expense and save it for yourself? $800 compounding at 8 percent for your 45-year driving lifetime would grow to over $300,000. Multiply that number by 2 if your spouse drives too. *Could $600,000 help fund your retirement?* What if I could show you a way to finance your purchases without transferring the interest to the automotive finance company?

The Challenge

How do I consolidate, and eliminate this debt forever?

Can I turn it into tax-deductible debt?

Step right up, step right up, and see the wonder of tax deductible interest that will amaze you. What if you could deduct all of that credit card and automobile financing interest? Turn your bad debt into good debt. Presto chango! Through the power of mortgage interest deductions all of this can be accomplished. Learn how to keep financing costs to a minimum by being on a cash basis for expenses except for your mortgage.

In Figure 8.2, we have traded bad (non-deductible ebt) for good (deductible mortgage debt). They are utilizing a cash-out refinance strategy to pay off their debts. They have now eliminated their non-deductible debt and created positive cash flow. The net result is a savings of $3,139 per month (or $37,668 per year). Even if they save this amount in an account that does not earn interest, they would have an additional $226,000 over 6 years. This side fund can pay off the original 15 year mortgage ahead of schedule.

Deductible Mortgage Debt

We believe that some people should consider having and keeping a mortgage even if they have the availability and resources to pay off their home. There are potential tax advantages that come along with it, if properly coordinated and integrated into a savings and investment program. This strategy may allow you to potentially recapture some tax dollars and interest expenses. Make sure to consult with your tax advisors before making any decisions. The right mortgage selected for the right duration and the right reasons can be a powerful financial tool, as long as you carry that mortgage with a disciplined approach to managing your debt.

Debt Snapshot

Type of Debt	Term (mos.)	Rate	Amount Owed	Old Payment	New Payment on Higher Mtg.	New 30 Yr. Mtg Rate
Mort-gage 1	180	6.5%	90000	1,600	1,011	5.5%
Mort-gage 2	360	9%	25000	500	0	
Home Equity Line	Interest only	5%	0	0	0	
Auto 1	60	5%	25,000	600	0	
Auto 2	60	6%	0		0	
Credit Card	open	14%	38,000	1,050	0	
Totals			178,000	4,150	1,011	

Figure 8.3   Debt Snapshot

Bad Debt (Nondeductible Debt) versus Good Debt (Deductible)

Whenever possible, try to use deductible debts over nondeductible debts. Learn how to lower some of your monthly payments. You will need to learn to turn bad debt, where interest is not deductible . . . into good debt, where interest is deductible. Pay yourself, not others. Identify your transfers, recognize problems, then reduce or eliminate them entirely.

Automotive Finance Alternative

Your automobile is one of the most expensive wealth transfers you'll ever make. Unlike your home, your car does not retain its value. Most car purchases are financed. You must pay back not only the principal but the interest. The interest paid to the automotive finance companies is not tax deductible.

When purchasing an automobile, the focus is usually on what auto payment you think you can afford each month, not the transfers you're making. The actual cost of owning cars over your lifetime is astronomical.

Let's assume that you're about 30 years old. If you want to buy a new car about every four years, you estimate you'll probably drive until you're 75. You believe that you can average about a 7 percent rate of return on your investments during that time. You estimate a cost of about $25,000 for each vehicle. We'll use a 6 percent loan interest rate.

Throughout your lifetime, you'll have purchased about 11 cars. What if you had been able to invest the annual interest saved on these vehicles? At 7 percent, the interest saved would have grown to over $400,000 by the time you were 75! Remember, this figure does not include the actual cost of the cars. After all those years of driving, and all of those car purchases, you'll end up with a used car worth about $10,000.

The interest paid is not tax deductible. If you could find a lending institution that would allow you to deduct the interest from your taxes, would you be interested in exploring that alternative?

First, you'll need to establish your own capital pools centered on the equity in your home, use it to make purchases, and most likely deduct the interest paid on those purchases. Purchasing a car using your equity line of credit would be an excellent option to recapture transferred interest. By using the equity in your home, you may be able to create more favorable lending terms for your purchase. If you pay cash, you can often negotiate a lower net purchase on the vehicle. You also pick up potential tax deductions.

Remember, a car is a depreciating asset. It loses value with each passing year. Why would you want to pay this loan off as fast as you can? Once it's paid for, it will only continue to lose value. First, we need to estimate the resale value of the car in four years. We only want to pay the car down to that amount. Why continue making monthly payments on something that will lose more value?

You create large opportunity cost by paying off a depreciating asset early. By purchasing your car using equity line of credit, you can adjust your monthly payments on this loan. The first couple of years on the loan, you would pay back the same payment as traditional financing. You are going to make this payment to a finance company anyway, now that you're paying it to yourself (with a deductible loan). Over time, you can find out what the residual or resale value of your car would be. You can then adjust your monthly payment so the loan balance doesn't go below the residual resale value of your car.

If you can adjust your monthly payment or bring the balance of your loan to the approximate future resale value of your car, you should do it. Your monthly car payment could be reduced from $400 to $300 per month (or even more). You can't make these adjustments using a traditional bank or lending institution, but you can if you use your own money. The bank's goal it to get all of the money back quickly. Your goal is cash flow management. If you sell the car, you can pay off the loan to yourself with the proceeds.

If you were able to save even $100 per month from your car payment or for even one year, at 6 percent interest you would have saved $1,272. A $200 per month savings translates into an annual savings of $2,544 that could be redirected into other areas of your plan.

Home Equity: Your Secret Weapon?

Home equity lines can offer you the ability to trade deductible mortgage based debt for nondeductible debts. Many families have turned to their home equity loans to provide superior lending terms to that of educational lending firms and automotive financing companies.

If used properly, you may be able to take advantage of better financing terms. Be careful not to overuse this privilege. Be sure to consult with your lending professionals to design an appropriate strategy. There are limitations on how much you can roll into your home equity loans, and some interest rates can be variable. You may be in for a surprise if the rate adjusts quickly.

Let's Review Your Credit Score

America was founded on the premise of equal opportunity and a level playing field for all. The credit system is no different. As we begin our financial lives, most of us don't have any credit at all. Therefore, we must establish credit. This is done typically through acquiring some sort of a loan, usually a lower balance credit card, a first automobile loan, or some small consumer loans. We all start with a clean slate and it is up to us to prove to the world that we are credit worthy. Most of us will rely on others' capital for the large majority of our lives. This means we will need to borrow money from others, typically banks and other financial institutions. The best way for the financial institutions to gauge whether or not to lend us money is by use of our credit score. Therefore, our credit score becomes one of the most important numbers that will ever be attached to us throughout our lives. We must protect it at all costs. If we do not, we will find ourselves locked out of many opportunities. A difference of only 100 points in our credit score can dramatically impact the prices and rates we pay on things like mortgage loans, automotive financing, school loans, and even the cost of insurance products. Take care to guard your credit score, monitor it, and make sure that the world knows that you are an excellent credit risk at all times.

Your Credit Is Key

One of the most important numbers in your life is your credit score. Creditors can wreak havoc on your credit score and your ability to build wealth. This will continue to plague your ability to build wealth for many years to come. Three little numbers (your credit score) can end up saving you hundreds, or even thousands of dollars? Lenders use credit scores to help them determine the *credit worthiness* of consumers applying for credit cards, lines of credit, or loans. Your credit score will probably be used for figuring out whether you qualify for credit, and if so, what terms and interest rates will you receive.

History of Credit Scores

Providing lenders with credit histories has created a billion dollar plus industry that keeps records on hundreds of millions of people. The information is collected and stored by credit bureaus that act as clearing houses for businesses that want to know what a customer's payment history is before they extend credit. At the center of the credit reporting system are the three national credit bureaus: Equifax, Experian, and TransUnion. These bureaus collect and gather credit information and make it available to businesses that subscribe to their service, as well as consumers who request copies of their reports.

Credit scores became widely used in the 1980s. Before credit scores, lenders used to physically look over each applicant's credit report to determine whether to grant credit. A lender might deny credit based on a subjective judgment that a consumer already held too much debt, or had too many recent late payments. Not only was this time consuming, but human judgment was prone to mistakes and bias.

Lenders used personal opinions to make a decision about an applicant that may have had little bearing on the applicant's ability to repay debt. Credit scores help lenders assess risk more fairly because they are more consistent and objective.

Consumers also benefit from this method. No matter who you are as a person, your credit score only reflects your likelihood to repay debt responsibly, based on your past credit history and current credit status. Lenders eventually began to standardize how they made credit decisions by using a point system that scored the different variables on a consumer's credit report. This point system helped to eliminate much of the bias that previously existed; however, it was still tied to intuitive measures of credit worthiness and was not based on actual consumer behavior.

Credit granting took a huge leap forward when statistical models were built that considered numerous variables and combinations of variables. These models were built using payment information from thousands of actual consumers, which made scores highly effective in predicting consumer credit behavior. When combined with computer applications, scoring models have made the credit granting process extremely fast, efficient and objective, while facilitating commerce and helping consumers quickly get the credit they need.

The Credit Modeling Process

Generally, credit scoring models review a set of consumers—often over a million—who open loans at the same time, and determine who paid their loans and who did not. The credit profiles of the consumers who default on the loans are examined to identify common variables they exhibited at the time they applied for the loan. The designers then build statistical models that assign weights to each variable, and these variables are combined to create a credit score. Models for specific types of loans, such as a car or home, more closely consider consumer payment statistics related to these loans. Model builders strive to identify the best set of variables from a consumer's *past* credit history that most effectively predict *future* credit behavior.

Risk Categories

When determining credit scores, lenders place you in a risk category that compares you to a large number of consumers with similar credit histories. This allows lenders to compare apples to apples, ensuring that your credit behavior is judged in a context that is relevant and fair. Your credit score is a fluid number, and changes as the elements in your credit report change. Your scores change over time, sometimes on a daily basis.

For example, payment updates or a new account could cause your score to fluctuate. There are many different credit scores used in the financial service industry. The score may be different from lender to lender (or from car loan to mortgage loan), depending on the type of credit scoring model that was used.

Who Uses Credit Scores and How Are They Used?

Banks, credit card companies, auto dealers, retail stores, and other lenders use scores to quickly summarize a consumer's credit history. This saves the need to manually review an applicant's credit report and provide a better decision. Many additional factors are used in determining risk, such as an applicant's income versus the size of the loan. Your credit score is a leading indicator of your basic credit worthiness.

What Information Impacts My Credit Score?

The information that impacts a credit score varies depending on the score being used. Generally, credit scores are affected by elements in your credit report, such as:

> Number and severity of late payments.
> Type, number, and age of accounts.
> Total debt.
> Recent inquiries.

How Do I Improve My Credit Score?

Paying your bills on time is the single most important contributor to a good credit score. Even if the debt you owe is a small amount, it is crucial that you make payments on time. In addition, you should minimize outstanding debts, avoid overextending yourself, and applying for credit needlessly. Credit applications show up as inquiries on your credit report, indicating to lenders that you may be taking on new debt. Use the credit you already have to prove your ongoing ability to manage credit responsibly.

How Often Does My Credit Score Change?

Your credit score is a fluid number that changes as your credit report changes. Therefore, any change to your credit report could impact your score. Sometimes these issues lag for years or decades and these issues can have devastating financial effects. It's critical that you are protected from creditors and bankruptcy. Review a copy of your credit report annually and be sure to check for inaccuracies. Better to find out before you need to apply for a loan. Guard your credit score as you would the health and safety of your family. It will more than return the favor.

If you're not on the path to financial success, you very well may be on the path to financial failure. Part of the job of your financial advisor is to make sure you understand which road you're on so that, if necessary, you can turn the steering wheel and get back on the road to building wealth.

Check Your Records

There are reasons to check your report. Credit information, which comprises an individual financial history, is an integral part of our modern life. Although it's most often used when someone applies for a loan, a credit report can also be important when you apply for auto insurance, home owner's insurance, renting an apartment, life insurance, or even when you apply for a job. I usually recommend that a consumer's credit report be reviewed at least annually to be sure that all information contained in the report is accurate and complete. Credit report agencies, commonly known as credit bureaus or consumer reporting agencies collect information on individuals from a variety of sources. Most of the data comes from a credit bureau's business subscribers, such as banks or other lenders. The information is obtained from public record. Credit reports don't really include any information about whether or not individuals are a good or poor lending risk. Credit bureau subscribers evaluate the information in the report using their own criteria.

A typical credit report may have some of the following information: personal identification data such as a Social Security number, birth date, current address, and marital status. Credit history, including your current and past creditors, credit terms, limits, and how well or poorly past debts have been repaid, inquiries, a list of requests for credit reports on the individual concerned, and public records such as information on bankruptcies or pending lawsuits, judgments, and other public records. Free annual credit reports are available once every twelve months from each of the three major credit bureaus: Equifax, Experian, and TransUnion.

Under rules of the Federal Trade Commission, the credit bureaus must provide a central access point where consumers may request a copy of their report, including an Internet Web site at www.annual creditreport.com, a toll-free number at 1-877-322-8228, and a postal mailing address. Incorrect or negative information can impact you and your score. You should review your credit report and make sure that you correct any incorrect or incomplete information. Consumers should contact the credit bureau in writing and explain as fully as possible that the information they believe to be incorrect. If requested, the credit bureau is required to investigate the items usually within 30 days after receiving a written request. As part of the investigation, the credit bureau will usually contact the lender or other information provider. Law requires the information provider to investigate the client's issue and report back to the credit bureau. When the investigation is complete, the credit bureau must provide the consumer a written report of the results. If it is found to be incorrect, resulting in a change to the credit report, the bureau will provide a free updated copy of the credit report to the consumer.

How do you correct errors? If you find an error in your credit report, you should notify the credit bureau that issued it. Some bureaus provide correction forms with their reports. You must also notify the creditor and request that the information be corrected. The Fair Credit Reporting Act says that the creditors must respond to your challenge, but the rules don't require them to change your report. Check your report 90 days after your request. If the mistake is still there, you have the right to make a 100-word consumer comment that must be sent out with the report.

Credit Cards

The use of credit cards has become a widespread and accepted part of our modern life. From its modest beginnings in the early 1900s, credit card usage has grown to the point where over 70 percent of American families have at least one general purpose card. Some have many more. There are many reasons individual consumers want to use a credit card. Some of the primary uses are safety, opportunity, leverage, and even guaranteeing personal identity. When used correctly, the use of credit cards allows a consumer to purchase goods and services without the need for a very large amount of cash. They also allow the customer to deal with short-term situations, like holiday purchases, emergencies, or medical expenses where paying cash may not be possible.

Credit cards also allow for payments of goods and services, for instance the telephone or the Internet, even internationally. Some transactions, such as renting a car, purchasing airline tickets, or guarantying payment at a hotel, might be impossible without the use of a credit card. Not all credit cards are alike and they vary in terms of the issuer, use, scope, and contract items. Some of the possibilities include bank cards, charge cards, retail cards, and secured credit cards are usually issued only by lending institutions, bank, savings and loan, or some other organization such as an airline, charity, or college group. Using these types of cards may allow the card holder to achieve other goals such as earning frequent flyer miles or making charitable contributions to the entity of their choice.

Interest Charges: Minimum charges may equal big interest. On some cards, even with a low balance such as $15, you'll still have to pay a minimum finance charge of 50 cents. While it doesn't seem like a lot of money, that's an annual interest rate of about 40 percent. Small amounts do add up for the credit card company.

Cash advances: Cash advances can also cost large sums; some bank also charge cash advance fees for money withdrawn from an automatic teller with your credit card. Don't forget, you should start paying interest on cash advances. There is no grace period.

Fees: In addition to an annual fee, many companies charge extra fees for special situations. For example, if you exceed your credit line, the bank may charge an overdraft fee, usually about $10 or $15 and if your minimum payment is due, there's often a late payment fee on top of that.

Finance charges: This is the interest charge on the amount you owe. Ironically, two cards with the same finance charge won't necessarily cost you the same interest even if you owe the same amount. That's because what you pay depends on how the company figures the balance on which they charge you interest. Make sure you pay close attention to how they're calculating your interest.

Minimum payments: These are typically due within 25 days of the closing date, although some banks have gotten a little cuter and shrunk the due date cycle. Sometimes, they even fall on a weekend. Generally speaking, you must pay at least 5 percent of the new balance or $10, whichever is greater. Whatever you don't pay will be typically carried forward and subject to additional finance charges.

When shopping for a credit card, you should compare the terms under which the card is offered. The devil is hidden in the details. Pay close attention to fees, average daily balance calculation rates, definitions of adjusted balance, interest rates on unpaid balances, Annual Percentage Rates (APRs), billing cycles, and periodic interest rates. Some cards offer great introductory rates and some may also offer other benefits such as cash advances, travel insurance, and discounts on telephone and lodging.

How Many Cards?

Keep the number of open credit cards to a minimum, ideally no more than one for personal use and one for business use. Why have 10 or more? That's just added temptation. Understand the terms in which your card is issued. Sign the cards as soon as they are received. Pay credit card bills promptly to keep interest charges as low as possible and maintain a good credit rating.

Authorize electronic payment of credit card bills from your checking or savings account to automate this process. Keep detailed records of credit card account numbers, expiration dates, and the telephone number of card issuers. The easiest way to do this is to photocopy the front and back and put it in a secure location. This can help you avoid unauthorized use and to protect you from credit fraud. Carefully review your statements each month, and keep customer copies of charge slips to allow for comparison with your monthly statement regularly.

The average American household has over $10,000 of credit card debt. If you only pay the minimums on these cards, it will take you nearly 60 years to eliminate this debt. Think of all of the interest that you will transfer in the process. All of those interest expenses could have been saved for yourself.

Did you know that each time you open a new trade line (credit card or loan), your credit score initially goes down? This is due to the fact that the credit bureaus have no way of knowing how that new trade line will perform. It's even worse if you have a relatively low credit limit on the card.

Example: A major retailer offers you a deferred or (no) interest teaser card with an introductory rate as low as 0 percent for a year (or two). If the balance is $2,000 and your purchase is only $1,500, many people think that is great. However, the credit bureaus don't know why you have the card. They just see that you have charged about 75 percent of the available credit. As a result, your credit score may go down, as your debt ages. Due to no fault of your own, you may actually be hurting yourself. In general, any time you are over about 35 percent of the available balance on a card, it can hurt your scores. First, make sure you only buy things that you have the money to pay for now. Next, if you must charge on a retail card, make sure the limit is high enough to keep your debt ratios in line. Make sure you understand what you are getting into. Otherwise, that 10 percent discount off your first purchase may end up costing you much more.

Chapter Highlights

➢ Understand how debt can prevent us from reaching our financial potential.

➢ Know the difference between good (deductible) debt and bad (non-deductible) consumer debt.

➢ Do you know your credit score? Make sure you review it at least annually and check for accuracy of reported records.

➢ Develop responsible habits for managing your use of credit cards.

CHAPTER 9
KEYS TO BUILDING AND
PROTECTING WEALTH

"The real voyage of discovery consists, not in seeking new
landscapes, but in having new eyes."

—Marcel Proust

The Challenge

How can you learn how to get your money to perform more
than one task at the same time?

Figure 9.1   Take the path less traveled!

Money Tactics

Understand Money! Don't fear it or continue to be mystified by it. Understand how it works, how to grow it, and how to control it. First, you will need to understand how to protect it from various wealth traps. Newton's third law of physics states that objects at rest tend to stay at rest and objects in motion tend to stay in motion. The same is true for money. Our platform allows you to use multiplier effects on your money by coordinating the most advantageous aspects of various financial instruments and integrating them into a cohesive mix of powerful wealth building strategies.

To achieve long-term success, you'll need to work with a financial professional who focuses on the principals of obtaining these multiplier effects, rather than one who only focuses on the accumulation of money method. You work too hard for your money and it's not fair for you if your money is not working as hard as you do.

As we discussed earlier, banks make money differently than us. You need to understand their model so you can employ it in your own life. This will be explained in further detail in another section. It is possible for you to derive a multiplier effect on your money in secure ways that have been shown to be safe and have proven the test of time. Some are guaranteed by financial institutions and banks, or even the government. The techniques are not that difficult to implement, if you follow our platform.

Coordination and Integration of Strategies

Our strategies are intended to help as many people as possible. They're not for everybody but they can be for anybody, specifically we want you to understand that you do have a shot to make a better life for yourself and to build significant or substantial wealth; however you choose to define your particular brand of success.

We believe the key lies in coordination of products and services with integrated strategies. You'll notice in Figure 9.1, it shows how the coordination of the moving parts in an expensive time piece or a watch work together to perform a precision movement.

Proper coordination of the parts is the only way that you can create a precision time piece based on a mechanical movement. If we opened the case, disassembled the moving parts and laid out all the pieces on a table, we would find that all we really have is a bunch of gears, cogs, and pins. Independent of each other, these pieces perform no real function whatsoever. They are worth only the commodity based price that each piece will sell for as a used watch part. Their highest value is only achieved, once they are combined to create an efficient movement. The same is true of financial strategies.

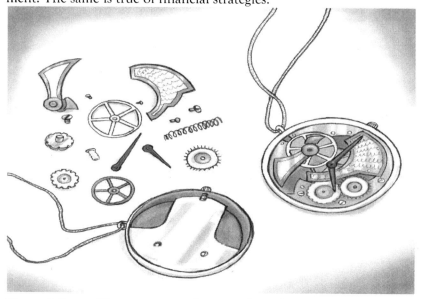

Figure 9.2   The sum is worth more than the parts!

The cogs in our prior example may represent various investments or businesses ventures. The gears could represent your real estate holdings and the pins may represent the cash flow into the model. The case provides protection for the movements so they remain integrated for maximum efficiency. The watch case may be viewed as representing your insurance protection products. If we're missing one of the components, the entire movement system will be diminished, and may not work at all. Similarly, when you are designing a wealth accumulation and protection plan, it is critical that you have all of the moving and fixed components included and coordinated properly.

Military Science Class

A brief lesson on land navigation. One of the essential tasks of soldiering is the ability to navigate across long distances, over and around mountains, and across rivers and valleys without straying too far off course. This is accomplished with a map and a compass. If you only check your bearings once as you set off on your journey, you may not end up where you intend.

During the course of our training, we traveled thousands of meters at a time through thick and densely populated forests and over mountains to locate our objectives (usually a handkerchief hanging from a tree attached to a glow stick) . . . a proverbial needle in a haystack! Imagine how easy it is to get lost or off course without frequently consulting your compass and map.

Financial plans should be used as maps and financial calculators as compasses. You need a map and a strategy to get where you are going, otherwise the terrain will whip you. You also need to set periodic reviews to adjust along the way. Most financial professionals fall woefully short in the follow up phase.

In the kingdom of lies, the truth is treason. When I was in the army, they taught us to look out for land mines. Now that we are in the business world, we see that there are financial land mines all over the place. Unfortunately, a metal detector can't always find them. We want you to build more money with less risk.

You must consider both your accumulated assets (old money) that represents your past decisions; and your new money that is represented by dependable income sources that you know are likely to continue. This is the money that you can either choose to spend or save. We also have a third category called sometimes money. This may include income sources such as: bonuses or commissions that you get from time to time, inheritance, and other windfalls.

How do we get more resources out of limited cash flow? The next step is coordination of the money. We want to take a look at money that is moving and migrating from one area to another to get the extra utility added to these dollars for a second or third use. If we can help you reduce taxes and costs at the same time, then we really hit a home run. Simply put, we want to shrink your expenses so you have more available capital for your goals.

Multiple Uses on Your Money

In order to fulfill your potential, it's critical for your money to get multiple uses and serve multiple purposes. In order for your money to grow rapidly, it needs to be able to perform more than one job at a time. Some of our clients have been able to get their money to perform two, three, or even four functions at the same time. This mindset can help your money perform much like the money of the financial institutions.

Financial institutions understand the principal of making their money work as productively as possible. This is nothing new. Since the invention of banking by the goldsmiths, efficient and effective use of money has consistently functioned as a time-proven strategy. Take a look at your current strategy, or lack of a coordinated strategy. Is your money working as efficiently as it should be? Have you built on your own cost recovery features? Have your current financial advisors taught you how to do this?

Figure 9.3   Which is better . . . new clubs or a better swing?

Clubs or the Swing?

For those of us who are washed up or retired athletes that are used to compete at a high level, we need something to do with our time. Golf serves that purpose for millions of us. In a billion dollar industry, it is outright laughable to consider that most golfers spend 10 or 20 times the amount of money on their equipment (or the clubs) versus coaching for the perfection of their swing. During my first lesson, my golf pro used compassion, and his sense of humor to humble me very quickly, he explained that carrying a bag with $3,000 worth of gold clubs only really insures that I'll hit the ball further out of bounds.

I am a lefty and had terrible slice. The only way I was able to cure the slice, was through proper coaching, and constant practice. This allowed me to correct my swing, which was much more important than purchasing a new club. How many golfers out there think they can fix their poor games by purchasing better and new improved clubs?

How many golf clubs and golf balls manufactures exploit these insecurities and fears, thereby causing the cycles to repeat over and over until the products of the golf industry became a multibillion dollar business?

Athletes and successful individuals both understand that the only way to reach your full potential is by controlling your environment and to focus on a process versus the products.

Money Decision Options: Process versus Product

The Keys to Building Wealth

A financial plan should serve as a blueprint that evaluates your current asset and debts and identifies the goals that you want or need to provide for. It typically lays out various strategies to help you pay for them. Developing a plan is the first step; sticking to it is another discussion.

Why have plans? Without planning, you run some potential financial risk. For example, you may not have enough in reserve to meet large future cost such as college tuition or a down payment on a home. You may also have to scale back future expected vacations or other lifestyle goals. It can help you manage the unexpected, providing a cash fund along with adequate health and life insurance coverage and to hedge against unexpected expenses or illnesses and it can provide money for special expenses that can help you afford the things that are important to you in life, such as education for your children, and travel expenses.

Financial planning in general, receives high marks. But financial planners can get mixed reviews. Make sure you're working with a planner that understands integration and coordination of the moving parts in your plan. People typically fall into different categories of how to plan money-based decisions. Some are more attentive to their finances, while others are just happy to pay the bills each month.

Our first category is what I would refer to as the default option. There are little to no decisions or planning. We refer to this as the glove box approach or proverbial junk drawer approach. This would be a scenario where a person may own several financial products without any real integration. He may own auto insurance, a retirement plan, an

IRA or a 401(k), mutual funds, some life insurance, group health in-surance, and so on.

The problem is that many people have no idea how these products impact each other: How their mortgage may be impacted by how they go about funding their 401(k). How their tax return may be impacted by whether they reinvest the dividends and capital gains or not. This is ground zero for planning. Not doing anything really isn't an option. It's obvious that you will not achieve a great deal of financial success and security under a continuous financial burden. Do whatever you can to avoid having the majority of your available money allocated to others, to both principal and interest payments. You must escape the yolk of consumer debt. Not having a plan is like the messy glove box in many people's cars. Let's get you off that path quickly and into some kind of planning.

Financial product-based planning is often like purchasing an economy car. You may decide that you need a financial product, but you've been taught to focus on the price. Consider your auto insur-ance. As an example, on the east coast where I live, we see commercials about cavemen and lizards that tell us that calling them "will save you a bunch of money on your auto insurance."

The commercials are humorous and they get people's atten-tion. Normally, after the commercial airs, people call in. The company representative will usually spreadsheet their prices against other carri-ers, you pick, and save money. This is how many people have been programmed to make general consumer purchase decisions.

They compare and contrast features, benefits, drawbacks, and ultimately, the price before making a decision. Unfortunately, that's not usually the best way for you to plan your finances. Usually, in mat-ters of finance, the solution with the least capital outlay is not the cheapest solution over the long run, and it's certainly not the best solu-tion.

Accumulation Plans and Needs-Based Planning

Next we examine what is commonly referred to as *needs-based planning*. Many financial professionals operate their practices on this platform. If you've ever worked with a financial advisor, an insurance agent, or stock broker, the discussion has probably centered on needs-based planning modules.

This discussion track centers on questions like:

How much money will you need to retire?

How much money do you think you need for your kids to go to college?

How much do you need to pay off your mortgage?

How much do you need to buy that car?

They will typically put you through a data collection exercise and what can often be described as a manipulative sales process designed to basically scare you into saving money or buying insurance.

Some even say things like:

"Don't you love your family?"

"How are you ever going to retire unless you save more money?"

"Don't you want to take care of them?" and

"What's wrong with you?"

When you get done with the process, many people typically buy the cheapest product that the salesman has to offer, because he's guilted you into a purchase. At the end of the process, the agent wants the whole process to begin again. He perpetuates his sales cycle by asking you for referrals!

They say things like: "I get paid in two ways, I get names of people that I help just like I helped you [yeah right] and I also get paid on the products that I implement."

Who the heck wants to go through that type of manipulative process and then have their friends and family experience the same painful exercise with this pit bull of an insurance salesman? That's why many insurance agents get a bad reputation. There is a better way to plan. All sales should be grounded in needs, but the data should not be manipulated. The more evolved agents, in the evolutionary sales chain, call themselves financial planners.

Modular Financial Planning

These guys are often experts at manipulating data. Their job is to give you many different variables to consider, and sell their services as your financial advisors. Usually their plans are situational in nature and are designed to sell products. This is different than comprehensive financial planning, which usually makes sense for clients with a net worth close to $5 million or over. The modular financial planner's basic formula is as follows.

They need to know what your assumption is for inflation, and if you don't have one, they'll give you one. It may just happen to work out that numbers they pick helps their argument for the products that they want to sell! They need to know how long you're going to be alive; you know that number right? We're also expected to know the day we're going to die. They need to know how much tax rates are going to go in the future. If you don't have a hotline to the IRS, they'll need to make an assumption for that. This will be based on what they assume (guess) the future of tax rates will be.

They also need to know what the financial markets are going to do. What's your assumed rate of return? Everyone thinks 8 to 10 percent returns in a single year is a reasonable assumption. The markets do perform at those levels on average (over long periods of time), but rarely has the market ever returned anywhere within the 8 to 10 percent range in a single year. That's like trying to guess right in Las Vegas! No wonder people are rarely happy with the stock market. They have the wrong expectations.

They'll also need to guess at many other variables, such as: How much money can you put away? How long will you work? (Many planners don't discuss the impact of a disability on your plan. They just assume you'll be able to contribute forever.) It's scary that if a couple of these variables are off by a little bit, it could mean the difference between you retiring in comfort, or working forever. Will you enjoy the retirement of your dreams, or will you need to move in with your kids one day?

If the plan falls short, you may have to reenter the workforce in your 70s, 80s, or beyond. (Asking customers if they'd like fries with their hamburgers, or becoming a greeter at Wal-Mart!) These are not the worst jobs, but probably not the job you want to have when you're 80. Armed with this knowledge, we can see that there may be some flaws in the traditional financial planning process.

Most of the plans sold, also carry a flat fee upfront, sometimes almost as much as the products sold. Additionally, the plan is technically wrong the day it's written, because all those variables are not static. . . . They move. They are constantly changing. Financial markets go up and down. People die at different times. Tax rates change. When we make assumptions, they may look good on paper, but if any of those variables change, we are left with an entirely different set of outcomes.

For clients with a net worth under $3 to $5 million, the traditional financial planning approach is rarely the key to building long-term wealth. It focuses on accumulating finite numbers as opposed to building as much wealth as possible. These plans are rarely monitored and regularly reviewed.

This brings us to economic based strategies. Work with professionals that can help you build wealth without setting any limits. You must begin to learn how to think like a bank. On the first day of business school, they told me two basic concepts that have kept me up at night ever since (1) Opportunity cost, previously covered; and (2) The effect of circulating capital. We were taught how to think like a bank and how to get multiple uses out of our dollars. This is an amazing concept and should be taught in all financial classrooms.

The ultimate goal is to help you understand how to build wealth without any limits and minimize your exposure to wealth-eroding forces. If your net-worth is over $5 million, you may want to consider a fee-based planning solution. It will likely be a comprehensive plan. Avoid financial plans that are centered around product purchases.

Your Engine Is Leaking Oil

Many people are spending more than necessary on their investments and savings plans. They're continuing to make regular capital contributions, as previously discussed, by throwing more money at the problem! Most people are trying to build their wealth by selecting better investment options, seeking higher rates of return, or simply by adding more money to their wealth accumulation vehicles.

The challenge with that *system* is all of the wealth traps on the road. These eroding forces often negatively impact our ability to build wealth. This is what I mean when I say that your financial vehicle is traveling down the road with one foot on the gas and one on the brakes.

You're putting quality premium gas (hard earned dollars) into your vehicle, thinking it's working properly. You've got 90 percent of the engine components working smoothly, but your engine may still leak oil. Unless you take your vehicle in for a tune up or have a mechanic look under the hood, it's difficult to determine where the inefficiencies lie within your engine. If left unattended for many years, that could cause breakdown in vital engine parts and ultimately, your engine may seize.

The same is true with your financial plan. Without attention to details or setting up regular reviews, your plan may go unattended and could result in unintended consequences. You should meet with your planner at least annually and speak with your advisors on a quarterly basis to address any material changes or issues that may impact your plan.

The first phase of the process is to stop the leaks. We want to identify the areas where you might transfer money and plug those leaks.

Step 1: Picture an engine filled with oil. The engine has a broken gasket and is slowly leaking oil. The first step is to plug those holes and make sure the oil level remains constant. The next step is to consider whether or not you want to add more oil (money).

Step 2: Once you capture the leaking oil and stop the leak, you can determine what to do with the excess oil that you've recovered. You have options. Remember, these are new options that we have created. They did not exist before. Do you want to hang onto your recaptured money, use them in your lifestyle (improved spending and cash flow), or do you want to invest them back into your savings platform? Will you put the oil back into your vehicle (perhaps for retirement savings?) or will you use it for current needs and wants?

Most financial experts suggest that a minimum of 10 percent of your gross income, pre-tax, be allocated for usage in your wealth accumulation plan. However, we've found that the best plans are funded with closer to 15 percent, or even 20 percent of your pretax gross income in an effort to be bulletproof. Our goal is to help you get an early start and have your money working for you, so that you are not working for money forever.

Chapter Highlights

> ➢ Understand different ways to plan your financial decisions.
> ➢ Is your wealth bucket leaking water? Take a look at how and where you may be transferring wealth.
> ➢ Understand the difference between having a planning process and buying products.

CHAPTER 10
THE FAMILY BUSINESS

"Two roads diverged in a wood, and I took the one less traveled by,
and that has made all the differences."
—Robert Frost

THE CHALLENGE

How do you get your household to run like a
business to maximize your income?

Economics is defined as the branch of social science that deals with the production, distribution, and consumption of goods, services, and their management. In the course of our economic studies, we learned about aggregate lifetime earnings of individuals. We learned that the average person works for about 40 years. Imagine if you were able to earn $100,000 per year? Your lifetime earnings would amount to $100,000 × 40 or about a total of $4 million of lifetime earnings! That amount may pass through your hands during your lifetime.

It sounds great, until you factor in the cast of characters who attempt to help themselves to a large part of your earnings with: taxes, fees, interest expenses, inflation, and even lawsuits. I remember imagining how wonderful life would be if we could find a way to keep most of it.

As far as we can tell, the most valuable commodity we have is our future potential. Specifically it is our ability to use our unique skills and talents to improve the world and change our financial futures by the application of our talents. For most of us, that future potential is valued as the sum of our future earnings. Said another way, our most precious asset is not our house, car, jewelry, or even our investments . . . it is our ability to earn a living and contribute to society. Reaching our potential and using our unique gifts allows us to lead a life of significance.

159

"I am worth more dead than alive." How many times have we heard someone say this? This is a ridiculous notion. What the person is saying is that their insurance death benefit amounts are larger than what they have been able to save. This is very common. Most people fail to build any significant wealth because they either do not save or because they don't have anything left to save each month. They are tricked into constant consumer purchases and they pay for these frivolous purchases many times over and all with interest expenses.

Our net worth is not defined by our bank accounts. Our worth is not defined by the sum of what we have managed to save. Our worth is at least our future earnings, plus what we have saved. This is our economic value to our families. Hopefully, those earnings will continue to increase over time. Why not make sure that your family gets this full replacement value, no matter what?

We insure our physical assets such as our automobiles, homes, boats, and jewelry without a second thought. We insure our businesses, factories, inventories, trucks, and buildings. How many of us insure our potential earnings? After all, this is more important than the other items?

It is our earnings that will allow us to build wealth, which can be applied to the development of a business. Once established, this business can ultimately provide us with ongoing revenue.

Consumer spending is the largest component of our gross domestic product. The consumer (individuals and families) drive our economy. The concept of the American family has changed quite a bit over time but the family household is still at the center of businesses, and remains the engine of industry and our economy.

The family should be viewed as both a social and an economic entity engaged in the basic functions of production, consumption, and exchange. Its purchasing decisions and activities fuel the nation's economy, while the family's financial interests must be protected.

The Family As a Business?

In considering our financial affairs, we frequently emphasize only our business or job (employment) and disassociate the concept of economics from our family life. The concept of making business decisions cannot end when you cash the paycheck. You need to conduct your financial affairs at home, with the same attention to detail that is paid at work.

We all know how to pinch pennies and shop for a deal, but economics and financial matters seem like a strange subject to many of us. We can't remember how many times people have told us "I am not good with money. It's not my thing." Few people are. We are not generally taught to focus on money issues. This is a skill set that needs to be learned and developed like any other. It's time to take charge and get involved in your money matters.

Most of us really have two business lives to consider. Our jobs and our household finances. Of the two, home and family are the most important. Remember, our jobs serve as a way to provide the best economic advantages to our family (business).

Along the same lines, a marriage is really a business partnership between two people. For years, we have taught this concept to young couples who are preparing to get married. In order to improve your chances of success, the marriage needs to be managed and protected. If we follow this economic analogy, we see that marriage is a partnership agreement that requires a plan, cash flow, and the protection of those finances.

Most couples quickly find out that they usually come from two different schools of thought on money. It is important to take stock of how each of you view and interact with money, and money-based decisions. If you have a singular vision and back that vision with the proper habits, you stand a better chance of financial success. Take the time to understand how money and bills are handled by each party, and try to create a common game plan.

Balance Your Checkbook Monthly

Do you balance your checkbook each month? Balancing your checkbook is one of the most basic habits for good money management, yet millions of Americans don't do it on a regular basis. Many people never record the pennies on the checks they write. Some guess at certain amounts, and other people only balance their checkbooks once a year when they do their taxes.

Balancing your checkbook each month helps you keep tabs on your cash flow, it also shows you the fees you're paying for bank services, and can warn you about potential problems such as overdrawing on your account. As banking services expand, these monthly statements have become important records for managing your daily finances. In addition to being a record of the checks you wrote, the statement can also show you your deposits and withdrawals. They may also provide helpful information such as when your CDs and time deposits will mature.

Some banks have even developed comprehensive master statements that show you all the accounts you have with the bank, including checking, savings, CDs, and even loans. The advantage here is convenience; you have a monthly snapshot of your dealings with the bank all on one document.

Here are a few reasons why you should balance your checkbook monthly. Balancing your checkbook is a method of verifying that your records using your checkbook register matches the bank's records as shown on your monthly bank statements. Typically, your bank processes thousands of transactions accurately but it can make mistakes. What if there's an error? In most cases, the bank statements are right, but you should compare your records (along with ATM receipts and your deposit slips), since errors sometimes do occur. Generally, you have about 60 days to report errors involving electronic transfers, but only 14 days for other kinds of mistakes. The sooner you notify the bank, the better off you are. If you don't balance your checkbook monthly, you might not find the error within the allotted 60 days. It's more likely that you may have made a mathematical error in your checkbook register that you're unlikely to find unless you balance your checkbook each month.

If you make a mistake or forget to post a debit card purchase, an ATM transaction, or another withdrawal in your checkbook register, you may start bouncing checks and incurring additional fees. These can often amount to $25 or more for each returned check and it may impact your credit score. If you don't correct this problem quickly, you can often incur a number of returned check fees. You might even incur more than one fee for the same check if the person re-deposits it, in hopes that your balance will now cover the outstanding debt.

If there is a problem at some point, it's much more difficult to sift through monthly transactions to sort through the problem. If you have balanced your checkbook each month, the most you'll ever have to do is look at your recent month's transactions. People sometimes make such a mess of their checkbook by not balancing it regularly that they have to close out their account or even open a new one. Unfortunately, the basic money management task of balancing our checkbooks is not taught in most schools and usually not even taught by our parents. If you're just beginning or starting out on your own, make it a point to balance your checkbook on a regular basis. This will serve as the backdrop to instilling good fiscal habits in your own family business. Once this is complete, it will be easier to review your family budget and make the necessary adjustments.

Time Required

About 20 to 30 minutes a month. Here's how to do it.

1. Reconcile all of your checks. Sort your canceled checks by check number or review the checks in numbered order shown on your statement. In your checkbook register, you would check off each canceled check returned to you or each check that appears on the check listing to make sure the amount you recorded is the amount that the bank shows.

2. Reconcile your deposit. In the same fashion, as we reconcile your checks, make sure the deposits shown on your bank statement are reported in your check register. Make sure to review your direct deposit amounts as well. Go through your deposit slips and paycheck stubs to make sure the bank statement shows all the deposits you have made. Check off the deposits in your check register the same way you did for your canceled checks.

3. Repeat the same process for your debit card purchases and ATM withdrawals.

4. Record any interest earned and review any bank fees. This can help you identify any fees or expenses that you may be paying (extra dollars in transferred money).

5. List your outstanding checks. These are checks that you did not check off your register, because they have not cleared yet. The same is true for outstanding debit purchases and ATM withdrawals.

6. Total the column of outstanding checks, debits, and ATM withdrawals and then repeat the same process for your outstanding deposit. This way you can keep accurate records of your money that will be in your account but have not yet cleared.

7. Record your ending bank balances, which are on your bank statement and then enter any outstanding deposits and checks.

Once this process is completed, calculate your balance. Just to-tal the lines on your check register plus any outstanding items. This should equal the balance on your check register. If it doesn't, do a quick check for math errors in your checkbook register, such as reversed numbers or by subtracting a deposit instead of adding it or vice versa.

Installing this process and adhering to it on a monthly basis is one of the best ways to make sure you stay on top of your finances and your financial situation does not run too far out of control.

Have a Budget

Business owners create detailed budgets each year. Family ex-penditures should also be budgeted in a true business fashion. The ba-sic purpose of creating a personal budget is to plan how your money will be spent. Given limited financial resources for all of us, a budget is a method of managing personal cash flow to meet both current obliga-tions, as well as providing for future spending needs.

Prepare a personal budget and use it as a family financial plan-ning tool. Properly used, a personal budget can ensure that income and expenditures both match in amount and timing. It can also serve to highlight potential cash flow problems, as well as identify opportunities to make better use of your current income. It also can serve as a yardstick to help measure your progress. By comparing your plan budg-et against actual results, you can see if progress is being made toward meeting your specific goals. This measuring process can often highlight areas where changes may need to be made.

Do whatever you can to lessen your consumer debt load. It be-gins with a well-written tracked budget. A budget can help you prevent impulse spending and afford a system to decide what you can and can-not afford. This process can also help you identify expenses that can be reduced or eliminated on a regular basis. Take time to write it down. You may be amazed by the money you spend without even thinking about it.

Communication, explanation, and understanding are critical to a successful family budget. Every member of the family needs to un-derstand what I am trying to accomplish and why it's important. This way, they can assist in helping the family meet its goals. Take time to explain the budget to each family member, and explain the financial realities that your family faces. Try to get everyone involved, and include the entire family in on the rewards whenever possible. Cooperation and commitment from every member are important, and they must not only understand the plan but buy into it as well. Make sure you buy into the overall goal or your family will see right through your stated intentions.

Steps to Prepare a Budget

There are a number of steps in preparing and using your personal budget. First, take a look at your past income and expenditures. This initial step is designed to help record information on past cash flow, taking a look at both income and spending. Ideally, a full year's worth of data should be gathered to even out the effects of varying income. Take a look at old paychecks, canceled checks, copies of bank statements, and your recent tax returns. You may want to also keep a spending diary for a short period of time. This will help you stay on track.

Establish goals and designate resources for specific purposes. Goals should be set with dollar amounts and a realistic time frame that each goal should be accomplished. Take a look at your available cash flow and earmark specific dollar amounts to dedicate toward meeting each goal. The goals should be simple; as easy as making ends meet each month, or they can be more complex and long-term, such as retirement planning or college funding.

Make sure that you maintain records. One of the most difficult parts of the budget process is to keep track of your income and expenditures. The more often you do this, the clearer your financial picture will become. Finally, use periodic reviews. Comparing your plan's budget with actual results can provide a great means of measuring progress toward an individual goal. The review will usually indicate if changes should be made from either: income, expenses, or both.

Expense Category	Estimated Monthly Expenses	Actual Expense	Revised Monthly Expense
Fixed Expenses			
1st Mortgage/Rent			
2nd Mortgage			

(continued)

(*continued*)

Expense Category	Estimated Monthly Expenses	Actual Expense	Revised Monthly Expense
Auto Payment 1			
Auto Payment 2			
Auto Payment 3			
Auto Insurance			
Homeowner's Insurance			
Health Insurance			
Disability Insurance			
Life Insurance			
Long-Term Care Insurance			
Student Loans			
Credit Card Payments			
Installment Debts			
Child Care			
Alimony/Child Support			
Utilities			
Cable Television			
Phone			
Cell Phones			
Internet			
Retirement Savings			
General Savings			
Total Fixed Expenses			

Expense Category	Estimated Monthly Expenses	Actual Expense	Revised Monthly Expense
Variable Expenses			
Water/Sewer			
Garbage Disposal			
Grocery/Food			
Lunch Meals			
Take Out			
Dining Out			
School Lunches/Milk $			
Gas for Cars			
Commuting Expenses			
Gym Membership			
Hair/Nails/Health			
Total Variable Expenses			

Figure 10.1

Expense Category	Estimated Monthly Expenses	Actual Expense	Revised Monthly Expense
Periodic Expenses			
Health Deductibles/Coinsurance/Prescriptions			
Clothing			
Car Repairs			
Home Repairs			

(continued)

(continued)

Expense Category	Estimated Monthly Expenses	Actual Expense	Revised Monthly Expense
Camp			
Holiday Gifts			
Birthday Gifts			
Doctor Visits			
Dentist Visits			
License Renewals			
Other Gifts			
Total Periodic Expenses			
Total Monthly Income			
Total of All Expenses			
Total Excess/Deficit			

Figure 10.2

Emergency expenses also need to be accounted for in your budget. These include unforeseen costs. Our short-term emergency funds and short-term savings need to be established and used for these purposes. Many of these expenses commonly involve things such as the replacement of major appliances, home repairs, automotive repairs, and unanticipated medical expenses.

Organizing and keeping your budget is very important and may become a constant source to better understand your journey to financial success. If you don't know where your money is going, what chance do you stand of ever being able to recapture these expenses and bring them back to the table for your own use?

Take a look at some of your more common household expenses. These areas may offer you an easy means of reducing your day-to-day bills that can then be used to either eliminate your consumer debt or saved to build your accumulated wealth. Some areas offer an opportunity for you to reduce your monthly expenses and free up some additional cash flow. These include things such as eating out for lunch each day, dining out for dinner, gifts to others, unnecessary trips or vacations, utility bills, such as cable television, telephone, cell phones, weekly dry cleaning and laundry bills, subscriptions to newspapers or magazines, non-generic prescriptions (if generic is available), clothing expenses, recreation, and entertainment. You must learn to control your spending or it will ultimately control you.

Flow of Money

While managing your cash flow and eliminating debt, there are points of control where we can increase, redirect, or stop the flow of money much like the lock system in a canal. An efficiently managed system requires that you understand how your money is flowing, where it's going, and how we can improve the flow to use these points of control effectively.

Our primary objective should be to have our money accomplish all that it can accomplish and increase our overall wealth by minimizing your wealth transfers. Make sure you exercise control by establishing specific targets for setting aside money before you spend any of it on your cash flow expenses. Always think about yourself first. After all, aren't you working for yourself and your family? This strategy can allow you to maximize control, increase potential growth, and minimize tax liabilities whenever possible.

Expenses and Savings

Family budgets should be arranged with respect to two distinct divisions. One part relating to expenditures now, and the other to expenditures allocated to meet future needs.

Present Needs and Wants

How much are you spending on basic living needs, such as housing, food, clothing, automobiles, utilities, and so on? How healthy is your emergency fund? Can you readily access 6 to 12 months worth of living expenses?

Future Goals

✓ What are you saving for future expenses, such as college funding, retirement planning, and so on?

✓ Is there a future purchase that you are saving toward?

✓ Have you protected your income and assets adequately?

✓ What are your household priorities?

✓ Where do savings and investing stand on your list of priorities?

✓ What are your short- or long-term goals?

✓ Do your children share your values related to money and finances?

✓ Are you saving 10 to 15 percent of your current monthly gross income? If not, what amount are you saving?

A Word on Kids and Money

Teach your children well and they will benefit for a lifetime.

If you want to teach your kids about money, it will serve you well to work off their own mini-budget outline. This way they can understand where money comes from and how much things cost. Quarterly or period-based budgeting is probably the best thing you can instill early on in a child's financial life. Give them small tasks to handle. Once they've established an annual budget you can break it down into quarterly or 12-week cycles. Once your child has proven they can make and manage their budget responsibly over that period of time, you may want to increase their funds for the following quarter. Some goals include: balancing their own checkbook or balance sheet, making systematic savings deposits, contributing a portion to charity or religious purposes, and maintaining or living within their budget.

There should be a direct correlation between how well they perform with a budget, managing their money, and how much independence they are given to spend their money.

Once you establish this budget, stick to it. When your child wants an outfit or an item for a special occasion, the first thing that you should ask them is: "Is it in the budget?" If not, teach them to start saving for it. It's okay to determine agreements on percentages that you and the child will pay, but the idea to bring home is the reality of how the money is earned, managed, and saved. This works much better than the old battle cry "Money doesn't grow on trees!" By empowering your children to make decisions about money, you will have a better chance of helping them understand the importance of good financial management.

It's important to have a review of the budget and at some point, you may want to introduce them to your family budget, so they can see where the money comes from. To keep telling them that money doesn't grow on trees has not proved to be an effective strategy in teaching kids fiscal literacy.

Make sure you give them the proper praise when it is earned and try to avoid using their allowance as a form of behavioral control or a punishment; this will defeat the purpose entirely. The purpose of their allowance and budget is to develop financial life skills. Stay focused on financial management and fiscal literacy and the rest will usually take care of itself. Make sure they understand how their budget impacts the entire family budget.

What are the financial values that you and your family hold dear? Your children should be clear on your personal family financial values and make sure their financially values are congruent and aligned with yours. Teach them what they will be able to do in the future if they're able to master money skills.

If you give a man a fish, he eats for a day. If you teach a man to fish, he eats for a lifetime. Once they've seen an outline of the family budget, they can see how their budget fits into the big picture and is easier for them to understand the needs of the family. They should understand how their brother's or sister's finances impact them. This type of process teaches them to share or potentially help each other out with any of their extra capital. This type of process can help them overcome their selfish ways and work toward team-based goals. The sooner you begin the process, the better off your family will be.

Protect Your Future at All Costs

Once you and your family have a handle on your spending habits, it's time to make sure that the plan will work under any circumstances. Where will the money come from to pay the bills if you can't work? Most times for young couples, there are no real investment assets to speak of when the marriage begins. The primary economic asset is usually their future income capacity of the working spouses. That value should be protected as carefully as our other assets.

It's an injustice to a spouse and the children (business partners) to start a family business with nothing more than hopes and dreams. The income earners capacity to earn must be protected at all times. A death or disability event can disrupt the cash flow of your family business at any time and many of the most serious financial problems arise at that time.

Imagine all that you have saved being depleted in a matter of months. How quickly could your savings, retirement plans, or other assets be depleted if you could not work?

Insurance is designed to meet such problems and make sure that your family will receive the full economic advantages. Death dissolves the family partnership agreement, but then what? Personal insurance for the family can come forward to meet those problems. It serves to keep the family estate, usually consisting primarily of the life value asset of the primary income earner(s), intact.

By protecting your income, you are able to guarantee that your spouse and children will receive your full economic value no matter what happens. Life insurance serves as a mechanism to pass on the full replacement value of the earning capacity to your family business. The problem with needs-only based planning is that it often focuses on the supposed needs of the beneficiaries as opposed to guarantying the full economic value of the insured's life.

Life and disability insurance should be a priority on the itemized budget. It should stand prominently, immediately after the necessities of life such as housing, clothing, food, and education. Many people do save money, but often to the exclusion of life insurance. The trick is to find ways to get your money to perform multiple tasks at once. As we continue our protection discussion in the next chapter, you will see the additional advantages of including insurance strategies in your accumulation planning. Life insurance is often viewed only as a protective measure, but can also serve as a dependable and convenient form of saving.

A Million Dollar Verdict?

My father is an attorney and I was raised on stories about lawsuits. Some of the cases are quite interesting. He would give us hypothetical scenarios and ask my siblings to determine a proper amount of compensation for the victims. We learned that the first consideration is usually not pain and suffering, it is the loss of earnings.

For example, if the disabled or deceased victim had been earning $50,000 per year and was 50 years old at the time of injury or death, he would likely be unable to perform his job duties and earn a living. In this case, he or his family would be out $50,000 × 15, which are the remaining years of his working lifetime (to age 65). The result is lost wages of $750,000 before adjusting for future wage increases, inflation adjustments, or raises. Next, other factors are added such as medical expenses (prior, current, and future estimates for care), pain and suffering, and/or punitive damages.

The idea is to properly compensate the injured party for their losses . . . not to make them lottery winners. Imagine if the injured party had been earning $150,000 per year, then we would need to triple the numbers. This is why we see multimillion dollar lawsuit decisions every day in our courts. If you were injured, you would probably want fair and just compensation. Conversely, if you accumulate wealth, it will likely come under attack by others. What if you don't die in an accident? Therefore, it will be critical for you to protect yourself accordingly (covered in a later chapter).

Human Life Values

In the financial services world, we call this compensation formula the human life value equation. Human life value uses a calculation method of insurance for the protection of human life values against all types of economic disruptions. My background training in economics has helped me understand the important role that permanent life insurance plays in providing financial security to the American family.

Life insurance has traditionally been viewed as an instrument to provide liquidity to beneficiaries for premature death related expenses, such as burial expenses, mortgage liquidity, outstanding debt repayment, and educational funding needs. The insurance industry has not done a good job of communicating the benefits of permanent life insurance to the consumer public. When used properly, the product can be used to accomplish much more.

Clearly, the ability to earn an income is by far your greatest asset. The money you earn is going to provide you with food, clothing, shelter, health care, transportation, insurance protection, education of yourself and your children, a vacation, and a retirement income.

The average income at age 65 can be illustrated by multiplying your current income, or the average of your current income to age 65. For example, if you are 25 years old, you would multiply the average current income by a factor of 40 to arrive at your lifetime earnings estimate. At age 30, you would multiply by 35, and at age 40, you would multiply by 25.

This table illustrates your lifetime earnings projection:

Annual Income $50,000 × 40 Working Years =
$2,000,000 Lifetime Earnings
Annual Income $75,000 x 40 Working Years =
$3,000,000 Lifetime Earnings
Annual Income $100,000 x 40 Working Years =
$4,000,000 Lifetime Earnings

During my risk management classes, I learned that in general, very small amounts of our human life values are currently covered with life insurance or disability income protection. Our earning power is an economic asset just like any other asset. It follows that we should also protect the monetary worth of our lives. These techniques and principles have been taught in our colleges and business schools for decades.

Chapter Highlights

➤ Run the family finances like a business.
➤ Balance your checkbook monthly and adhere to a budget.
➤ Understand the flow of money.
➤ The value of human life.

CHAPTER 11
INSURANCE STRATEGIES

"The reason that worry kills more people than work
is that more people worry than work."

—Robert Frost

The Challenge

I want to protect myself, my family, my business, and my assets. How can I bulletproof my plan and get most of my premiums back?

More money, more problems. Once you manage to build a little wealth, you will need to consider how you want to protect it. Wherever wealth accumulates, someone will try to steal it.

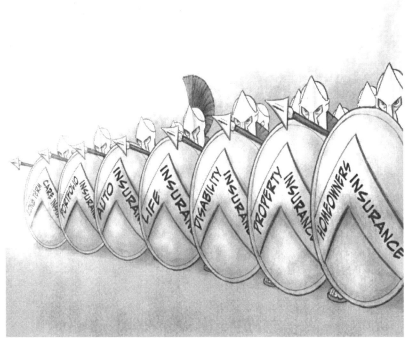

Figure 11.1   The Phalanx of Protection.

Phalanx Overview

In ancient times, battles were won or lost based on the competency of military leaders. One of the greatest military civilizations in history dates back to ancient Greece. The Greek empire thrived as a civilization because of their superior military campaigns. Their Phalanx became the most formidable military formation of the ancient world. Phalanx was comprised of columns of soldiers who would line up with interlocked shields on the battlefield to create an impenetrable wall comprised of shields and spears.

Their defense was virtually impenetrable, because of the interlocking fashion of their shields. When the soldiers fought together as one single unit, they were usually unstoppable.

The most famous battle in the ancient world pitted the east against the west in the Battle of Thermopile. During this battle, three hundred elite soldiers from the Spartan Army faced off against hundreds of thousands of Persians. They used their famous Phalanx formation as their defense. Over the course of several days, the small three hundred man army held its ground against one of the largest armies ever assembled in the history of the world.

Hire a Few Spartans

Imagine the security that would come with being surrounded by an army of the greatest warriors ever to walk the face of the earth? Lucky for us, we don't have to worry about foreign invaders trying to steal our possessions and burn our villages to the ground. We do have many other perils and wealth eroding factors that can impact our ability to build and protect our wealth. That is where our insurance-based strategies come into play. We must build strategies to protect us from unforeseen events.

Your Insurance Phalanx

Our insurance programs must be strong enough to protect us from any potential peril that might come our way. It is in the coordination and integration of your insurance and protection strategies that you can develop as an effective risk management plan. Once you have the interlocking protection in place, you can use it to help other areas of your plan come to life.

Figure 11.2   Build a high wall of protection around your own city
of wealth. The Trojans understood this concept.

Only once you have a sound foundation of risk management
and protection strategies in place, can you build your wealth worry free.
My goal is to work with you to create an effective risk management
program that can work in a coordinated fashion to help you maximize
your protection, while minimizing your out-of-pocket outlay. In this
fashion, you can create a virtual Phalanx of protection around your
wealth. Once this is done effectively, the next step is to use cost recovery strategies to help you recapture the capital that you are spending in
order to protect your financial interests.

Risk Management and Protection

Many pay a little so that a few get a lot when they need it.

Insurance allows us to eliminate risk in our economic affairs.
Insurance may be defined as a means of reducing uncertainty with respect to personal and business affairs. The elements of risk or uncer-

tainty are universal in our economic life. We use insurance as a way to deal with risk.

How Much Do I need?

In general, you should purchase all of the insurance that you can get, and all that company will issue. It is impossible to leave your family rich, by buying too much life insurance; it is impossible to make yourself rich, by buying too much disability insurance; and it is certainly impossible to get back twice the value of your home, or other valuable asset, by over insuring it. The system does not allow you to do that. Therefore, anyone who buys less than the maximum available coverage may end up cheating themselves. Insurance products are designed to make sure that what you want to occur will actually happen in your darkest hour. It's impossible to buy too much insurance. Therefore, you should have the maximum protection available, and should seek to find ways to get others to offset or minimize your out-of-pocket cash outlay.

Insurance costs can end up consuming a large portion of a family's disposable income. When we consider that the average family may spend well over $2,000 a year annually on auto insurance, $500 to $1,000 on home owner's insurance, another $500 or so for an umbrella policy, several hundred dollars to well over $1,000 annually for term life insurance policies, not to mention the cost of annual health insurance, we must examine what the true cost of these plans represent.

Imagine for a moment, if you didn't have to purchase any insurance at all, and instead, you had the luxury of being able to save all your money for the future. That could easily represent several thousands of dollars that could potentially be compounded at interest for you to use at some point in the future. From our earlier discussions, we realized that even $4,000 or $5,000 a year compounded annually over a large period of time could one day grow to nearly $1 million.

However, we must consider the possibility that if there were a major claim from a hurricane, tornado, or automotive accident, there could be devastating financial consequences. In fact, some or all of our wealth could be eliminated in a matter of moments. Therefore, the best course of action seems to be to cover the largest claims and managed the catastrophic coverage, while minimizing your out-of-pocket outlay wherever possible. Ideally, we should try to self-insure the smaller claims that can help lower our premiums. This premium savings can be recaptured to be saved elsewhere for our financial priorities.

Imagine if we could eliminate even $1,000 a year in unnecessary costs of insurance, and reposition that somewhere else within our financial model for future growth. The results could represent exponential savings for you and your family to recover over your lifetime, regardless of what the stock market is doing. This is the goal of a well-orchestrated, coordinated insurance program, designed to provide you with catastrophic coverage, while minimizing your annual out-of-pocket outlay.

Let's talk about the origins of risk management and insurance. If we travel back in time, we see that there was once a time when people had no insurance to protect their personal assets. The industry had not been invented yet. This was not a period of economic growth. Industry and commerce typically only occur in a secure environment. In the period before insurance protection, the progress of the primitive commercial societies was stifled. People were paralyzed by fear, and made their financial and risk decisions based on fear and superstitions.

We now live in a world where risk can be transferred. The creation of our modern insurance industry has allowed us to make better decisions surrounding our money and our property. By running efficient business models, insurance companies allow us to shift specific risks away from ourselves into a pool of capital of individuals that agree to help each other should a loss should occur. When a loss occurs, the pool is used to compensate its claimant for their loss.

Unfortunately, many Americans have been taught to view insurance as a necessary evil and a bad investment. This is a pessimistic view of insurance. It is important to understand that insurance is designed to ideally reimburse the owner for the full replacement value of any insured item that is lost or destroyed. Basically, many people pay a little into a fund, so that a few can get everything back when they need it.

What Will You Get Back If You Have an Accident?

How have you insured your automobile? If one was totaled in an accident or stolen, would you rather have the full replacement value of the vehicle paid to you, or would you be happy to receive just enough money to buy another lesser vehicle? What if the new vehicle is much less valuable than the car that was totaled? It may get you to and from work, but you just might prefer to park it around the block where no one at work will see!

What about your home? If your home were destroyed in a fire, tornado, hurricane, or some other peril, would you want the insurance company to pay you the full value of your home, or only build you a new home that will serve your basic living needs? What if your house was destroyed and they only wanted to provide you with a replacement shack?

Figure 11.3   Are you insured for full replacement value?

If you were to die prematurely, how much do you want your family to have? If you died in your sleep and your guardian angel allowed you to come back down to earth to place as much money in a checking account as your family would need to replace you . . . what would that amount be? Would the number be closer to an annual income for as long as you would have been working or would you want them to receive only what they need for basic survival and nothing more?

How about your income? If you became disabled or could not work, would you prefer to have your full income replaced or a fraction of your current earnings? Perhaps just enough to meet your minimum survival needs? This is the same result as having your paycheck cut in half by your employer. Few would stand for that.

Unfortunately, many people are more focused on their basic needs when justifying the amount of their insurance purchases, as opposed to focusing on the full replacement value of their prized assets.

How have you made your risk management decisions? Many people have insured only small amounts of their income and assets. Some people don't believe in insurance, or limit their coverage in an attempt to lower their bills. Please understand that it doesn't have to be this way! You can achieve both goals without very little out-of-pocket expense . . . maybe no additional expense at all.

You can do this by recapturing the dollars that you are transferring, and then by redirecting those dollars back to fund your risk management needs. What if your risk-management decisions come back to haunt you? Will you feel penny wise and pound foolish if (or more likely when) one of these perils actually occurs? You may end up cheating yourself, your family, or your business in your moment of need. Make sure you focus on achieving full replacement value coverage.

You get what you pay for! Almost every time we look for a cheaper alternative, we end up buying something with fewer benefits and less intrinsic (real) value. In our purchasing decisions, if we always buy based upon price first, we will end up with a house filled with inexpensive junk! There are many people that can tell you the price of everything, and the value of nothing. Steer clear of these individuals.

They are cheapskates who die with a bunch of garbage in their house and a few extra bucks in a low interest savings account at the bank. Whenever you can, buy insurance products that replace the full value of the assets and the income that you want to protect.

Once you accomplish this you can select the appropriate coverage that will make your life whole if that risk or peril actually came to be. No one complains when the insurance company sends a check equal to or greater than the value of the loss incurred. There are creative ways to cover your maximum loss without having to pay enormous premiums.

Beware of Madison Avenue

Don't be fooled by low-priced teaser ads. It is difficult for us to get through a night of television without being exposed to multiple insurance advertisements. At first glance, it may seem that one insurer is actually offering the coverage at deep discounts from another insurer when in fact if we peel back the layers of the onion, we see that there may be major differences in the policies. Make sure to perform a side-by-side analysis of the coverage. You may quickly discover the reason for the savings (less coverage or low introductory rates that may soon skyrocket).

Deductible Tactics

Deductibles—every policy has a deductible which is an amount you pay for a loss before the coverage kicks in. These deductibles may vary from a few hundred dollars to a few thousand dollars. You can reduce the cost of your insurance by taking a larger deductible but you will have to pay the amount of any potential losses up to that deductible. Work with your personal CFO to design a strategy that creates the proper balance for each.

You may be able to redesign your current coverage to create similar or larger savings. One strategy is to insure the large risks and minimize the premiums at the same time. This can be accomplished by underwriting the smaller risks yourself. In general, it can make sense for you to keep your deductibles high on your casualty insurance policies (auto and homeowners). The deductible represents the amount that you will be responsible for paying before the insurance company pays for the balance of the damages. Higher deductibles will usually lower your premiums.

You don't always need to cover your first dollar of loss. There are many ways that you can adjust your deductibles accordingly. The concept is that by increasing your deductibles you will free up dollars that can be saved to cover the gap between your original deductible, and your new (higher) deductible. Every year that you don't have a claim, your side-fund is growing. Over time this can add up to very large sums. If you don't have the difference saved, hold off on this strategy. If you are diligently saving money in another area, you will soon be able to take advantage of this strategy. Remember, we are trying to coordinate different aspects of your finances.

Many people carry very low deductibles on their insurance products, often $250 or $500. This is usually a function of not having many other assets when we first obtain the coverage. Many people don't review their deductibles annually. As your savings and other assets grow it may make sense to raise your deductibles to $1,000 or even as high as $2,000 per incident. Unfortunately, most agents don't teach this philosophy. Most offer quick, cookie-cutter solutions.

Here's a quick example of how premium savings can add up over time.

Age	Year #	Annual Savings	Cumulative Amount Saved	Opportunity Rate of Return	Cumulative Opportunity Cost	Cumulative Account Value
30	1	$500	$500	8.00%	$0	$500
31	2	$500	$1,000	8.00%	$40	$1,040
32	3	$500	$1,500	8.00%	$123	$1,623
33	4	$500	$2,000	8.00%	$253	$2,253
34	5	$500	$2,500	8.00%	$433	$2,933
35	6	$500	$3,000	8.00%	$668	$3,668
36	7	$500	$3,500	8.00%	$961	$4,461
37	8	$500	$4,000	8.00%	$1,318	$5,318
38	9	$500	$4,500	8.00%	$1,744	$6,244
39	10	$500	$5,000	8.00%	$2,243	$7,243
40	11	$500	$5,500	8.00%	$2,823	$8,323
41	12	$500	$6,000	8.00%	$3,489	$9,489
42	13	$500	$6,500	8.00%	$4,248	$10,748
43	14	$500	$7,000	8.00%	$5,107	$12,107
44	15	$500	$7,500	8.00%	$6,076	$13,576
45	16	$500	$8,000	8.00%	$7,162	$15,162
46	17	$500	$8,500	8.00%	$8,375	$16,875
47	18	$500	$9,000	8.00%	$9,725	$18,725
48	19	$500	$9,500	8.00%	$11,223	$20,723
49	20	$500	$10,000	8.00%	$12,881	$22,881
50	21	$500	$10,500	8.00%	$14,711	$25,211
51	22	$500	$11,000	8.00%	$16,728	$27,728
52	23	$500	$11,500	8.00%	$18,947	$30,447
53	24	$500	$12,000	8.00%	$21,382	$33,382
54	25	$500	$12,500	8.00%	$24,053	$36,553
55	26	$500	$13,000	8.00%	$26,977	$39,977
56	27	$500	$13,500	8.00%	$30,175	$43,675
57	28	$500	$14,000	8.00%	$33,669	$47,669
58	29	$500	$14,500	8.00%	$37,483	$51,983
59	30	$500	$15,000	8.00%	$41,642	$56,642

(continued)

(*continued*)

Age	Year #	Annual Savings	Cumulative Amount Saved	Opportunity Rate of Return	Cumulative Opportunity Cost	Cumulative Account Value
60	31	$500	$15,500	8.00%	$46,173	$61,673
61	32	$500	$16,000	8.00%	$51,107	$67,107
62	33	$500	$16,500	8.00%	$56,475	$72,975
63	34	$500	$17,000	8.00%	$62,313	$79,313
64	35	$500	$17,500	8.00%	$68,658	$86,158
65	36	$500	$18,000	8.00%	$75,551	$93,551

Figure 11.4   Potential Insurance Premium Cost Recovery Table

Don't sweat the small stuff! Work with an expert or team of experts to help you design and coordinate your risk-management strategies. One size does not fit all! Each plan is like a fingerprint and no two are exactly the same. Choose strategies that are suitable for your financial situation to find creative ways to finance these premiums. The best plans will include provisions that attempt to recapture these premiums and expenses over time.

If you find that you don't have the right amount of coverage in place, your savings from your deductible changes may allow you to increase your policy limits. If you could purchase the maximum amount of insurance with very little (or nothing) additionally out-of-pocket, what would stop you from buying the best policy available on the market? Keep in mind that this policy would also typically provide the greatest amount of coverage and additional benefits. Work with a professional agent that can help you make informed decisions.

Coordinate and overlap different coverage types to provide for maximum protection from all risks. If possible, self-insure the smaller to allow for the greater insurance protection.

When most people think about insurance, they think of property and casualty insurance. Most Americans purchase this type of coverage first (auto, homeowner's or renter's insurance). Unfortunately, many Americans also judge the insurance industry by their experience with these carriers. There are actually many types of insurance to consider. Accidents can also cause your wealth to be transferred. Our father was an attorney and we were able to hear and see daily third-party accounts of people who had been in an accident and whose lives were altered (usually negatively), whether they caused the accident or not.

Types of Insurance

➤ Auto and Home Insurance
➤ Health Insurance
➤ Disability Income Insurance
➤ Life Insurance
➤ Long-Term Care Insurance

Some were impacted, because they were in an accident at the fault of someone else. We want to make sure you're protected in either scenario. You can be impacted by something that a coworker, spouse, or child is involved in. You could be impacted by an act of your own. Due to no fault of your own, someone or some entity could sue you and attack your wealth. Take steps to protect yourself.

Property Insurance

Homeowner's Insurance

Homeowner's Insurance is insurance protection for the investments in your home. It also protects you if you are sued for damages or injury you caused. Be sure you have the right amount and type of coverage in place so you can collect when there is a loss.

Generally speaking homeowner's insurance covers your house and its contents, including your personal possessions and valuable articles against damage or loss. If you rent, you can also obtain insurance for your home contents. There are also special policies for condos and co-ops. Coverage, policies vary in the kinds of perils or hazards they cover and how they compensate you for a loss.

A standard or *named perils* policy provides limited protection; it lists the specific perils such as fire or theft which may be covered. Broad coverage gives you insurance for all types of losses except those specifically excluded from your policy. You can also get a special insurance rider for valuable articles such as jewelry, artwork, collectibles, etc. This will also carry the separate premium. The insurance industry codes homeowner's policies from H01 to HO8 to reflect the range of coverage. The broader the policy the higher the premium you will pay.

What is excluded? Virtually no policy covers losses resulting from things like war, police action, wars, acts of God, nuclear explosions, and so on. You may be able to get a rider or endorsement to your policy to cover situations that are normally excluded such as floods and earthquakes which will generally pay extra premium for this type of coverage.

First review your existing policies to determine if the proper type of coverage is in place. Will your current coverage replace your current home? In the event of a claim, how much of your home would be replaced?

Do you have full replacement value or a lesser amount of coverage in place? Some clients are also covering the land when it may be unnecessary. You will need to review it if your replacement coverage costs or ATV coverage is in effect. Have you considered the need for an inflation-adjusted rider? You should review your disaster insurance program and determine whether it is necessary or appropriate, including flood insurance, hurricane insurance, tornado insurance, earthquake insurance, and so on. Have you coordinated your liability coverage with an additional umbrella liability policy? The worst time to find out is after you place a claim!

Liability coverage—this coverage can protect you if you are sued for causing property damage or injuring someone. Extra or excess liability increases the amount of coverage and may give you additional protection for a wider range of activities such as your role in community or government organization.

Liability insurance includes insurance products that protect your assets and income. Some examples of liability insurance include auto insurance, homeowner's insurance, and umbrella liability insurance.

Liability claims can result from a car accident, property related accidents, swimming pool accidents, slip and fall accidents on your property, icy walkways and steps, driveway injuries, snow mobile accidents, ATV accidents, fist fights, road rage, animal bites, and other wacky accidents. As the son of a prominent personal injury attorney and an emergency room nurse, we were raised on weekly stories of unbelievable accidents and perils. It was better than watching *Ripley's Believe It or Not!* These were wild stories of crazy accidents and sudden death but they were real stories! These real life experiences cemented in our minds; the absolute need for proper insurance plans.

Standard liability insurance policies max out at about $300,000 of liability insurance coverage per individual that you injure, and about $500,000 per incident (if more than one party is injured). Most home-owner's insurance policies cover about $500,000 of liability insurance. If your assets exceed these amounts, you may want to consider purchas-ing a separate liability policy (or an umbrella policy). Umbrella policies are designed to provide extra protection if you are sued above your ba-sic policy thresholds. These policies begin at about $1 million. It sounds like a huge number, but accidents can often result in claims that exceed several million dollars of damages.

Next comes professional liability coverage. Any doctor who has practiced medicine for a few decades can tell you that it's rare to prac-tice medicine for that long and not get sued, often due to no fault of their own. Some people just want someone to sue. Maybe they saw a commercial, have a grudge, lost a job, or feel that they have been wronged in some way by society. We are a great nation with far too many whiners. There will always be a greedy bump and bruise attorney waiting to fan the flames of anger and file a complaint.

If my father took all of the silly cases and frivolous lawsuits that walked into his office, he would probably be a very rich man. He has managed to be an advocate for victim's rights with legitimate claims, while avoiding the temptations of a quick buck and fast cash. He knows that in the end, we all pay. Eventually, if we get tired of higher premiums as the result of increased lawsuits, the pendulum of justice will swing the other way. A jury of insurance premium paying peers will eventually turn their backs on all claimants and the attorneys if the sys-tem gets too far off course. For this reason and many others, he is my hero. Lawsuits and accidents can happen at any time. Make sure that you are taking the proper steps to protect your wealth properly.

5 Minute Insurance Check-up

Take a few minutes to answer the following questions about your current coverage.

✓ Is the cheaper alternative actually better?

✓ What are the differences in coverage?

✓ How long will this coverage last?

✓ Are there any hidden fees, deductibles, coinsurances, or exclusions?

✓ Do my premiums remain fixed or will they definitely or possibly increase over time? If so, how?

✓ Are there any benefits on the new policy that are likely to cost more or provide fewer benefits than my current policy?

✓ Will I need to add riders to have similar coverage to my current policy?

✓ Is it clearly in my best interest to switch coverage?

Many factors must be considered before an informed decision may be reached. Property and casualty insurance plans must be coordinated and integrated properly.

The most common type of casualty policies are auto and home insurance. Almost everyone has a car in their household. Most of these cars are insured for collision, liability, and comprehensive coverage.

Auto Insurance

Auto Insurance Savings Ideas

Consider the following when reviewing or shopping for your auto insurance needs. In general, try to ask for higher deductibles whenever possible. These costs are unrecoverable, so it's wise to minimize them in any way you can. Consider dropping collision and comprehensive coverage on older cars worth less than $5,000 to $10,000, depending on your cash levels in other areas.

Discounts

Remember to inquire about discounts for things like low mileage, and student, safety, and driver training courses. Some carriers also offer discounts for anti-theft equipment, airbags, and other vehicle features. Sometimes you can achieve discounts for more than one line of coverage with the same carrier such as auto, home, recreational vehicles, and so on. However, you should avoid duplicating coverage such as medical and life coverage in your auto policy, where you may own it separately elsewhere. There is little benefit to this additional coverage that can often increase your premiums unnecessarily.

Type of Vehicle

Some people figure out that they can afford the auto payments before they figure out the cost of the insurance. Remember, the real cost of the vehicle includes he cost, financing, insurance, gas, and maintenance. Some people are quickly surprised to see that the real cost is more than expected. Compare various insurance costs before purchasing the car, as cars are typically rated according to make and model, and prices may vary dramatically.

You should review whether your state mandated levels are met by your current policy and whether those levels are also adequate for your current wants and needs. Review the potential benefits of lowering your premiums by raising your deductibles to free up capital for other insurance needs. You should review your coverage and make sure that it's provided for uninsured and underinsured motorists. Review if all owned vehicles are included in the policy or only the specific vehicles attached to each individual policy. You should review with your financial representative whether it is appropriate to remove collision coverage on older or later model vehicles.

Review the liability coverage limits to make sure they are adequate and of a level of that can be coordinated with your other umbrella liability policies. You may want to determine if medical payment benefits are an appropriate addition to your policy.

Health Insurance

Health insurance can be one of the most confusing and expensive types of insurance. Insurance companies, employers, and health care providers continue to create more options that can end up adding to the overall confusion in this arena. Some of the most common choices include individual health plans, group insurance (HMO, POS, and PPO plans), managed care platforms, and association programs. Health insurance carriers make their money through administration of claims, assuming risk, and managing the spread between risk and actual claims.

Health insurance is one of the largest expenses facing Americans and it is equally important for you to figure out how to coordinate your benefits here as well. Should you take an HMO, POS, PPO, or another plan design? Should you opt for low deductibles or a high deductible health plan? Is there actually a way to beat the system or hedge your risks? Maybe you can coordinate the coverage with other benefit plans to create some efficiency. A good planner can help you decide what strategy is best for you and your family.

Many of us have some type of health insurance coverage, though more and more families are without health insurance than ever before. Most covered individuals and families have either company sponsored health plans offered from their employer; or government sponsored coverage from Medicare or Medicaid. Private health insurance coverage makes up the balance.

Every year, plan designs and coverage features are changing. It seems that higher medical expenses and increased premiums coupled with lower benefits are an annual painful event. When will it end and how much of our income does it ultimately consume?

Selecting your health care plan offerings should be an annual ritual. Examine your personal usage over the prior year(s) and try to anticipate any upcoming medical expenses that may be foreseen for you and your family. Take steps to design a plan to protect your family and yourself without breaking the bank.

It is not always necessary to purchase the most expensive plan (usually a PPO). Sometimes your doctors and specialists are participating in the other plan offerings (POS and HMO). Plan ahead, and make a few phone calls to see if your doctors participate with the alternative carriers. These plans may offer similar coverage at reduced costs. It is also important to understand which benefits may be reduced or eliminated on your plan elections.

Be sure to examine which hospitals participate in your plan as well. Some plans exclude specific hospitals and cancer centers. Pay close attention to the maximum plan coverage limits. Try to pick a plan that provides at least $1 million in lifetime benefits. A major health issue can wipe out your accumulated assets pretty quickly.

Cost Recovery Ideas

There are many factors to consider. It is difficult to anticipate life's challenges. When it comes to your health, you can never have too much protection. Make sure you have the right coverage in place when it counts? Almost all health insurance companies pass costs onto consumers from their plans with two basic charges. The charges include the calendar year deductible and coinsurance (out-of-pocket expense). The calendar year deductible is an initial amount in medical expenses that you agree to pay before the insurance company incurs any financial liability. In general, you should apply the same strategy to health insurance as your other insurance risks. Your focus should be to cover those risks that could be financially detrimental to your wealth building process. You may want to select overall limits that are as high as possible; take advantage of managed care networks for quality treatment and cost savings.

If you are not taking large amounts of prescription drugs on a regular basis, look for prescription drug plans with higher copayments and generic drug savings or mail-order options. Why pay three co-pays if you can purchase your prescriptions every three months in larger quantities? If possible, purchase your health insurance as part of a larger group to take advantage of additional cost savings. Unless your family is subject to very high medical expenses, you should generally choose deductibles and coinsurance limits that are as high as you can reasonably manage.

Once you've built wealth in other areas, you should consider increasing your deductibles, which will also allow you to potentially recover costs over time. If your family requires some sort of professional medical assistance more often than most, a lower deductible may be a better choice. The same rationale applies to the stop-loss or coinsurance expense, which includes all out-of-pocket expenses. In general, you can lower your premiums by accepting some financial risk.

Even when you qualify for Medicare, it's not free. You pay a monthly fee and you will likely need supplements that you pay for. You also get to pay for your own prescription plan! At the rate we are going, your entire Social Security check may be needed just to pay for your prescription drugs! Thank god we are all living longer. We get to provide the politicians and the drug companies with more of our wealth. While the medical and pharmaceutical fields have been successful in extending life . . . the quality of your own life is up to you. You will need to allocate future savings dollars to help offset this expense. Coordination of your retirement savings strategies and your future medical insurance needs are critical components in a well-designed retirement plan.

In general, you should consider increasing your annual deductibles on these plans. Most people end up paying at least a part of their deductible. As you model your annual cost of health care, you should probably add the cost of your deductible to the annual premiums as part of the annual total cost of your plan. If you don't reach your full deductible, you have managed to save some money on the plan.

Disability

What if you could no longer work? If you became sick, hurt, and couldn't work how would you survive? More importantly how can you protect yourself? One of the most unfortunate losses in life is the ability to earn a living. In one moment, you can lose your ability to pay for everything. How long could you live on your savings before they're depleted. How long can you maintain your standard of living? Maybe three or four months. . . . Then what?

Does Money Grow on Trees?

If you have an asset, you usually insure it. Imagine for a moment if you had a magical money tree in your backyard that provided you with money each and every week. At the end of each week you would visit your tree and it would hand you twenty $100 bills. You would have your $2,000 for the week and you would go about your business. I wish I had a tree like that! What if that tree were to die? That would be quite an inconvenience. Would you take steps to insure or protect that magic money tree at all costs? Without question, most of us would. We would insure it just as we would insure our homes, automobiles, or any other of our possessions.

In reality, that machine is you; your ability to work and earn an income that provides the capital makes your world go around. Without you, the flow of money breaks down. Your most valuable asset is your ability to earn an income and serve as an economic asset for yourself and your family. Therefore, as we build or create a coordinated strategy of wealth building and protection, it's critical that we take steps to insure the money tree. If you are disabled and your ability to earn money is lost, then what?

Permanent Disability: The Economic Death

This event is viewed as the nightmare scenario for many people. Although not dead, you have effectively been removed for the workforce and your productivity for dependents and business associates disappears. However, you still exist as a consumer. This will likely cause new financial burdens. Medical expenses and other special maintenance needs may also persist, often over a long period of time. These new expenses can eat up even the limited financial family resources that may have been accumulated. This event is by far one of the worst potential perils.

Who will pay your bills? Maybe you could borrow the money you need. Don't bother going to a bank. They won't look at someone who has no ability and no income to repay them. How about your relatives or friends? This kind of charity has limits. Maybe your spouse, if you have one, can get a second or third job. Perhaps you will have to sell off some of your assets. In most cases, the forced sale of an asset generally means a reduced value for that asset. You could always apply for Social Security benefits, but you must satisfy a five-month wait and may be unable to perform any job. The only answer is to protect yourself.

Do you insure the goose or the golden eggs? I'd say insure both, but losing the goose would be much worse than losing an egg or two. The goose represents your future, the ability to create more eggs. You can insure your home by purchasing a disability income policy.

Protect Your Income: Insure the Golden Goose

W.W.Y.D.I.Y.I.S.T? ®

What Would You Do If Your Income Stopped Today?

How would the "movie in your mind" of your own life change?

Figure 11.5   How would an interruption in income impact you?

Disability Income Insurance

If you are now earning $8,000 per month, how would you manage on $3,000 per month (or less)? If your employer cut your income in half, you'd probably quit. With a disability you can't quit.

Job A or Job B?

Let's say you're interviewing with me today. I have two jobs to offer you. You get to choose one.

1. The first job pays you $100,000 per year as long as you show up for work. But in the event that you become sick, hurt, can't work, we'll pay you nothing.

2. The second job pays you $98,000 per year, but in the event that you become sick, hurt, or can't work, we will pay you 60 percent of your salary or roughly $59,000 for the rest of your working career until age 65. With that in mind, which job do you want?

The prudent person would answer; well I'd like the second job, especially when they consider the statistical likelihood of becoming disabled during their working years. The risk is far greater than losing their home to a fire, or having an auto accident that wipes out their vehicle and totals it. The statistics are alarming and approach roughly 30 percent of all Americans.

The question that I would normally then ask is, which job do you have? Most people have the first job. Some people have group disability insurance through their employer that usually only covers a very basic amount of their income. Usually, it does not cover their bonuses or any commission income above their base income levels. They have a lot less than they think. The worst time to find out about it is when they go to make a claim and find out that they're not going to get enough; sometimes it's not even enough to cover your monthly bills.

The next question is which job do you want? Well, we all want the second job. If I can show you a way to turn back the hands of time to the day when you signed up for your actual job and get you job number two would you be interested?

You can have job number two by simply completing this disability income application and seeing if you qualify.

How can I Purchase Disability Insurance?

Types of Coverage

Many people are under the impression that they are all set when it comes to disability coverage. Generally, disability coverage comes in a few basic types: workmen's compensation, group disability coverage, and private disability coverage.

Workmen's compensation is only available if you're injured or disabled while on the job. If you work a typical 8-hour day, who covers the other 16 hours of the day? Coverage is limited to very small monthly benefit amounts, usually under $1,000 per month.

Group Insurance

Your employer may cover you under a group disability policy. It's important to know when these benefits begin, the definition of disability, and how much you are entitled to receive and for how long.

Many group policies are limited in their coverage. The amount of your coverage is usually tied only to your base salary. It does not usually cover your total income from things like commissions or bonuses.

Taxes

Some group employer-paid policies are taxed when the benefits are paid.

Integrated

The benefits are often tied to any government benefits that you may receive. Whatever amounts you receive from the government will be subtracted from your monthly benefits.

Definition

The definition of disability may be very weak. If you are able to perform a lesser paying job, you may not qualify for coverage.

Portability

If you leave your employer, it is unlikely that you would be able to continue that coverage.

How to Start Your Review

Make sure that your coverage is coordinated and integrated properly in an effort to maximize your coverage, while minimizing your out-of-pocket expense and cost. The best way to begin is to audit your

voluntary and group coverage to make sure that you are covered properly. From there, you can identify any gaps in your current coverage
plans or areas that may need to be bolstered or bridged accordingly.
Typically, group coverage falls in one of two classifications, either short-
or long-term disability. Both of these products have their place, but can
often provide a false sense of security for participants.

Short-term disability can last anywhere from a handful of weeks
up to approximately two years, though some plans offer longer coverage. Long-term disability can last until age 65, 67, or even longer, but
also typically does not have some of the bells and whistles that an individual policy might offer.

Private Insurance

The purchase of an individual supplemental policy is often necessary and the best strategy to purchase this type of coverage is from
an employer's plan that offers discounts on the retail rates. Many employers offer supplemental buy up insurance. Much like your umbrella
liability policy, this private disability policy is designed to pick up where
your group insurance falls short. By purchasing it from an employer
sponsored program, you can often realize 10 to 15 percent discounts
off the regular retail premiums. Make sure that you work with a professional to design the proper income replacement strategies.

There is a limited number of companies that sell disability coverage. The strength of the coverage will be based on the definitions of
coverage in the policy. The more coverage and benefits the higher the
premium. There may be caps or limits on income coverage. It may not
cover specific occupation classes, or what is known as our own occupation rider.

The coverage should be for your occupation, not any occupation. This means if you're a doctor and become disabled, you could get
a job teaching, and still receive disability from your former occupation.
Some policies would withhold benefits for this disability because of
your ability to perform any job regardless of what it is.

In selecting the right type of coverage you will want to focus on
three criteria. Try to strike a balance in coverage between costs, benefits, and contract coverage language. Find the balance. Usually, you are
picking the contract with the best two out of three included.

The coordination of these various benefits is critical to helping
you maximize your coverage while also identifying any gaps or holes
that may exist in your current coverage. The group platform is typically

easy to qualify for but may not cover things like bonuses, commissions, and other variable forms and sources of income on an annual basis.

Your income is your most valuable asset. Without it, you're in big trouble. You can spend your entire life building your wealth and lose it in an instant. An accident, illness, stress-related impairment, cancer, heart attack, and stroke can disrupt and affect your financial picture. Nearly half of all home foreclosures are due to disability. Don't leave yourself and your family exposed in the event of a disability. Relying on luck or dumb luck is not the solution.

Long-Term Care Insurance

Americans are living longer than ever before and long-term care is quickly becoming a growing concern. Things that used to kill us, no longer do. People survive heart attacks, strokes, and even cancer at an ever increasing rate. What was a death sentence only a generation ago has become a mere chronic condition. Unfortunately, with an increase in longevity comes an added expense. As people live longer, it stands to reason that they will grow older than in the past. When you get old, you get sick. As you become sick you may need care. That care costs money. How will you pay for your care?

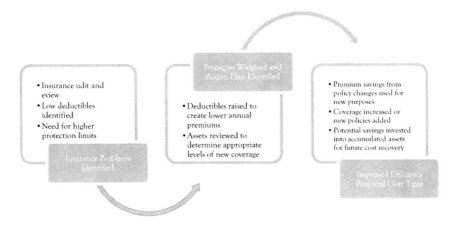

It is important to ask questions and address some important issues. What are the chances that you or a family member may need long-term care? Who will care for you and how will you pay for your care? It could be you, your spouse, a parent, or even a sibling.

Normally the need for long-term care results from a lengthy chronic illness. However, something as unexpected as an accident or injury could also result in the need for long-term care. It could happen to anyone at any time.

How can I afford the Insurance?

Practical Exercise

Look for creative ways to find the money to fund your coverage needs. You may be surprised how easy it is to identify existing resources.

Self Assessment Exercise

✓ Do you have an updated and valid will, health care proxy, power of attorney, trusts, and so on?

✓ Do you have an umbrella policy?

✓ Have you reviewed your homeowner's and auto policies?

✓ Do you have disability income insurance?

✓ Do you have health insurance? Is it the right option?

✓ Do you own all the life insurance you can buy?

Chapter Highlights

➤ Understand the role that insurance plays in the protection of your wealth.

➤ Seek ways to build cost recovery mechanisms into your insurance programs.

➤ Maximize your coverage wherever possible.

CHAPTER 12

LIFE INSURANCE

THE BEATING HEART OF YOUR FINANCIAL STRATEGIES

"Education is the ability to listen to almost anything without losing
your temper or your self-confidence"
—Robert Frost

Let's talk about your life insurance. There are few financial discussions surrounded by more opinions and misinformation than this topic. If all the stories you've heard about permanent life insurance turned out not to be true, when do you want to know? We don't think life insurance is the only financial product that you should own, but if we could only pick one—life insurance would be near the top of the list.

In reality, this is the only financial product that can guarantee what you want to happen, actually will happen—no matter what. One of two things will happen. You will either live past normal retirement (age 65 to 70) or you'll die before. Life insurance policies can help with both. Life insurance is the only product that can create a significant and substantial estate, immediately.

Once you are approved by the carrier and pay your first premium, you are covered. If you die in the first year, or in five years, your family is covered. If you didn't save enough in your 401(k) plan, your spouse will be able to use the death benefit to cover the shortfall (if you have a large enough policy). If you haven't saved enough in your child's college fund, the death benefit can also cover the gap. The same is true of the death benefit for replacing your income (depending on how much of your income you cover), and other savings goals. What other savings product can do all that?

Any other accumulation vehicle is dependent on you making regular contributions (or a substantial lump sum investment) over long periods of time. This approach requires you to continue to be gainfully employed (avoid becoming disabled), and also requires the financial markets to perform favorably.

In the more likely event that you don't die before you retire, permanent life insurance can also build cash values that can be used to offset your other accumulation needs. Life insurance is an excellent place to save and accumulate wealth for the long-term. Over long periods of time, many permanent (lifelong) contracts can perform at internal rates of return north of 5 percent tax-free. Many carriers have been paying dividends for over 100 years—some are approaching 200 years! Take a look at their historical dividend schedules. Many people focus only on the short-term savings aspects when comparing life insurance as an investment vehicle with other asset classes.

Generally speaking, permanent life insurance is a hybrid product that starts off as a means of protecting your income. Over time, the savings component kicks in and begins to add a secondary benefit to your program. Remember, it's not only what you earn that counts, it's what you keep!

What long-term rate of return would you need to earn in order to outperform these returns on an after-tax basis year in and year out? Many investment programs will outperform life insurance rates of return on a pre-tax basis. They may also outperform the cash value growth on an average basis. They will not usually outperform life insurance dividends consistently on an annual basis. This is the secret of cash values when coordinated into your plan. The reasonable predictable nature of life insurance dividends (from reputable carriers with 100+ years of consistent dividend histories), can help provide a layer of security in your overall wealth accumulation plans.

Life insurance should not be used as your only investment vehicle, but it certainly has its place in the lineup. Life insurance cash values can be used as a place to access capital during periods of corrections in financial markets. By using cash values in this manner, you offer your other investments the chance to heal or recapitalize themselves. The more cash values you have amassed, the longer they will last. Again, if you die before you complete your savings goals, you also have an instant estate (the amount is up to you).

A well informed wealth builder understands how to use life insurance to make his or her financial life a success. We have done extensive research and have determined that we are all going to die. It would be nice if your life insurance protection is there when it happens. By following this logic, you can leave peace of mind to your family and insure your legacy—no matter what!

If something has no value, you don't insure it. You definitely have a value. How much of it you choose to insure is up to you. Unfortunately, there seems to be more confusion than clarity on this topic. Consider the following:

If you didn't come home tonight, how would your family be impacted, how would your business be impacted, and what would the outcome be? How would your legacy be impacted? Will your children be able to continue to go to the same schools with their friends? Will your spouse be able to continue to live in the home that you built together? What about your business or your employees?

If you were going to die tomorrow, how much life insurance would you buy? Most of us would buy all we could get, especially if we didn't have to pay for it. Premiums would not matter since the rate of return would be enormous in one day. Most people don't have any problem owning life insurance. They just don't want to pay for it. The trick is to use the recovered costs from other areas of your plan to fund your insurance purchases. If there were no additional out-of-pocket outlay, we would want our families to have the maximum amount possible.

What would you call someone that deserted his family with no money and piles of debt? What you would call someone who left their family with no money and a lot of debt, but who left because he died in an accident (or in his sleep)?

We may have more pity on the second fellow, but end results would be the same. What if this father died in the middle of the night but left his family a substantial life insurance policy? He left his final love letter to his family. His insurance contract allowed him to be there in sickness and in health, in life and in death. He was able to fulfill his promises and obligations to his family and make sure that the checks kept coming throughout their lives.

Life insurance has no substitute. Not to insure adequately through life insurance is to gamble with the greatest economic risk to your family and your business. The bet is a particularly selfish one, as in the event that the bet is lost, it falls upon your family. Failure to safeguard dependents on the loss of your current income is little short of a crime.

Life insurance is the opposite of gambling. Its purpose is to create certainty for us out of the greatest uncertainty where we are confronted. One of its primary objects is to guarantee income to those who may not be allotted the time to accumulate on themselves. It guarantees the full estate you had set out to accumulate, but were prevented from completing because of an untimely death.

Public Opinion

Where does the negativity surrounding life insurance come from? The financial media offers lots of information about life insurance and how to determine the need for it. Very little of their information is useful or accurate. These sound bites and quick reports are filled with financial myths and rules of thumb. Some of these financial experts claim that you may not need any life insurance at all, especially if your kids are grown. It is impossible to shrink a subject of this complexity down to a 30-second discussion. It seems like most of the advice is based more on opinion than fact.

What if you could put your money into a contract that would provide the following benefits: a competitive rate of return, unlimited investment options, disability waiver (self-funding if you become disabled and cannot work to fund it yourself), liquid for removing your cash values quickly, tax-free estate to your heirs, collateral for loans, tax deferred growth, tax-free access to your gains (from policy loans), protected from creditors, tax-free death benefits, no mandatory distribution age on your investments, and a product that creates an immediate estate? This sounds like a product that can create financial security and peace of mind along with tax advantages.

Life insurance can accomplish all of this and more. I know of no other product that does all of this. It's like the putter in your golf bag. It may not be the sexiest club in the bag, but you use it on every hole and it is one of the most important clubs to your game. An insurance contract is nothing more than a legal document; it's an agreement to pay benefits in the event of loss in exchange for a premium. We don't know why the public has such an issue with life insurance as an accumulation vehicle. We should all own life insurance. As covered earlier, we all have a value and our value to our families must be insured.

How Did We Get Here?

Life Insurance Myths

The first myth about life insurance is when you buy it, you are primarily buying death protection. That is completely wrong. Anyone who proposes that does not understand the value of permanent life insurance. It is the foundation for future success. This myth is partly due to the effort of advertising by major insurance carriers.

Through the first half of the twentieth century, life insurance stood high on the list of family financial priorities. It was used as a multipurpose savings and protection product. In the 60s and 70s, it changed in public perception. Major carriers pushed their low-cost term life insurance rates and emphasized death benefit protection in their advertising campaigns. This approach still lingers today.

As a result, an uninformed public began to view life insurance as physical death protection or as a philanthropic act of the insured. He or she typically chose an arbitrary death benefit amount that seemed like the right figure. Rarely were the innocent parties (spouses, children, business employees) consulted on the plan design and amounts. Many even went so far as to see this as some sort of gift or donation to their families.

Today, we are more informed about life's risks. We know that insurance can serve many different purposes. Unfortunately, the life insurance industry has a long way to go in repairing its image in the marketplace. At present, life insurance for each American family averages only a few years of income (if that). Most of the coverage is provided from group life insurance contracts. If we deduct annual installment debts, the average life insurance per family would average a little higher than one year's income.

Currently, a very small percentage of the nation's disposable personal income is spent on life insurance premiums. It seems that consumers spend more money on just about anything else. We spend more annually on any of the following categories: alcoholic beverages, tobacco, travel, spectator sports, electronics, toys, sporting goods, and cosmetics. This distribution of current family expenditures raises the question of whether the family's right to life insurance protection is properly met. The trick is to purchase as much coverage as possible, and find a way to get your premium dollars back—with interest. Permanent life insurance allows this to happen (over time).

How much should you purchase? This is a very easy calculation. The insurance company will not insure you more than your future income potential. We suggest that the ideal amount is the maximum amount that the insurance company will offer. As discussed earlier, this amount is roughly equal to your current annual income multiplied by your remaining working years (many carriers max out at 15 to 20 times your current earnings). What beneficiary would want less money than what the deceased was worth? Why would the beneficiary only want what they needed to make ends meet?

Types of Life Insurance

Types of Insurance

➢ Term Life Insurance
➢ Whole Life or Permanent Insurance
➢ Universal Life Insurance
➢ Variable Universal Life Insurance

Term Life Insurance

Many people believe that term life insurance is the cheapest policy to own. We think that it is the most expensive form of insurance to own. Some carriers provide misinformation to get their point across. They don't tell you that 95 percent or more of all term policies never pay any claim. Life insurance is limited to death benefit protection only when you buy some of the lesser products these insurance experts tell you to buy.

Most people will not die before they retire. Therefore, the need for premature death benefit protection is not as great as the need for ultimate death benefit protection. Insurance companies know from actual calculations that the term life insurance policies will not result in many death claims. Most policies do expire or lapse. The only way you can win with term life insurance is to die young, and you will lose a substantial amount of money, one way or the other. Who wants to win that bet?

That is not to say that term insurance has no place in people's insurance portfolio. It does, but only for a very short period of time and for a very specific purpose. Take a look at the following calculation to illustrate this concept further.

Age	Year #	Annual Expense	Cumulative Expense	Opportunity Rate of Return	Cumulative Opportunity Cost	Cumulative Total Cost	Net Value of Term Insurance Death Benefit
30	1	$1,000	$1,000	7.00%	$0	$1,000	$300,000
35	2	$1,000	$2,000	7.00%	$70	$2,070	$297,930
36	3	$1,000	$3,000	7.00%	$215	$3,215	$296,785
37	4	$1,000	$4,000	7.00%	$440	$4,440	$295,560
38	5	$1,000	$5,000	7.00%	$751	$5,751	$294,249
39	6	$1,000	$6,000	7.00%	$1,153	$7,153	$292,847
40	7	$1,000	$7,000	7.00%	$1,654	$8,654	$291,346
41	8	$1,000	$8,000	7.00%	$2,260	$10,260	$289,740
42	9	$1,000	$9,000	7.00%	$2,978	$11,978	$288,022
43	10	$1,000	$10,000	7.00%	$3,816	$13,816	$286,184
44	11	$1,000	$11,000	7.00%	$4,784	$15,784	$284,216
45	12	$1,000	$12,000	7.00%	$5,888	$17,888	$282,112
46	13	$1,000	$13,000	7.00%	$7,141	$20,141	$279,859
47	14	$1,000	$14,000	7.00%	$8,550	$22,550	$277,450
48	15	$1,000	$15,000	7.00%	$10,129	$25,129	$274,871
49	16	$1,000	$16,000	7.00%	$11,888	$27,888	$272,112
50	17	$1,000	$17,000	7.00%	$13,840	$30,840	$269,160
51	18	$1,000	$18,000	7.00%	$15,999	$33,999	$266,001
52	19	$1,000	$19,000	7.00%	$18,379	$37,379	$262,621
53	20	$1,000	$20,000	7.00%	$20,995	$40,995	$259,005
54	21		$20,000	7.00%	$23,865	$43,865	$0
55	22		$20,000	7.00%	$26,936	$46,936	$0
56	23		$20,000	7.00%	$30,221	$50,221	$0
57	24		$20,000	7.00%	$33,737	$53,737	$0
58	25		$20,000	7.00%	$37,498	$57,498	$0
59	26		$20,000	7.00%	$41,523	$61,523	$0
60	27		$20,000	7.00%	$45,830	$65,830	$0
61	28		$20,000	7.00%	$50,438	$70,438	$0

(continued)

(continued)

Age	Year #	Annual Expense	Cumulative Expense	Opportunity Rate of Return	Cumulative Opportunity Cost	Cumulative Total Cost	Net Value of Term Insurance Death Benefit
62	29		$20,000	7.00%	$55,369	$75,369	$0
63	30		$20,000	7.00%	$60,644	$80,644	$0
64	31		$20,000	7.00%	$66,289	$86,289	$0
65	32		$20,000	7.00%	$72,330	$92,330	$0
66	33		$20,000	7.00%	$78,793	$98,793	$0
67	34		$20,000	7.00%	$85,708	$105,708	$0
68	35		$20,000	7.00%	$93,108	$113,108	$0
69	36		$20,000	7.00%	$101,025	$121,025	$0
70	37		$20,000	7.00%	$109,497	$129,497	$0
71	38		$20,000	7.00%	$118,562	$138,562	$0
72	39		$20,000	7.00%	$128,261	$148,261	$0
73	40		$20,000	7.00%	$138,640	$158,640	$0
74	41		$20,000	7.00%	$149,744	$169,744	$0
75	42		$20,000	7.00%	$161,627	$181,627	$0
76	43		$20,000	7.00%	$174,340	$194,340	$0
77	44		$20,000	7.00%	$187,944	$207,944	$0
78	45		$20,000	7.00%	$202,500	$222,500	$0
79	46		$20,000	7.00%	$218,075	$238,075	$0
80	47		$20,000	7.00%	$234,741	$254,741	$0
81	48		$20,000	7.00%	$252,572	$272,572	$0
82	49		$20,000	7.00%	$271,652	$291,652	$0
83	50		$20,000	7.00%	$292,068	$312,068	$0
84	51		$20,000	7.00%	$313,913	$333,913	$0
85	52		$20,000	7.00%	$337,287	$357,287	$0
86	53		$20,000	7.00%	$362,297	$382,297	$0
87	54		$20,000	7.00%	$389,058	$409,058	$0
88	55		$20,000	7.00%	$417,692	$437,692	$0
89	56		$20,000	7.00%	$448,330	$468,330	$0
90	57		$20,000	7.00%	$481,113	$501,113	$0

Figure 12.1   Term Life Insurance Costs

As you can see from Figure 12.1, the best time to own term insurance is the first year (if you die). Every year after, the premiums are invested by the insurance carrier for their use. Therefore, the real return of the death benefit decreases as well annually. Once the policy expires (in year 20 in our example), your premiums are lost forever . . . along with the lost opportunity costs on those premiums. By life expectancy, the premiums have grown to hundreds of thousands of dollars. If you lived to reach 90, your premiums will have been worth about $500,000 to the insurance company. This is true even if you die sooner since the capital continues to grow for the insurance company long after you leave this earth.

Term Life Explained

Let's take a look at term life insurance. Term life insurance may seem cheaper than permanent insurance. Term insurance can be a recoverable expense. With purchasing term insurance, the actual calculation cannot be completed until the death of the insured. At that point, you can compare the premiums paid versus the benefit received to determine the value that was either gained or lost. You must also factor the money the premiums could be earning if you had invested them elsewhere. This opportunity cost is very costly over time.

Remember, with each premium paid, the policy takes on additional cost and returns fewer benefits. This is due to the fact that the insurance company is keeping the premiums and investing them for the insurance company! You are spending more each year, and they are on the hook for less. Since most people cancel or drop their policies before they die, this money stays on the books for the insurance company. On average, less than 5 percent of all of these policies pay out any death claims. That's worse than the slot machines! Some experts put the payout rate at closer to 2 percent of all policies. Compare this to the permanent life policies that will all pay out if they are in force at the time of death.

Term life insurance provides a death benefit in exchange for premiums paid as long as the insured dies within the specified period of time. The cost of the term insurance increases with age. Usually, teaser rates for 10, 20, or even 30 years are offered. Many people find that they must drop the coverage at the point when they need it most. In year 31, the premiums could be 2 to 10 times the original rate. At this point, all premiums usually end and the insurance company liability ceases immediately. However, the opportunity cost of the money you paid out in premiums continue to accrue forever. If the money was paid out in premiums has been invested, it would still be accumulating wealth for you instead of the insurance company! Take a look at the following table.

Cost of Term Insurance

Many people do not calculate the time value of money on the premiums spent when looking at the true cost of owning term insurance. You must factor in not only the premiums, but also what those premiums would have been worth if you had taken the risk and invested the money yourself. We are not suggesting that people take the risk of not owning insurance, but rather that they understand the true cost of owning term insurance. Remember that by buying permanent insurance and investing in the term makes much more sense than buying in the term and investing the difference!

Client #1: Buy Term and Invest the Difference
Assumptions: 7Percent Returns, 32 Percent Combined Federal and State Tax Bracket
Term Insurance: $250,000 Annual Premiums: $1,000
Investing $5,000 in a side fund annually
Result after 30 Years: Total Account Value: $472,000
Taxes Paid on the Annual Dividends and Gains: $113,700
Opportunity Cost Lost on the Taxes: $115,500
Cost of Term Life Premiums $30,000
Opportunity Cost of Term Life Premiums Paid: $64,400
Total Costs to Grow the Account: $323,600
Net Wealth after Costs: $472,000 - $323,600 = $148,400
*You invested $5,000 30 years = $150,000!

Client #2
Permanent Insurance: $250,000 Annual Premiums: $6,000
Investing $0 in a side fund annually
Result after 30 Years: Total Cash Value: $323,700*
Taxes Paid on the Annual Dividends and Gains $0
Opportunity Cost Lost on the Taxes: $0
Cost of Term Life Premiums Recovered: $30,000
Opportunity Cost of Term Life Premiums Recovered: $64,400
Total Costs: $0
Total Balance: $418,100 You invested: $180,000

Which client would you rather be? Which client are you now?

Which Policy Is Best?

Remember, the best policy is usually the *best for the consumer*, not for the company. Don't be fooled by the difference between cheap premiums and real value. The best policy is generally the most expensive policy from a cash flow standpoint. This would be the one with the highest annual premiums, the lowest sales loads, and the lowest initial death benefit, while still meeting the guidelines of a life insurance contract. Few people seem to grasp this point.

It's interesting to note that the federal government decides how much you can place into an insurance contract. Since the federal government is involved in this decision, we would need to ask why. There must be tax advantages if a government controls the contribution limits and the amount you can own. Government regulations draw a direct correlation between premiums and the face amount of a policy in order to keep the life insurance from being taxed like other financial vehicles. Life insurance is too often sold to the public as an expensive item to be placed in your safety deposit box until death. We view it as a banking tool or an effective parking place for you to build wealth.

You have the opportunity to borrow against cash values at very low costs, compared to other financing options. You can invest virtually anywhere you wish once you've accumulated cash values and maintain your life insurance benefit when you need them most. We know of no other financial vehicle that can afford all of these opportunities in one place.

Permanent Life Insurance

Permanent life insurance can offer a competitive intermediate and long-term rate of return on the cash values. Your premiums and interest compounded on a tax-deferred basis, which helps avoid increasing taxes under the current tax law. These assets are generally protected from creditors in many states, where the assets are held in cash values. Death benefits can increase significantly over time and may also carry tax advantages. Permanent protection can also help in the settlement of your estate. Finally, you retain the opportunity to assign your equity as collateral for other loans if necessary. This can help you minimize those unnecessary interest costs in other areas of your financial life.

Select a carrier that consistently receives top ratings from major rating agencies. Usually A, double A, or triple A ratings. Focus on a firm that does not have an investment strategy dramatically different from the rest of the industry, and has a strong record of investment performance as measured against the industry. It should provide consistently strong performance to the policy holder, and generally a high cash value performance and low expense loads.

Insurance companies set limits on the maximum amount that they will insure. For most companies, the maximum is a factor of age and generally be anywhere from 10 to 20 times your income (some higher). Net worth must be considered as well. Most people view insurance simply as an expense. We are all conditioned to spend as little as possible on expenses, especially on expenses where we see no immediate gains. But this approach to insurance can be very limiting and misleading to us. In order to understand why this is not true, you need to examine a couple of different types of insurance.

One of the greatest benefits of a permanent life insurance policy is that once you've accumulated some cash value in your contract, you have secured the best means of minimizing wealth transfers to others. Use quality permanent insurance to minimize the needs to borrow funds from someone other than yourself. This can allow you to take advantage of more attractive yields elsewhere. The key to this process is discipline, and a commitment to manage opportunities effectively.

Whole Life Insurance

What is whole life insurance? Whole life is cash value insurance that stays in effect as long as premiums are paid. This is different from term insurance that provides coverage for a specified term only and must be renewed on a regular basis. Premiums are paid for the whole life of the insured person, continuing until he or she dies or to a specified maximum age.

There are different variations of whole life insurance offered by some carriers. Some are limited life policies where premiums aren't paid over the insured lifetime but for only a limited period. When that period is over, the insurance remains in effect with no further payments. Some of the typical pay types include 10-year pay periods, 20-year pay periods, and life paid up at age 65. Simply put, a 10 pay policy means that premiums are paid for 10 years, 20 pay for 20 years, and so forth. The payment period for a life paid up at 65 is the number of years between the policy's issue date and when the insured reaches age 65.

The whole life or cash value life insurance policy has several characteristics that differentiate it from term life insurance. The protection continues for a lifetime as long as the premiums are paid and the policy doesn't lapse due to excessive loans. Premiums, except for limited pay policies are paid for as long as you live. Premiums remain level throughout the payment period and part of each premium goes toward a cash value that gradually increases over the life of the policy. The net cash values are available to the policy owner in the form of policy loans and surrender values. This is the secret to building wealth inside an insurance contract.

Cash value insurance policies also have non-forfeiture options to ensure that the owners won't lose or forfeit all their money paid into the policy if they aren't able to continue paying premiums. In short, whole life insurance never has to be renewed as long as the scheduled premiums are paid on time. The policy owner has predictable level premiums along with a savings element that is a feature of the policy in the form of accumulations in cash value.

Guarantees

Whole life insurance offers guaranteed premiums for the life of the contract. Unlike other products, they never go up. The contract also guarantees a death benefit that will never go down. In fact, most of the time the death benefits will continue to rise. The contracts offer a guaranteed cash value as well. There is a minimum guaranteed cash value that accrues over time, and a current assumption value based on dividend performance.

Savings Components

Part of your premium goes to cover the cost of the insurance, while the balance goes into the savings component of your contract. This feature allows whole life insurance to operate as both a savings and protection vehicle. Term Life insurance does not have any savings vehicle components. It is a pure cost. It is like renting versus owning your life insurance.

Tax Favored Growth

If you access your cash values from a loan arrangement, there are no taxes due. There are no taxes due on an insurance policy loan, just as there are no taxes on loans made with other financial institutions. However, if you surrender your policy when a loan is outstanding, a taxable event may occur. The savings component or *cash value* increases tax-free until the policy cash values exceed the premiums paid into the policy. At this point, the cash value grows on a tax deferred basis. These values can be accessed from the policy tax-free from policy loans. You don't even have to apply for these loans. Just call up the company and they'll send you the money. Upon your death, the total gains are paid tax-free to your beneficiaries no matter how much the gain is over the premiums paid. These loans do charge an interest rate, usually close to or even below the crediting rate of the insurer. Work with your financial professional to examine the benefits and drawbacks of properly using policy loans.

Figure 12.2   Permanent Life Insurance Hidden Benefits

Dividends Make the Difference

Each year, whole life insurance carriers declare their dividends. The amount of the annual dividend from year to year is unknown and can vary widely from carrier to carrier. The carrier uses a series of formulas to determine the proper dividend amounts. These formulas are comprised of annual claims experience, expense management, and the investment performance of their underlying general accounts.

Usually, at the time the policy is issued, the company makes a projection of these dividends based on its current financial position. The dividend is not technically guaranteed. It may be higher or lower than what the company has projected for that year. Some agents have been known to focus only on the current dividend rates. This can lead to skewed expectations.

Ask your agent for a copy of the dividend history of the insurance carrier. This way you can see a better picture of the company's past performance in good markets and bad. Most insurance companies have paid dividends consistently for over 100 years.

Keep in mind that once the dividend is paid to you, it cannot be lost or taken away. It is guaranteed to remain in your policy. That is much different from dividends on investments, which if they are reinvested can be lost to the future market declines. This feature allows us to use insurance cash values to add a layer of security to our savings and growth strategies. It is not uncommon to see older whole life insurance policies with hundreds of thousands or even millions of dollars in cash values (most of these gains qualify to be accessed tax-free).

A whole life insurance policy provides wide flexibility. You could borrow money from your policy; or you could use your cash value as collateral for a loan. The cash value is exempt from many creditors. In most states, life insurance cash value is not exposed to a liability judgment. However, you should check with your insurance company to see if this is true in your state.

Initially, many people fail to see the advantages of owning whole life insurance. They often focus on the premium compared to the low premium for term life insurance. Don't discount the savings aspect. Hopefully now you can see the difference. Our financial lives are largely a gamble. Life insurance serves as a measure of safety to withstand the unusual financial strains on your family or your business.

How can I pay for it?

Whole life or permanent life insurance is often quickly dismissed by the public as an expensive way to fund their life insurance needs. Actually, there are ways to fund your policy premiums with little or even no out of pocket expense. You might already be spending these dollars in other areas. Remember our chapter on taxes. Perhaps using some or all of your annual interest and dividends can cover the difference. By using this approach you may be able to grow those dividend and capital gains in a tax favored environment, eliminate (or minimize) your costly term-life insurance premiums, and create a death benefit that will be in force for life. Consider the following practical example.

Universal Life Insurance

Universal life insurance is a hybrid product that combines term life insurance with a small savings component. It typically has a lower premium than whole life insurance. Additionally, it can offer a more flexible design that can allow you to adjust your premium payments. This feature may allow you to purchase more death benefit protection for the same price as whole life insurance. This type of product can be appropriate for individuals who are more focused on the death benefits of the contract than the accumulation of cash values, and for clients who are older.

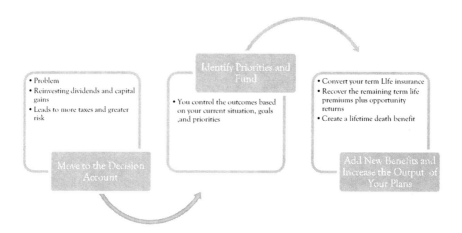

Figure 12.3   Find the money to fund your priorities.

The product operates on the premise of assumptions versus guarantees. Unlike whole life policies, universal life policies do not participate in the dividends of the insurance company. They typically receive a crediting rate on the cash component. If the crediting rates remain high then you may not need to pay many premiums in the future. If the crediting rates adjust downward, you may need to pay more to keep your insurance in force. The absence of guarantees and dividends are a disadvantage to this type of contract. If you choose to pay lower premiums than the scheduled premiums, it can end up reducing your ultimate death benefits and even risk a policy lapse (depending on crediting rates).

In general, these types of policies are suitable for people who are interested in a long-term death benefit protection. The insurance industry positions these policies as a more permanent form of term life insurance. There are even riders you can add that will guarantee a death benefit regardless of the crediting rate.

You will not be excited about the cash value growth from these products. In general, this is not the type of policy that you would use to supplement your savings or retirement planning goals.

Variable Universal Life Insurance[*]

This product is built on the same chassis as Universal Life. It is designed to provide death benefit protection while also offering the potential for long-term cash value accumulation. With variable universal life, you have the ability to invest your underlying cash values as you see fit. A variety of funding options are generally available for these policies, which reflect the performance of underlying investments such as stocks, bonds or real estate securities.

Since these funding options are professionally managed, there are fees and expenses associated with them which will be clearly detailed in the product's prospectus.

You also have the option to borrow money from your policy. Loans and withdrawals will reduce your policies cash value and death benefit. Additionally, if the market corrects while you have a loan out, the loaned amount will not be available to benefit from the correction.

---

[*] Please see the financial disclaimer on page 348 for more information.

This product is generally viewed as a more risky proposition then Whole Life since the policy premiums, death benefits, and cash values are not secure. Success and failure is a function of the financial market performance and your funding levels.

Integration and Coordination: Hidden Benefits, Living Benefits, and Make Your Plan Jump to Life in Three Dimensions!

How Long Will I Need Life Insurance?

Let's talk about the living and death benefits of life insurance. Many people are under the false pretense that life insurance is only required until their families are grown. Others believe that once their children are out of college or once the mortgage is paid off that life insurance will no longer be necessary.

We believe that life insurance really serves as an extended warranty that surrounds your financial vehicles until the day you die. We all feel safer buying a used vehicle, if we know that if something goes wrong, there is a safety net. The problem will be repaired. There will be someone there to fix it and it's someone else's problem (and expense).

Imagine if we could have this peace of mind in our financial lives? We make rash decisions at times, ignoring the impact of our financial decisions on other parts of our plans. By having insurance in place, and knowing that there will be an ultimate payout, we can make financial decisions with less stress.

The classic example looks like this. Sometime before retirement (the sooner the better), both spouses purchase a permanent life insurance policy on each other and name the other as beneficiary. This would be separate from any estate tax planning policies.

Let's assume that you have one pool of capital comprising your financial retirement assets. The value will increase or decrease based on what the financial markets are doing. Most retirees are scared to look at the television to see what the markets did each day. Their financial futures are tied to the ups and downs of the stock markets. This is not an ideal retirement scenario.

No matter where you are in the investment cycle you know odds are one of you will pass away before the other and when that happens, there will be a capital infusion from the death benefit to re-capitalize your wealth (if you own a permanent insurance policy). In other words, the bucket will fill back up (at least partly) from the insurance proceeds.

If you both live too long and outlive your primary bucket of assets, you will still probably have a few additional sources of capital. Remember, the life insurance contracts have been building cash values that can be accessed to offset your income needs. These values are largely determined by the amount of premiums you paid and the length of time that you paid in. The earlier you purchased these policies, the more likely you are to have larger cash value reserves.

Finally, you may want to consider the equity in your home. Your home may be paid off or very close to being paid off at that point. An insurance plan opens more doors because the proceeds can make sure that you won't unintentionally disinherit your children if you use the equity in your home. Life insurance will eventually pay off those debts on your ultimate demise.

This allows you to spend the time you want with your family in the lifestyle that you're accustomed to, and you'll worry less about running out of money. The top fear among most senior citizens is not death, but outliving their income and outliving their assets. As a result, they begin to spend less during the years when they should be enjoying their golden years.

Many seniors are living like paupers or significantly decreasing their lifestyle to make sure they don't run out of money. As they age, the amount of time between market corrections and recoveries seems longer and longer. It is easier to stay fully invested when you are young. Try doing it at age 75! Consider what a different world that would be if they had permanent insurance in place on each of them? That's the ultimate retirement do-over.

Mortgage and Debt Cancellation

The majority of bankruptcies are owing to a force beyond the control of the party failing. Mortgage liquidation often leads to substantial reductions in the family estate at an unfortunate time.

Transfer of the mortgage responsibility to the mortgager's heirs, usually their wife and children, also seems unfair and often results in foreclosure on the mortgage on the home or small business establishment. Make sure to hedge the mortgage obligations on the life of the mortgager by using a life insurance contract. Don't transfer the responsibility of repayment that is really the mortgager's to the dependent members of your family.

Chapter Highlights

➤ You get what you pay for: Understand the different types of life insurance.
➤ Understand the benefits that permanent insurance can provide.
➤ Review potential cost recovery methods.

CHAPTER 13
SAVING VERSUS INVESTING

Saving is not investing and investing is not saving. They are two mutually exclusive events. These two words are often used synonymously, but could not be more different from each other. Savings is defined as accumulating money, and in general, these assets are typically insured, guaranteed, or earn interest at a relatively constant basis and are usually readily available for use with a few stipulations.

Saving versus Investing: Don't invest what you can't afford to lose—in the short run. My goal is to help you control your money. Once you have highlighted and eliminated many of your wealth transfers, you should see an increase in your current cash flow. We also believe that you should be saving as much as possible into your financial plan. Most Americans fail to achieve any significant financial wealth because they don't save enough. We've got one of the lowest saving rates compared to the rest of the developed world, and that is not a good picture for the future of America or the long-term wealth of our country. We need to start saving money; more importantly we need to start saving money in the right places. Where you build wealth has more to do with what you end up with than just selecting better investments. P.S. The likelihood of actually putting money in the best investments at the right time is not strong for any of us. Your plan is going to be impacted more substantially by the coordination of your money than by products you invest in. Creating the right environment for your money to grow is essential.

Where Should You Save?

History of Savings Rates

Unfortunately, today most people save less than 3 percent of their income. Combined with an average inflation rate of about 3 or 4 percent per year, it's no surprise that people struggle to make financial progress. This is the definition of financially treading water. We have become a buy now, pay later society. This behavior needs to change immediately. Otherwise we are doomed, and the silent partners win.

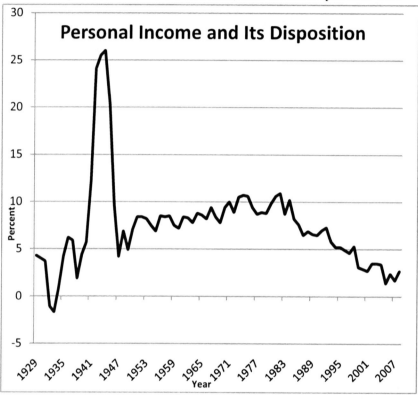

Personal Income and Its Disposition

Source: U.S. Bureau of Economic Analysis

Figure 13.1   Personal Savings Expressed as a Percentage of Income.

As represented above, our national personal savings rates are a disgrace. Personal savings has dropped to an abysmal number, less than 2 percent. In fact, for many segments of our population, it's actually a negative number, meaning that the mirage of future prosperity is now being paid with borrowed money. Our current wants and desires trump our goals and long-term ambitions. Worse, these numbers include the high income earners and baby boomers, many of whom are shoveling their incomes into retirement plans. When we exclude the billionaires, millionaires, super rich, very rich, wealthy, and high income earners, we see an even scarier picture.

The average American is not thinking about saving. We are wondering how to put gas in our car at $4.00 per gallon! In fact, most people's savings accounts in America are actually negative. In other words, if Americans earn $70,000 in household incomes, many spend close to $75,000 on goods and services (if not more). We don't think it's because we don't want to save any money. Everyone over the age of 12 knows that it is important to "save for a rainy day." Let's examine why we can't save.

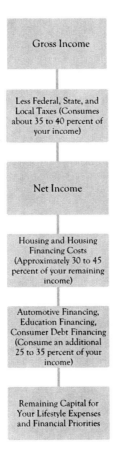

Table 13.2   Typical Cash Flow Table

The taxes always get paid, because they are confiscated before most of us can spend them! Taxes are generally taken right out of our paychecks. Financial institutions take most of what remains with financing charges and interest, the balance is often spent on frivolous consumer purchases.

Meanwhile, real wages in America have declined; young couples living on one income have a lower standard of living than most of their parents did, and the percentage of Americans who own their home is falling. A few decades back, moms started working to provide extras for the family, such as better vacations, holiday gifts, and so on. Today, inflation and taxes have eroded wealth so rapidly that two incomes are required just to make ends meet. More families are renting because they have to instead of by choice. Households with only one income is no longer normal; they are the exception.

Daycare has replaced family dinner. Mortgage foreclosures are increasing at an alarming rate, the number of families in the middle class is decreasing. Average savings accounts are smaller, and our average family debt continues to rise. Additionally, the number of people below the official government-defined property level continue to grow at an alarmingly rapid rate.

The percentage of our senior citizens working beyond age 65 is one of the largest growing segments of our demographics. The number one fear among them is not death, public speaking, or public nudity, it is outliving their assets! They don't want to find themselves becoming a burden on their children or grandchildren because of stock market corrections or unforeseen major medical bills. However, most seniors and emerging retirees still have large amounts of their money at risk in the markets.

Personal bankruptcies are approaching record levels; more and more Americans find themselves with an empty pot instead of a pot of gold, by the time they reach age 65. Don't let this be your financial future, take some steps to coordinate and integrate your strategies today. It begins with a savings plan.

Minimum Savings

Why should I save and how much is the right amount? You should start by defining a number that you plan to save regularly. Work toward a goal. We suggest having the equivalent of 6 months of bills saved in the bank (or in liquid accounts). We believe that you should be saving a definite amount from what you earn each month, and you should define and understand what that minimum number is. Pick a number and try to stick with it for a few months. Once you are comfortable at this level, see if you can increase the amounts. Have the conviction to stay on course, no matter how difficult it gets. Your emergency account will help you survive short-term setbacks and allow you to take advantage of any opportunities that come your way.

You should also know where you stand financially. You should be able to understand whether you'll be okay today, and in the future. Will you be ready for retirement or are you on your way to a second career in the fast food industry during your golden years? Take stock of your current position, and take action.

Why travel the same path with the others who are also grasping at straws and hoping to win the lottery or betting on stock market success? To be financially successful, you need to get off the current path and get on the road less traveled. This can be the road of financial freedom and independence.

Small amounts add up over time. Start by saving something: $1 to $5 per week for a few months. Once you master this level of savings, bump it up. Keep it up if you can. Continue to increase your savings in small increments until you are able to save 10 to 15 percent of your gross income each year.

Savings Strategies

What does $100 per month grow to at a specific interest rate and for a specified number of years?

Examples: A Tale of Two Investors: The Cost of Waiting

Client A: Starting the plan at age 22, saves $4,000 for 10 years at 8 percent. Total Contributions $40,000.

Age	Annual Savings	Rate of Return	Total Account Value
22	$4,000	8%	$4,320
32	$4,000	8%	$62,582
52	$0	8%	$629,741
62	$0	8%	$1,359,564

Client B: Waits 10 years and then invests $4,000 from age 32 until age 62. Total contributions $120,000.

Age	Annual Savings	Rate of Return	Total Account Value
22	$0	8%	$0
32	$4,000	8%	$4,320
52	$4,000	8%	$197,691
62	$4,000	8%	$489,383

Figure 13.3   The Cost of Waiting

Please be aware that it is not important to focus on the actual rate of return for this example. We are simply illustrating the time value of money growth. We are highlighting the cost of waiting. The differences will vary depending on the rate of return.

As you can see, Client B never catches up with Client A, despite the fact that he or she put more capital into the plan. Therefore, starting early and often is one of the keys toward building long-term wealth.

Just Starting Out?

Building wealth is not impossible. Anyone can do it. If every person just saved $100 a month from ages 23 to 65, and invested their money into relatively safe financial products, he or she would have about $1,000,000 by age 65. Today, less than 1 percent of Americans age 65 or older have created that much cash or other liquid assets. Worse, many people lose at least $100 a month, every month, and they don't even know it. Search for these elusive dollars and put them to work for yourself!

Small amounts can add up pretty quickly. If you are young or just starting out, try starting with a small monthly amount. If you are lucky enough to have money left over at the end of each month, start to save $50 or $100 per month. If you don't have any money available at the end of each month, you may need to revisit your budgeting. Trace your spending habits. Can you eliminate $2 to $3 per day and save it for yourself?

You may need to try some of these time-tested, belt-tightening tactics. Bring your lunch to work (even a few days per week). Brown bagging your lunch can save you $5 to $10 per day depending on your habits. What about bringing your own coffee to work, eliminating some of those magazine subscriptions, or buying a few less rounds of beer on the weekend? Review your cable bill, phone bill, and utilities for potential savings as well. You don't have to live like a pauper, but if you want to build wealth, you will need to develop some discipline and a few basic savings habits. The sooner you begin, the better off you'll be.

Pay yourself first. Most people end up paying all of their bills each month. They also end up finding ways to spend all of what remains (and then some). By creating a forced savings account (bill), you stand a better chance of achieving your long-term goals.

Once you've created a savings strategy, you'll begin to accumulate funds. When you have larger amounts of cash on hand, all types of different opportunities appear and you can negotiate very favorable purchase prices on your consumer goods. Plenty of life's problems would disappear if this understanding was generally accepted and practiced widely among our population. Remember, whatever you do is going to be measured against what other people are doing financially.

Small Amounts Do Add Up

Examine the small things you can do on a regular basis that can impact your wealth. Here's an example of silly spending. What is the cost of coffee over our lifetime (besides what it does to our body and mind over the long run)? What is the financial cost of a daily cup of coffee? If we take an average of $2 per cup, seven days a week, that amounts to $730 per year. Remember, we need to calculate the opportunity cost loss on those dollars. What if we compounded these dollars at an 8 percent rate of return?

Instead of buying coffee every day, if we worked out, got our endorphin levels up, and were able to save the money into a Roth IRA at an 8 percent rate of return, we could build close to $90,000 in new wealth just from our recovered coffee cost over a period of 30 years!

The Real Cost of Smoking . . . $600,000?

What about our cigarettes? Millions of Americans smoke cigarettes every day, and from what we can tell the ad campaigns don't have much effect on people quitting smoking. If we can clearly illustrate the financial pain (or the financial cancer of smoking), maybe that will help save a few lives. Let's take a look at that. We don't know how much a pack of cigarettes is today in your state, but here in New Jersey with the state taxes included, it costs about $8 a pack. Let's calculate the cost of the road to an Iron Lung one day. By smoking one pack a day, seven days a week, the cost is $56 a week.

We will round it down to $50 per week. That comes to $200 a month, or $2,400 a year. If you can find a way to quit, this cost can be recovered and saved somewhere. If you are a 20 year old who is smoking, there are potentially 600,000 reasons ($) why you should quit.

Age	Annual Savings	Rate of Return	Total Account Value
25	$730	8%	$788
35	$730	8%	$11,421
55	$730	8%	$89,312
65	$730	8%	$204,240

Age	Year #	Annual Expense	Cumulative Amount Saved	Opportunity Rate of Return	Cumulative Opportunity Cost	Cumulative Account Value
22	1	$2,400	$2,400	7.00%	0	$2,400
23	2	$2,400	$4,800	7.00%	$168	$4,968
24	3	$2,400	$7,200	7.00%	$516	$7,716
25	4	$2,400	$9,600	7.00%	$1,056	$10,656
26	5	$2,400	$12,000	7.00%	$1,802	$13,802
27	6	$2,400	$14,400	7.00%	$2,768	$17,168
28	7	$2,400	$16,800	7.00%	$3,970	$20,770
29	8	$2,400	$19,200	7.00%	$5,424	$24,624
30	9	$2,400	$21,600	7.00%	$7,147	$28,747
31	10	$2,400	$24,000	7.00%	$9,159	$33,159
32	11	$2,400	$26,400	7.00%	$11,481	$37,881
33	12	$2,400	$28,800	7.00%	$14,132	$42,932
34	13	$2,400	$31,200	7.00%	$17,138	$48,338
35	14	$2,400	$33,600	7.00%	$20,521	$54,121

Age	Year #	Annual Expense	Cumulative Amount Saved	Opportunity Rate of Return	Cumulative Opportunity Cost	Cumulative Account Value
36	15	$2,400	$36,000	7.00%	$24,310	$60,310
37	16	$2,400	$38,400	7.00%	$28,531	$66,931
38	17	$2,400	$40,800	7.00%	$33,217	$74,017
39	18	$2,400	$43,200	7.00%	$38,398	$81,598
40	19	$2,400	$45,600	7.00%	$44,110	$89,710
41	20	$2,400	$48,000	7.00%	$50,389	$98,389
42	21	$2,400	$50,400	7.00%	$57,276	$107,676
43	22	$2,400	$52,800	7.00%	$64,814	$117,614
44	23	$2,400	$55,200	7.00%	$73,047	$128,247
45	24	$2,400	$57,600	7.00%	$82,024	$139,624
46	25	$2,400	$60,000	7.00%	$91,798	$151,798
47	26	$2,400	$62,400	7.00%	$102,424	$164,824
48	27	$2,400	$64,800	7.00%	$113,961	$178,761
49	28	$2,400	$67,200	7.00%	$126,474	$193,674
50	29	$2,400	$69,600	7.00%	$140,032	$209,632
51	30	$2,400	$72,000	7.00%	$154,706	$226,706
52	31	$2,400	$74,400	7.00%	$170,575	$244,975
53	32	$2,400	$76,800	7.00%	$187,724	$264,524
54	33	$2,400	$79,200	7.00%	$206,240	$285,440
55	34	$2,400	$81,600	7.00%	$226,221	$307,821
56	35	$2,400	$84,000	7.00%	$247,769	$331,769
57	36	$2,400	$86,400	7.00%	$270,992	$357,392
58	37	$2,400	$88,800	7.00%	$296,010	$384,810
59	38	$2,400	$91,200	7.00%	$322,946	$414,146
60	39	$2,400	$93,600	7.00%	$351,937	$445,537
61	40	$2,400	$96,000	7.00%	$383,124	$479,124
62	41	$2,400	$98,400	7.00%	$416,663	$515,063
63	42	$2,400	$100,800	7.00%	$452,717	$553,517
64	43	$2,400	$103,200	7.00%	$491,464	$594,664
65	44	$2,400	$105,600	7.00%	$533,090	$638,690

Figure 13.4   Cost of Smoking

Without driving yourself crazy, try to examine the little areas where small things add up in your own financial decisions.

Find the Money

You have more than you think. Let's examine the money that the habitual lottery players spend on weekly lottery games. These people dream of winning a million bucks. The average person could actually amass $1 million by age 65, if they could recapture the money they gamble away and save it. This is the money they are spending on lottery tickets, overpriced coffee, silly magazines, and cigarettes, and so on . . . about $75 per week. If they saved this money systematically in a side fund, they could accumulate a small fortune.

They could be among the few Americans that amass over $1 million by age 65. This is an easy concept, yet it requires discipline, knowledge, and courage. Just like our favorite characters in *The Wizard of Oz*, you'll need courage, a heart, a brain, and someone to help you take the road less traveled; a path that leads toward the accumulation of your own wealth.

A New Perspective

Imagine for a minute if you were lucky enough to be able to keep every penny of your lifetime earnings. What if you could choose to spend it as you wish without paying any taxes? What a wonderful situation that would be.

Next imagine if you and your spouse had a combined income of $100,000 a year. From ages 25 to 65, you will have worked 40 years and a total of $4 million will have passed through your hands. It would be great if you didn't have to pay for housing, clothing, food, other consumer decisions, or taxes. Unfortunately, we live in a world where you have to consider the impact of these costs on our wealth.

It's critical that you make all consumer purchasing decisions with a strategy in mind. You need to begin thinking in a way that allows you to understand the true costs of your items. Every purchase contains sets of costs. The first is the after-tax earnings required to make the exchange for the purchase of the item. The second is the lost opportunity costs of those dollars.

For example, a $700 television purchase doesn't just cost you $700. It costs you the time that you had to put in to make $1,000 that allows you to pay $300 in taxes, in order to net the $700. Once the trade is completed, you have traded your money for a new television.

However, the cost of that television also includes the opportunity cost lost on those dollars spent. If you didn't spend them on your television, then you would have them to save or invest. Those same dollars could have potentially earned a rate of return for many years.

Age	Annual Savings	Rate of Return	Total Account Value
25	$4,000	8%	$4,320
35	$4,000	8%	$62,581
45	$4,000	8%	$197,691
55	$4,000	8%	$489,383
65	$4,000	8%	$1,119,124

Figure 13.5   Savings Slide

If you and your spouse purchased that television on New Year's Day to watch some ball games, at age 25, you traded the opportunity to grow that money for the rest of your life. Let's take a look at what $700 would grow to at a compound rate of return of 7 percent for those remaining 40 working years.

This is the amount that has been transferred to the television retailer if they look after their dollars wisely. This is the reason that corporations spend millions of dollars to advertise their products! You can now begin to calculate the total cost of your consumer decisions. Our closets are filled with clothing and shoes that go unworn most of the time. How many pairs of shoes do we really need? Some of us probably have canned goods in the pantry that date back to the Carter administration. Even a $1 can of peas can end up costing $40 over our lifetime. The effects are devastating and you need to start thinking about your consumer decisions in this context.

You now know the importance of saving. I am reminded of a lesson that I learned years ago in the military and it stuck with me. Once all the information is in, it is time for a decision. I was taught that in the Army's officer corps, and it is something that I have carried with me and served me well throughout my life, those who procrastinate, who delay and put off making important decisions, financial or otherwise, leave themselves open to a variety of problems and forces beyond their control. Confront your financial obstacles, design a plan, and take action. Are you ready to commit?

Age	Cost of Item	Rate of Return	Total Account Value at the end of year
25	$700	7%	$749
35	0	7%	$1,377
45	0	7%	$2,708
65	0	7%	$10,482

Figure 13.6   The Full Cost of Consumer Purchases Examined

$10,500: That's almost fifteen times the original amount spent.

Investing Strategies

Why Invest? It seems like a lot of risk. Why should I consider investing at all? Investing incorporates different factors of risk as a means to drive up your potential returns. We all know that there is usually a direct correlation between risk and reward. In general, it is also understood that sometimes there is the possibility that you will lose money. Investments are usually accepted or declined based on the risks involved.

People generally only invest their money if they believe there is a possibility that the rate of return on their money would be greater than it would be in an otherwise guaranteed account at a lower rate. People need to understand what the differences are between saving and investing.

If you don't like to have any losses when it comes to your money, you may want to employ some other strategies rather than just buying investment products. In general, all stocks, bonds, and mutual fund investments will probably lose some value at some point in time. The key is to have this (or other pools of) money available and intact when you need it.

Unfortunately, the imperfect nature of life is such that we can't control where these investments will be in their lifecycle when we need the money. What do you do if the stock market does not perform as expected in the year when you want to purchase a home or vacation property, retire, your child needs their invested dollars for educational expenses, or you get divorced, lose your job, or become disabled?

What would you do if the stock market and the real estate market are both down the year that you lose your job, retire, or get divorced? Sometimes the fishes and loaves fail to multiply to meet our required needs. This is why we save for a rainy day.

There a few time-proven strategies designed to smooth out the bumps in the road of investing over a period of time that include the following.

Dollar Cost Averaging is a timing strategy of investing equal dollar amounts regularly and periodically over specific time periods (such as $100 monthly) in a particular investment or portfolio. By doing so, more shares are purchased when prices are low, and fewer shares are purchased when prices are high. The point is to smooth out the total average *cost per share* of the investment with normal volatility. This strategy is touted as a way to give the investor a chance to lower the overall acquisition cost for the shares purchased over time; however, in a steadily rising market, this can also cause an increasing cost basis on the purchase.

When using a cost-averaging strategy, the investor decides on three parameters: the fixed amount of money invested each time, an investment frequency, and the time horizon where all of the investments are made. With a shorter time horizon, the strategy behaves more like lump-sum investing. Some studies have found that the best time horizons in the stock market, in terms of balancing return and risk, has been 6 or 12 months. In short, cost-averaging offers an option to investors who are facing the decision of either investing a lump-sum or investing smaller amounts over a defined period of time. Cost averaging is not a suitable substitute or alternative for systematic long-term investing.

Asset Allocation is an investment strategy that seeks to reduce the investment risk while maintaining a desired rate of return by spreading an individual's investment over a number of asset classes. It takes advantage of the tendency of different asset classes to move in different cycles, and therefore helps smooth out the ups and downs of the entire portfolio while decreasing volatility.

Stocks, bonds, and cash or cash equivalents are the investments that are normally used as underlying asset classes. Depending on the individual's needs or preferences, tangible assets such as real estate or precious metals and other commodities may also be included in the mix. The asset allocation process normally begins with an analysis of the historical levels of risk and return to reach the investment side being considered.

These historical values are then used as a guide to structure a portfolio that matches each investor's individual goals and overall risk level. There is no single asset allocation model to fit every investor or each stage of the person's life. Asset allocation decisions are usually individual in nature and involve carefully answering a number of key questions.

For example, what are your investment goals? Why are you investing? What's the primary need for income? To pay for current living expenses or as a source of emergency funds? Are you accumulating money for some future need? If so, what is your time horizon? When will this money be needed? At retirement, immediately, or to pay for a future expenses, such as college education? What are your liquidity needs? When will you need this money back? Or how quickly do you think you'll need to be able to recover your investments and turn it back into cash?

Additional Asset Allocation Considerations

Risk tolerance: How comfortable are you with the inevitable ups and downs of the financial markets?

Tax impact: Will the investment added to your overall income tax burden or help mitigate taxes?

Economic Environment: What is the state of current economic conditions? This would include factors such as interest rates, state of the economy, and current inflation rates. These are all essential factors to consider in your overall asset allocation.

International Investing: What about international investments? How comfortable are you investing in foreign markets? Over time financial markets, individual's goals, and situational changes. Periodically, an investor should review his or her situation to ensure that past investment allocations are still appropriate. If not, you should make adjustments with your financial professional.

Many variables are combined to formulate an analysis and recommendations that should be specific to your individual needs. One size does not fit all. Asset allocation neither assures a profit nor protects against any loss in declining markets. In fact, if you plan on investing money, you must be prepared to endure losses, at least in the short run, and possibly over the long run as well. However, it has proven to be one of the more defensive styles of investing to allow you access to multiple asset classes and to improve your odds of success. By using a segmented and coordinated plan comprised of different asset classes for different purposes, you can build a tiered program that will help you weather any storm.

It's also important to coordinate your asset allocation across all of your accounts in order to avoid any overlap between accounts. Some of your accounts may own the same type of investments. Make sure that your retirement savings account holdings are also coordinated with your personal accounts.

Rebalancing the Portfolio: Portfolio rebalancing neither assures a profit nor protects against any loss in declining markets, but it has proven to be an effective way to manage the portfolio over time, in an effort to attempt to mitigate risk.

The Rule of 72: How long will it take to double or triple your investments? The Rule of 72 is a quick mathematical rule of thumb that helps in estimating approximately how many years it will take for an investment to double in value at a specific rate of return.

The Rule of 72 states that if the number 72 is divided by an interest rate, the result is the approximate number of years it will need to double that investment. For example, at a 1 percent rate of return, an investment will double in 72 years, but at a 10 percent return, it will take only 7.2 years to double. This is a helpful rule in trying to figure out how quickly your accounts may increase exponentially. As a quick rule of thumb, $10,000 invested at a constant rate of 10 percent would double every 7.2 years. Therefore $10,000 would become $20,000, then $40,000, and then $80,000 in about 22 years.

The *Rule of 115* is similar to this rule in that it allows one to estimate how long it will take an investment to triple in its value. If you divide 115 by an interest rate, this will result in the approximate number of years needed to triple an investment. For example, at a 1 percent rate of return, an investment will triple in approximately 115 years, but a 10 percent rate of return will take only 11.5 years to triple, and so on. *Please note that these are not exact formulas. They are used for quick rule-of-thumb guess-timates only. They are about as accurate as the average return formulas that they are based upon. Use them with caution.*

Inflation

Unfortunately, the opposite is also true. These rules can also tell you how long before a given item will double or triple in price, at an estimated average rate of inflation. Therefore, if the current infla-tion rate is 3 percent, you can take that estimated average inflation rate, divide it into 72, and see that it will take approximately 24 years before those prices double. These are guidelines and not hard, fast rules. They're used primarily to help you quickly gauge what your long-term needs may entail.

Types of Investments

There is no limit on places to put your money. Some places carry more inherent risks than others. In the pyramid of wealth build-ing that we talked about earlier, the foundational strategies include products like savings accounts, treasury bills, fixed annuities, money markets, money funds, and traditional life insurance or cash value ac-counts. As we work our way through different investment classes, we see things like government, corporate and municipal bonds, converti-ble bonds, conservative mutual funds, balanced accounts, utility stocks, energy stocks, retirement plan assets, and so on.

The more aggressive or growth-related assets include things like investments in real estate, limited partnerships, equity-based partner-ships, growth stocks, mutual funds, variable life insurance, and variable annuities. Under the speculative category, we see products such as oil and gas exploration, commodities, gemstones, options, precious metals such as gold and silver, artwork, hedge funds, and venture capital funds.

Which Vehicle Is Best?

As we examine the different places we can put our money, which place is best? We first need to create some selection criteria for our decisions. How can we simplify the process? There are many places for us to put our money: the financial markets, mutual funds, stocks, bonds, real estate, our businesses, municipal bonds, CDs, permanent life insurance, retirement plans, and so on.

If we could only pick one of them, what would it be and why? We must first establish criteria for what we want our investments to accomplish. Most of us are tax sensitive, so we may want some tax-deferral or tax-free growth. Products like an IRA, Roth IRA, and retirement savings plans can offer some of these advantages. Certain vehicles offer some tax deferral, but also limit what we can put in (and dictate how long it must remain there). Where do we put our dollars beyond those limits? We certainly don't want to be limited in terms of what we can contribute to our investments.

Most of us also want to earn a good return on our money (or an internal rate of return). We like guarantees if we can get them. Sometimes there is a trade-off between returns and guarantees. As business owners, we also want protection in place from our creditors and potential lawsuits, or bankruptcies.

We also want to keep our dollars liquid. We may need them for an opportunity or in an emergency. We definitely need to make sure that we are getting more than one use on our money. If our money only accumulates in one place, we don't get a second, third, or fourth use out of it. Ideally, we'd like to pass our wealth on to our heirs in the most efficient means possible. We want our money to be free of any estate taxes, fees, and expenses that can encumber an estate when it transfers to our heirs.

We'd like someone else to contribute to our plan if we're unable to work. If e became sick, hurt, or can't work, we don't want the gasoline to stop going into our financial vehicles. We want someone else to keep funding our plans for us.

How many benefits do you derive from each product? Ideally, we want products that can offer multiple benefits. We are looking for the financial world's Swiss Army Knife. How many uses are you getting out of each of your current products?

Usually picking only one product is not the best plan. Over the years, we have struggled to find a product that does it all. The one that comes closest is dividend-paying permanent life insurance. It is truly the Swiss Army Knife of the financial services world, as it accomplishes most of the above, if not all, at varying times. If life insurance were the only product that you used, you would not fail financially. This is due to the fact that life insurance policies, unlike many other investment products, offer guarantees. Permanent life insurance, commonly referred to as whole life, offers two different types of insurance on your investable dollars. Most contracts offer a guaranteed minimum rate of return that is generally somewhere in the range of 3 to 5 percent compound over time, and a current dividend assumption schedule which is not

Product	Tax Deferral	Tax Free	Rate of Return	Guarantees	Creditor Protections	Unlimited Contributions	Wide Selection of Investments	Collateral	Estate Tax Free to Heirs	Liquid	Disability Waiver
Stocks and Bonds											
Mutual Funds											
Real Estate											
Business											
CDs											
Municipal Bonds											
Permanent Life Insurance											
Retirement Plan											

Table 13.1   Which Product Is Best?

guaranteed because it is based upon the dividend payment and the performance of the insurance company over time. However, even though it is not guaranteed, many of these carriers can provide historical dividend information going back for over a century. Unlike many equity based products that measure their performance on an average return basis . . . life insurance companies provide detailed records of year by year dividend payments. Very few other financial products come close to that type of a historical performance track record. While I do not believe that life insurance should be the only product in your portfolio, I do believe that if it were the only product in your portfolio (if you could only pick one), it represents a very compelling alternative investment category to the typical equity based investment options.

If life insurance were the only product that anyone owned, a few investments may beat it over time. A handful of investors would miss out on tremendous gains, and some might miss out on long-term average rates of return greater than the cash value growth. However, if life insurance was the only product that you used to build wealth, nobody would fail. As long as you stuck with the program over the long run.

In reality, you will probably need to purchase multiple financial products to help you reach your different objectives. Table 13.1 is designed to give you the framework to make informed decisions about the benefits of your financial products.

One way to improve investment returns is to reduce your expenses. The greatest expense that most investment portfolios incur is taxes. Remember, it's not what you earn but what you keep that matters. Your portfolio should be carefully constructed to minimize wealth erosion due to taxes.

Managing Your Plans

Make sure you work throughout the year with your personal CFO and your tax advisors to create a coordinated and integrated plan designed to maximize your after-tax performance. This should all be part of your annual tax strategy as it relates to your financial plan.

Wealth is specifically amassed by focusing on after-tax returns as opposed to pre-tax returns. The next critical step is objective selection of investment managers to execute your asset allocation plan. Selection should be based on the quality of the investment team, not necessarily the name of the firm. Pay close attention to relative performance, fees, and expenses. Take a look at how they performed over long periods of times—three, five, or ten years since inception. Also be aware that these numbers may vary widely.

Be aware as you make your investment decisions that some advisors will try to compare historical returns that sometimes include the performance of a previous manager. Historical returns alone do not guarantee success and may even be misleading. Before you make any final decisions on your financial services firm, you must consider performance and the ongoing monitoring of your individual portfolio. It is important that as a client, you always have access to timely information regarding your portfolio. You should not have to wait until the end of the month to review the performance of your portfolio. Timely information is critical to your decision-making process.

It's also important to understand how the absolute return of your portfolio compares to the targeted rate of return for your money. Additionally, it is important to understand how the manager that you are paying to oversee your assets is performing compared to their relative benchmarks and other managers within their defined space.

Your advisor should provide you with printed copies of reports on your portfolio on a regular basis. It is also important to rebalance or reallocate your portfolio from time to time, depending on changing issues ranging from your family's ongoing cash flow needs to more macroeconomic trends that may be impacting your overall wealth.

Eliminate the Greed Factor

There is definitely a potential greed factor when it comes to investing. Everyone would like to become rich and get rich quick. Investing is more about experience and timing of the markets. Develop a plan and create definite timelines for each asset classification and each financial goal. Set short-term (performance) and long-term (accumulation) goals for your money.

Make sure to reallocate annually and monitor those assets that have underperformed and outperformed their benchmarks. What goes up must come down. Decide when to sell—before emotions enter the equation. If your goal was to earn 10 percent on an investment, and it is up 20 percent, maybe you should consider selling. Many different factors will need to be considered before making a decision, but a solid game plan can help you stay grounded when emotions race.

Make sure to reallocate annually and monitor those assets that have underperformed and outperformed their benchmarks. What goes up must come down. Decide when to sell—before emotions enter the equation. If your goal was to earn 10 percent on an investment, and it is up 20 percent, maybe you should consider selling. Many different factors will need to be considered before making a decision, but a solid game plan can help you stay grounded when emotions race.

Taxable Equivalent Yield Table

Taxable Income (Joint)	$125,000	$250,000	$400,000
Approximate Combined Federal and State Tax Rates	33%	38%	40%
Tax Exempt Yield (%)	Equivalent Taxable Yield (%)		
2.50	3.73	4.03	4.16
2.75	4.10	4.43	4.58
3.00	4.47	4.83	5.00
3.25	4.85	5.24	5.41
3.50	5.22	5.64	5.83
3.75	5.59	6.04	6.25
4.00	5.97	6.45	6.66
4.25	6.34	6.85	7.08
4.50	6.71	7.25	7.50
4.75	7.08	7.66	7.91
5.00	7.46	8.06	8.33
5.25	7.83	8.46	8.75
5.50	8.20	8.87	9.16
5.75	8.58	9.27	9.58
6.00	8.95	9.67	10.00
6.25	9.32	10.08	10.41
6.50	9.70	10.48	10.83
6.75	10.07	10.88	11.25
7.00	10.44	11.29	11.66
7.25	10.82	11.69	12.08
7.50	11.19	12.09	12.50

Table 13.2   After-Tax Equivalent Yields

* Table 13.2 lists the approximate taxable equivalent yields for those filing a joint return with the listed net taxable income. The individual who purchases investments exempt from federal and state income taxes could potentially realize the approximate after tax yield for the corresponding interest rate. Many factors may influence the actual taxable equivalent yield that you may realize, including the alternative minimum tax. Individuals should consult their tax advisor on an annual basis to determine their tax situation. While every effort was made to provide accurate information in this table, its accuracy is not guaranteed.

Short-Term, Mid-Range, and Long-Term Goals

An important rule for building wealth is to be able to distinguish between long-term and short-term strategies. Just like the game of golf, different clubs are used for different areas of the game. Short-term instruments are used for things like emergency funds, deposits on major purchases such as vehicles, unplanned expenses, and down payments on real estate, homes, and other major purchases. Long-term goals should be designed to build wealth and capital through regular deposits over time that may or may not be readily accessible, and to earn second and third uses, depending on the products chosen to fund these long-term needs.

If people regularly save 10 to 15 percent of their monthly income and lived on the other 85 percent of their income, they would probably avoid many financial challenges in life. You can spend more of the remaining 85 percent on your wants, if you limit the impact of your silent partners on your finances.

Time for a Change?

When should I cut my losses and change my strategy? How will this impact me? Imagine that you're in an elevator on the thirtieth floor of a building and you're trying to get to the fortieth floor and for some reason the elevator keeps going down but it stops at each floor during its descent. You're in an elevator that is going down, but you still have some choices. You can choose to get off and take another elevator. Now you find yourself at the twentieth floor. Would you get off?

Figure 13.8   *"Going Up, Down, or Standing Still?"*

What if for the last 6 months you've been trapped in a (financial) elevator that has been going down? Now you are on the twentieth floor, why on earth would you wait until that same elevator goes all the way back up to the thirtieth floor before you do anything about getting off? Each day, the elevator stops at a new floor and at the end of each day you have the opportunity to step off that elevator into the central corridor of the elevator banks and choose a different elevator.

Some of these other elevators (products and strategies) can even guarantee that you won't go any lower, and still give you the opportunity to go back up just as rapidly as the current elevator that you're on.

This is the decision that investors face in a down market. Many of their current brokers offer little more advice than "Hang in there and hold on, markets usually come back," and "If you sell now you really create a loss" or . . . "It's only a real loss if you sell, it's just a paper loss right now"—nothing could be further from the truth in terms of the reality of how money works.

During a down market, many investors want to wait until the market comes back before they make a move with their finances. Usually, they focus the discussion on real versus apparent losses. We certainly understand and appreciate the psychological effect of creating a real loss. However, there are different types of accounts that follow different rules. Qualified retirement plans don't usually have tax ramifications until you take distributions. Therefore, why would you not be concerned with where your money is heading next? The past is irrelevant relative to how your money will grow today and tomorrow. Why wait till the account comes back to a certain level before making a change? What if other investments can get you back quicker?

All of your investment decisions should be made based on your master plan and strategies. Investments need to be considered relative to other investment opportunities at all times. Additionally, attention should be given to the tax ramifications (or benefits) of selling and changing products.

Diversification, Guarantees, and Layered Strategies

Let's draw another analogy. Imagine that you're in an elevator and you're on the thirtieth floor of a building when you hear a loud snapping noise, and all of a sudden you begin to hear screeching and you feel the elevator in a free fall descent. Since you have thirty floors to travel, there is some time to press the call button for help. When you ask for help, the man on the other end tells you "Hang in there, it usually stops, and sometimes it even goes back up." How would you feel? This is the classic example of investing in the market without a safety net. When investing without any of your assets guaranteed, you run the risk of being at the mercy of the market. What is earned can quickly be snatched away.

Now, imagine that you're in a different elevator. You hear a snapping noise again and you feel the elevator shake and begin to slide a little bit, and the man comes over the intercom and tells you "Don't worry; we've had an interruption. There are four different cables holding up your elevator car. One of them has snapped and caused the elevator to shake and drop a little bit. However, it appears we have the situation stabilized, but even if the other three cables break, which is very unlikely, you will experience a very quick drop. It will be very rapid very scary, much like a theme park like Disney Land or Universal Studios. But, at the end of the ride, we have a gigantic spring able to withstand the weight of over ten cars. That spring will bounce you back up again. It will be a wild ride; you'll go up and down and up and down, eventually coming to a rest at exactly the place where you started to fall and maybe even substantially higher than that." Which elevator would you prefer to be on?

This is the type of financial plan that you can create by using a series of coordinated products. Some of these products will need to be held for a long period of time. Others will allow immediate access to your money, and others still will be designed for midlife goals. The important thing is that they work together to provide you with additional benefits and new guarantees if possible. By the way, there are products and features that allow you to build a solid base of bricks beneath that spring and continue to ratchet it up each and every year once you hit new peaks in your own financial elevator. Guaranteed contracts, annuities, insurance contracts, and insured municipal bonds can offer different layers of guarantees to a segment of your overall portfolio.

You can develop strategies that are designed to not only make sure that you succeed in your own financial elevator, no matter what the financial markets do, but that also gives you the opportunity to profit and live your life free of any worry about what outside forces will do to your money. You'll also be able to sleep well at night, not worrying about the financial devastation that goes on from time to time in the financial markets.

Chapter Highlights

➤ Understand the difference between saving and investing.
➤ Create a savings goal and define your own personal monthly minimum savings target.
➤ Understand how you can begin to recover costs and turn them into savings.
➤ Strategy and Process is more important than product selection when selecting investments. Design strategies that are not only diversified but also layered to allow for maximum flexibility.

CHAPTER 14
REAL ESTATE AND
MORTGAGE STRATEGIES

"A man builds a fine house; and now he has a master,
and a task for life; he is to furnish, watch,
show it, and keep it in repair, the rest of his days."

–Ralph Waldo Emerson

The Challenge

How do you purchase a $350,000 home while transferring the least amount of wealth possible?

Options

Option 1: Pay Cash: $350,000 paid.

Opportunity Cost lost on $350,000 invested for 30 years at 6 percent = Total Cost of $2,010,220.

Opportunity Cost lost on $350,000 invested for 30 years at 8 percent = Total Cost of $3,521,930.

Financing Alternative

Down Payment: 20 percent down = $75,000.

Finance the difference with a 30-year fixed rate mortgage in the amount of $280,000. This note carries a principal and interest payment at 6 percent of $1,678 per month (plus property taxes and insurance). Total payments are equal to $604,000.

Opportunity Cost lost on a $75,000 down payment invested for 30 years at 6 percent = Total Cost of $430,760.

Opportunity Cost lost on a $75,000 down payment invested for 30 years at 8 percent = Total Cost of $754,700.

Real Estate Overview

Your home is part of your accumulated assets, and is a major portion of your lifestyle. How you pay for it can dramatically influence the wealth you transfer away? It also represents a major lifestyle decision. If you want to pay off your home early, you'd probably want to do it in a way that would transfer the least wealth possible in the process.

Transfers are inevitable, no matter how you pay for your home. You may save interest by prepaying your mortgage, but you also lose potential interest because those dollars are not earning interest. If you finance your purchase, then there's the obvious wealth transfer in the form of interest payments. If you pay cash for your home, you have wealth being transferred because your money is no longer earning interest for you. Our focus is to help you achieve the best use of the money you are spending on your home, with the least out-of-pocket costs along the way.

Real Estate Strategies

There are many ways to own real estate. You can purchase a home to live in (owner occupied), a vacation home, an investment property, a share in a real estate investment trusts (REITs), or a time-share.

Understand What You Can Afford

You need to stay grounded in reality. Meet with professionals who will show you what you can afford and have them show you how they arrived at their conclusions. Otherwise, you could be stuck with a home that you cannot afford.

If you are sick and don't like the diagnosis, you can always see enough doctors for different opinions until you meet one who is willing to say that you are healthy—or at least not as sick as the last guy he saw! This does not make you a healthy person.

Work with mortgage planners and real estate professionals that will tell you what you need to hear—not what you want to hear. The best offense is a good defense. Your home can function as the financial engine of your plans. You don't have to make your dream home your first purchase. Start at a reasonable level, you can always trade up. As a general rule of thumb, housing-related expenses should not exceed 33 percent of your annual income, and total debt service payments (autos, credit cards, school loans, consumer debts, and so on) should not exceed 50 percent of your annual income. Remember, another 25 to 35 percent is confiscated from taxes. That doesn't leave much for heat, electric, TV, internet, phones, household spending, or your savings program. If you cripple yourself with housing payment debts, you may not be able to save at all!

The Down Payment

In order to get into the real estate game, you're going to have to secure a down payment. Typically, banks will require approximately 20 percent of the purchase price as a down payment. Some programs are offered with little to no money down. For our purposes, we will examine the more traditional 20 percent down payment method. Simply put, if you purchased a $300,000 property, the bank will typically require a down payment of $60,000.

How will you be able to secure such a large amount of capital unless you purchase a property? The best way to save for this event is to minimize your housing expense outflows with a coordinated financial housing plan. Few couples would argue that they have ever saved more than when they were saving up to purchase their first home. The biggest challenge is to save a down payment. It's obvious that you'll need to save some money. Some of the best ways that you can do this would be to encourage others to join your venture, either directly as partners or indirectly as tenants.

One option is to partner with roommates, friends, or family members to pool your capital in an effort to secure a down payment more easily. The second option might be to delay the instant gratification of moving into an apartment and rather opting to live at home. This would give you to the opportunity to save, which would have otherwise have been transferred to rent in your own capital account. From there, you have choices. You can then choose to use your saved capital as a down payment on the property that you now own and control.

You'd be in control of potential tax benefits and you would be building equity in a property as opposed to building equity for someone else who owns the property you are renting. As a quick example, if your monthly rent was costing you $1,500 per month. On an annual basis, that would cost you $18,000. If you're able to save that money and earn some rate of return, you may be able to capture close to $20,000 in one year by not renting. Add to this disciplined savings strategy a second business partner (or part owner) on your property and you may be on your way to building wealth in the real estate game.

Once you've secured the property, you may want to consider having roommates or friends live in the property with you in an effort to decrease your monthly outlay. A $1,500 rental payment is a pure cost. A $1,500 mortgage payment carries with it a potential mortgage interest deduction. That may bring the total net out-of-pocket cost down to around $1,000 to $1,200 per month. That number can be cut in half again by adding a roommate or a tenant to that property. You may be in a position where you can offset or find an additional $500 to $800 per month that can be recapitalized somewhere else on your financial model. Structuring your programs in this fashion may open new opportunities for yourself to build wealth more effectively. Ready to test the waters?

Property Selection

Once you have your down payment saved, you be able to start house hunting. Get prequalified for what you can actually afford—not what you want. Real estate can be an emotional process, especially if it's a purchase for your primary residence. Remember, your home is a place to live. First and foremost it is a lifestyle asset before it is an investment. What if the value never appreciates? Would you still buy it?

Financing Strategies

There are many ways to finance real estate transactions. Is there a right choice? There are so many choices, is it even possible to make the right one? Making the right choice can be very confusing. Many options reduce the interest rate on a mortgage by expediting the mortgage payments.

While transferring less interest is desirable, there are other issues that must be included in our thought process as well. In our review, we want to help you develop a selection process designed to find the right strategy for you (with the least wealth being transferred along the way).

There is a great deal of misinformation concerning this topic. Many people make the decision based on what they have heard, and not necessarily what is correct. As we go through this discussion together, we're going to examine both the concepts, as well as the numbers and help you gain a better understanding of how your mortgage may affect your wealth. If what you believe to be true about your mort-

248 | Ivy League Wealth Secrets

gage and how it affects your ability to accumulate money turned out
not to be true, when would you want to know?

There are several reasons to have a mortgage, and many reasons not to
have one.

1. The first is simple, if you don't have enough money, you'll need to
    borrow it from someone else.

2. The second is that you have the money, and could pay cash, but
    because of the current tax treatment of interest on mortgage loans,
    you may be better off to take the deduction and keep your money
    invested in other areas.

3. The third reason is to carry mortgage is the spread. The spread is
    the difference between the percentage that you can borrow money
    and what you can earn on your money.

There are many ways to finance the cost of your home. If banks
made the same amount of money on every type of mortgage, how many
options do you think they would have? Probably only one! Obviously,
the banks make money in different ways on different programs. Some
products allow them to make more, some less. Wouldn't it be nice to
know which ones make them more and which ones made them less, so
that you can make your decisions accordingly? It's like having the other
team's playbook!

There are many choices available. The most expensive way to
acquire a home is to pay for it upfront with cash. If you were lucky
enough to have enough cash to buy a home without a mortgage, you
would be using the most expensive approach. Many people are surprised to hear this. The additional expense is due to the opportunity
cost associated with the loss of use on those funds (see Chapter 5 on
opportunity costs).

Since you paid cash, the bank now has that money available to
use for its investing opportunities. However, you no longer have those
dollars available and you can't earn anything extra with them. Only the
bank can use them now.

Generally, using a mortgage and paying for it over the longest
period of time possible would be the most advantageous. Don't con-
fuse this with taking on more debt or risk than necessary. What is the
difference between having $100,000 invested in conservative areas with
a corresponding mortgage; and not having the $100,000 invested but
being mortgage free? Being debt free is a state of mind. You are debt
free when you have the ability to write a check and pay off the debt—

not when you terminate the repayment schedule! By keeping your mortgage in place, you pick up mortgage interest deductions and create more liquidity, access, and control over your finances.

> Thinking of paying cash for your purchase?
> Before you do consider this:
>
> A lump sum of $300,000 invested at a compound rate of return of 6 percent for 30 years could potentially grow to $ 1,723,047. A 30 year mortgage loan amount of $300,000 at a rate of 5.5 percent would cost a total of $1,556,000. That represents a difference of $167,000 over the life of the loan. Plus the potential mortgage interest tax deductions!

This is due to a combination of factors such as potential tax benefits, opportunity costs, and paying back with cheaper dollars (inflation effects). This is contrary to what the public is trained to believe, but our evidence is clear and overwhelming to support it. There are three reasons why this is true:

1. You receive a tax deduction for the interest you pay on the loan. *Tax Benefits*: If you are concerned about your current tax liability and maximizing your opportunities, then this discussion may be helpful. There are individuals who care nothing about the potential tax benefits associated with carrying a mortgage. This discussion is geared toward those who would like to consider options available to reduce their taxes, as well as maintain the use of their money.

2. If you have a fixed rate mortgage, over time you pay the mortgage back with money that is not only tax deductible, but you are using future dollars that are cheaper because of inflation. Inflation eats away at the purchasing power of our money. Having a fixed payment helps us over time.

3. By opting to use a mortgage, you do not suffer as large an opportunity cost as a person who buys the house using all cash. You have your money available to work for you and sometimes you're able to receive a higher rate of return on that money than the rate that you're paying from your mortgage interest. In this strategy, you control the money. You can use them as you see fit, and your

money is more accessible than if you pay for the house with cash. You can also choose to terminate the loan agreement at any time by simply sending the bank a check. You're in control here—not the bank!

Remember, once you pay for the house in cash, the money is now trapped in the home. In order to get it out, you have to beg a bank for access to your own money! You have to either apply for a new mortgage or a line of credit on the property. This process is slow, and costs money for application fees, expenses, and other costs. In this case, you are not in control. The bank will decide if they feel like lending you your own money! What if you lose your job or become disabled?

You can opt to try to sell the property and get your money back as well. This will depend on you making a decision to sell your home. There are some potential negative personal feelings attached to this type of decision. Additionally, you need to hope that the real estate market is strong when you decide to sell. The sale may also result in expenses: realtor's commissions, fees, bank costs, potential repairs, inspections, advertising expenses, and so on.

All of these factors will decrease your profits. What if you need the money when times are tough? What if you need the money when you are disabled or unemployed? The bank will probably respond to your loan application along these lines: "You have been a great customer. You paid your mortgage payments on time, you made extra payments, and you completed the mortgage early. We're not sure you can pay us back. After all, you're (unemployed, disabled, have poor credit, and so on). Sorry . . . have a lollipop."

Large Down Payment on the Purchase of a Home

We agree that putting more than the minimum required down on the purchase of a home reduces the interest you will have to transfer to the bank during the financing period. Before doing this, you should also calculate the interest lost by having your money locked up in your home. Once the money is in the house it earns zero interest. When you consider the time value of money, large down payments must be viewed in a different light. Perhaps you can invest the lump sum and direct the interest earnings into municipal bonds, permanent insurance, or another asset.

Paying Cash for a Home

Few people actually have this option, but many believe this is a good thing. Most of the people who actually do this would receive little or no tax benefit by carrying a mortgage because of their income level. The tax benefit is just one consideration. The spread is even more important. You may miss out on higher returns by keeping your money working for you.

We Want to Pay Off Our Home Quickly

The fastest way to pay off your mortgage is to write one huge check. The fastest way to build enough capital in your bank account is to save. Will it be easier to save with a larger 15-year mortgage payment or a smaller 30-year mortgage payment? Could you save the difference in a side fund?

The Impact of Inflation on Payments: Use it to Your Advantage

Remember when you purchased your first house? You wondered how you would ever make the payments. Over time, making the payments on the loan was easier to handle. One of the reasons is the impact of inflation. The money we have today is our most valuable. Future dollars will be worthless due to the impact of inflation. Since, you can lock in your mortgage for 30 years, you will benefit by not prepaying your mortgage with inflated dollars. Instead, keep your money invested with the opportunity to perhaps keep pace with or ahead of inflation. The dollars you have today are your most valuable. Use them wisely.

# of Years	Mortgage Payment Amount	Inflation Rate	Future Payment Effect in Today's Dollars
10	$2,000	3%	$1,475
20	$2,000	3%	$1,088
30	$2,000	3%	$802

Table 14.1   Benefits of paying over time with inflation eroded dollars.

Down Payment: What Is the Cost to You versus the Potential Earnings for the Bank?

Here's how it is growing for the bank:

➢ What is the time value of money?

➢ Do you earn interest on your down payment? No.

➢ Is your down payment accessible? No.

➢ What would your down payment be worth today had you been able to keep it and invest it for yourself?

We need to consider the opportunity cost on your down payment.

# of Years	Down Payment Amount	Rate of Return	Total Future Value
10	$60,000	7%	$118,029
20	$60,000	7%	$232,181
30	$60,000	7%	$456,735

Table 14.2   What is your down payment worth . . . for the bank?

Many people believe that paying cash for their home is a good idea. This would be the equivalent of the largest down payment possible. Since the home appreciates the same as if it's completely financed or if it's paid in cash. We have to consider the cost of having our money tied up in our homes.

Here's a quick example:

$300,000 Cash Paid for a Home versus Investing at 7 Percent Growth
Total Opportunity Cost lost after 10 years: $590,000
Total Opportunity Cost lost after 20 years: $1,160,905
Total Opportunity Cost lost after 30 years: $2,283,676

Of course, to be fair you must also account for the costs associated with carrying a $300,000 mortgage during that time (net of the tax benefits). I will provide several examples.

Home as an Investment

Many people think that their home is their greatest investment. Is your home a good investment? Let's take a look at the true rate of return of your home. First, remember your home is a place to live! It can also provide you with a way to accumulate some long-term wealth. However, there have been periods of time where owning a home provided little or no appreciation or equity growth. Let's examine.

My Home Is My Best Investment?

Current Value of Your Home: $450,000
Purchase Price: $175,000
Owned for 20 Years
Value of Improvements (paint, carpet, landscaping, pool, furnished basement, addition, and so on): $40,000
You Have Earned a Gain of: $235,000 (net of you original cost and the cost of improvement)
Rate of Return of Your Home as an Investment: 3.76 percent
How does this compare to your other investments and the overall inflation rate?

Many people feel that their home is their best investment and a good place to park their money. Take a look at your numbers and see how your house is really holding up as an investment. How does its performance compare to your other investments? It's possible that you do have large gains in your home, but you may be forced to sell or refinance to access the money. Both of these strategies have elements of risk and uncertainty. If your home appreciation values don't keep up with the returns that you could receive from your other investment opportunities, then prepaying your mortgage may not be prudent. We also need to subtract the real estate commissions and closing costs from the amount you sell your house for to get a better picture. To be fair, you must also account for transaction fees and taxes on your alternative investment choices as well.

Home Equity Access

If you already paid cash or shelled out a huge down payment for your home, you may still be able to get it back. Depending on your ability to service the mortgage payments, you may want to consider an equity out refinance or a home equity loan (usually fixed interest rates), or a home equity line of credit (usually variable rates).

Mortgage Spreads Examined

There may be a significant difference between how much you have to pay to finance your home, and what you may be able to earn with your money invested. It costs the same to live in your house whether you finance it or pay cash.

We must also consider the possible opportunities if we can earn more return with our money than it costs us to borrow those dollars. If we can accomplish this, then we must consider making a lower down payment than 100 percent on our purchase. Shorter loan periods give borrowers the perception that they save more interest. While they do save interest, they lose interest as well. Many of the mortgage payment strategies focus on minimizing interest payments over the life of the mortgage as their goal. The shortest mortgage payment plan would be a cash payment. As discussed earlier, this is usually the most expensive option.

The interest associated with your mortgage is only one element that should be considered. By looking at both ends of the spectrum, you can get a better feel for the overall picture. Most people choose the shorter loan period due to the interest they think they will save by doing so. If interest saved were the only goal, then paying cash for your home would be an even better alternative. By paying cash, we do save the interest we would have otherwise given to the bank. The other side of the coin is that we no longer have our money invested, so we are also losing interest.

15- or 30-Year Mortgage: Which Is best?

The best 15-year mortgage is a 30-year note where you save and invest the difference and pay off your house in 15 years with one big initial check. Generally, this option gives the greatest tax benefits while carrying the mortgage. A 30-year mortgage puts you in control, since you have the option to pay the 30-year mortgage off early if you choose. Using the 30-year option provides you with options that are not available with a 15-year mortgage.

The 30-year mortgage option offers the greatest tax benefits while carrying the mortgage. It also provides an opportunity to continue the mortgage if interest rates rise in the market in the future. Many people pay off their mortgage in 15 years, only to pull out the money in the future at higher rates. You may also be able to earn more on your money than the mortgage is costing you in interest (net of deductions). People who are looking at a 15-year mortgage option will be amazed that there are more tax benefits in the first 15 years of a 30-year mortgage than there are in the entire 15 years of a 15-year mortgage. A 30-year mortgage is more appropriate than a 15-year mortgage for most people.

Many people think that once they get their home paid for they will be able to save more money. All things being equal, if you save and invest the difference between a 15-year mortgage and a 30-year mortgage, you would have the same amount as someone who paid off their home in 15 years and began saving and investing their entire monthly payment (assuming the same interest rates each year).

Option 1: 15-year Mortgage:
    Loan Amount: $300,000.00
    Term of the Loan: 15 years
    Interest Rate: 5.750 percent
    Monthly Mortgage Payment: $2,491.23

Option 2: 30 Year Mortgage:
    Loan Amount: $300,000.00
    Term of the Loan: 30 years
    Interest Rate: 6.000 percent
    Monthly Mortgage Payment: $1,798.65

Payment Difference: $692.58 per month or $8,310 per year.
Side fund potential growth
$8,310 invested at 6 percent for 30 years would grow to $696,472.
$8,310 invested at 6 percent for 15 years would grow to $205,052.
$8,310 invested at 8 percent for 30 years would grow to $1,016,811.
$8,310 invested at 8 percent for 15 years would grow to $243,712.

Another major consideration is that the person with the 30-year loan had the potential to access their money for the entire period. If they save the difference, they will have accumulated additional capital that can be used to make new financial decisions. If it is prudent for them to pay off their home in 15 years, they may still have that option available.

It makes even more sense to lock in the longest loan duration period if mortgage interest rates are low. This way we can maximize our tax benefits and pay the note off with inflated money in the future. Most people would agree with this assumption, but some comment that this strategy works only if you are disciplined enough to save and invest the difference between the 30- and 15-year mortgage. While this line of reasoning seems correct, there are few who are more disciplined in the second 15 years, to save and invest their entire house note than they are to save the difference between the two payments. In other words, if you can't save the difference now, how will you ever save the entire amount in the future?

There is really no mathematical reason for anyone to have a 15-year mortgage. However, this is not to say that you have made a financial mistake by paying on this schedule. Some people prefer the peace of mind that comes with a fixed 15-year mortgage payment plan. Paying your home off in 15 years is another issue that does not require you to have a 15-year note. When you consider the tax benefits available in the 30-year loan option, the rate of return required on the difference between the two mortgage options may well be within your risk tolerance levels.

It may be possible to pay your 30-year note off sooner than 15 years, assuming you want to have your home paid off, which would be better than a 15-year note. If you were going to choose a 15-year mortgage so that you can get your home paid off as fast as possible, then choosing the 30-year option and investing the difference may work out even better.

In order to accomplish this goal, you must be an honest with yourself. You must resist the urge to spend the payment differential (savings) on consumer purchases. Instead, you must save these freed-up dollars where they can accumulate to provide you with additional options.

Tax Advantages

Which one of these two paid the most in taxes over the 30-year period? The one with the 15-year mortgage! There are more tax deductions in the first 15 years of a 30-year loan amortization than there are in the entire 15 years of a 15-year mortgage. See below.

Amortization Tables: 30-Year Mortgage

Loan Amount: $300,000.00

Term of the Loan: 30 years

Interest Rate: 6 percent

Monthly Mortgage Payment: $1,798.65

Total Interest Paid over the Life of the Loan: $347,514.56

15-Year Mortgage Plan Alternative

Loan Amount: $300,000.00

Term of the Loan: 15 years

Interest Rate: 5.75 percent

Monthly Mortgage Payment: $2,491.23

Total Interest Paid Over the Life of the Loan: $148,421.45

You will need to select somewhere to put the difference between the two payments. In general, relatively liquid, low-risk investments make the most sense. The stock market is probably out. Don't bet your bricks on the performance of the financial markets. However, you will need to achieve a rate of return greater than or equal to the net carrying cost of your mortgage rate (the rate adjusted for your mortgage interest deduction).

Permanent life insurance may be a good place to put the saved difference between the two mortgage options, especially when you factor in a tax savings at interest, as well as the term insurance premiums replaced along with interest. If you have term insurance or mortgage insurance, then purchasing permanent life insurance may reduce or eliminate the need for term or mortgage insurance. You can now save these premiums as well.

Amortization Table

Year	Loan Balance	Yearly Interest Paid	Yearly Principal Paid	Total Interest
2009	$296,315.96	$17,899.78	$3,684.04	$17,899.78
2010	$292,404.71	$17,672.56	$3,911.26	$35,572.34
2011	$288,252.21	$17,431.32	$4,152.50	$53,003.67

(continued)

(*continued*)

Year	Loan Balance	Yearly Interest Paid	Yearly Principal Paid	Total Interest
2012	$283,843.60	$17,175.21	$4,408.61	$70,178.87
2013	$279,163.07	$16,903.29	$4,680.53	$87,082.16
2014	$274,193.86	$16,614.61	$4,969.21	$103,696.77
2015	$268,918.16	$16,308.12	$5,275.70	$120,004.89
2016	$263,317.06	$15,982.72	$5,601.10	$135,987.61
2017	$257,370.50	$15,637.26	$5,946.56	$151,624.87
2018	$251,057.17	$15,270.49	$6,313.33	$166,895.36
2019	$244,354.45	$14,881.10	$6,702.72	$181,776.46
2020	$237,238.32	$14,467.69	$7,116.13	$196,244.14
2021	$229,683.28	$14,028.78	$7,555.04	$210,272.93
2022	$221,662.27	$13,562.80	$8,021.02	$223,835.73
2023	$213,146.53	$13,068.08	$8,515.74	236,903.81
2024	$204,105.57	$12,542.85	$9,040.97	249,446.66
2025	$194,506.97	$11,985.22	$9,598.59	261,431.89
2026	$184,316.36	$11,393.20	$10,190.61	272,825.09
2027	$173,497.21	$10,764.67	$10,819.15	283,589.76
2028	$162,010.76	$10,097.37	$11,486.45	293,687.13
2029	$149,815.85	$9,388.91	$12,194.91	303,076.04
2030	$136,868.78	$8,636.75	$12,947.06	311,712.79
2031	$123,123.17	$7,838.21	$13,745.61	319,551.00
2032	$108,529.76	$6,990.41	$14,593.41	326,541.41
2033	$93,036.26	$6,090.32	$15,493.50	332,631.73
2034	$76,587.15	$5,134.71	$16,449.11	337,766.44
2035	$59,123.50	$4,120.17	$17,463.65	341,886.61
2036	$40,582.73	$3,043.05	$18,540.77	344,929.66
2037	$20,898.41	$1,899.49	$19,684.32	346,829.15
2038	$0.00	$685.41	$20,898.41	$347,514.56

Amortization Table

Year	Loan Balance	Yearly Interest Paid	Yearly Principal Paid	Total Interest
2009	$287,016.61	$16,911.38	$12,983.39	$16,911.38
2010	$273,266.69	$16,144.84	$13,749.92	$33,056.22
2011	$258,704.98	$15,333.05	$14,561.72	$48,389.27
2012	$243,283.54	$14,473.33	$15,421.44	$62,862.59
2013	$226,951.62	$13,562.85	$16,331.92	$76,425.44
2014	$209,655.47	$12,598.61	$17,296.15	$89,024.05
2015	$191,338.16	$11,577.45	$18,317.31	$100,601.51
2016	$171,939.40	$10,496.00	$19,398.76	$111,097.51
2017	$151,395.34	$9,350.70	$20,544.06	$120,448.21
2018	$129,638.36	$8,137.78	$21,756.98	$128,585.99
2019	$106,596.85	$6,853.25	$23,041.51	$135,439.25
2020	$82,194.97	$5,492.89	$24,401.88	$140,932.13
2021	$56,352.42	$4,052.21	$25,842.56	$144,984.34
2022	$28,984.12	$2,526.47	$27,368.30	$147,510.80
2023	$0.00	$910.65	$28,984.12	$148,421.45

The saved premiums may be recovered to offset the new permanent insurance premiums. If you choose to invest these savings, you will also earn interest. The interest earned on the mortgage insurance premium savings must be factored in along with the opportunity cost recoveries. Remember, there are more factors to consider than just the monetary benefits. Liquidity and access to your money over the 15 years are some benefits to consider. Since we do not know what is ahead economically, the control of your money provides you with more potential options in the future. When comparing the options of choosing between a 30-year fixed rate mortgage and a 15-year mortgage, we must also recognize that the real benefit of a 15-year mortgage is that the mortgage will be paid off in 15 years as long as you can handle making those payments.

Therefore, there is no real mathematical reason to have a 15-year mortgage. We do recognize the fact that there are many emotional and other reasons for using this type of a strategy. Most of the arguments against a longer mortgage duration argue that human nature gets in the way. They argue that people will not save the differential between their two payments. This can be accurate. Therefore, I would suggest if you're going to use this type of a strategy and you're committed to making a 15-year mortgage payment (that you can really afford), you may want to consider creating a bill for yourself. This can be done by paying not only your 30-year mortgage payment, but also making a separate payment to another financial institution. It could be done using a bank program, a mutual fund family, or one of our personal favorites, dividend-paying permanent life insurance policies. Over time, these policies or side funds can grow and accrue interest that can be used to surrender your remaining mortgage debt.

Also consider the event of a disability. I have seen this scenario play out in real life too many times. Imagine that you've been paying your mortgage on time and you are in year 12- of a 15-year mortgage. You suddenly have a terrible accident and are placed on disability. Most people do not own sufficient personal disability insurance. At some point, you will need to be wheeled in to see the banker where you will beg for mercy. You may argue that you've paid your mortgage on time or ahead of time every month for the past decade. He will likely respond by saying something along the lines of "You have been a great customer, and we do appreciate the fact that you've paid on time. But given your current circumstances, we're not so sure that you can pay us back. We'd like to help, but unfortunately the bank is not in a position to lend to those who are out of work."

How would you be able to access the equity built up in your home, short of selling the property? I know most people believe that the real estate market will remain strong and robust forever. If we examine the historical performance of the real estate market, we will see that it moves in a system of peaks and valleys over long periods of time (similar to other financial markets). It's quite possible that some people could be negatively impacted by declining real estate values in their time of need. With millions of Americans at risk, odds are that some people will have equity trapped in their homes that is inaccessible at their moment of need.

When this occurs, those people will be out of luck. I would much rather be in a position where I have control and access to liquidity of my money than being at the mercy of a bank underwriter's decision to allow me to refinance my property. I don't want to hope that someone will purchase my home to bail me out of the jam. Once people know your story, they're quick to try to take advantage and may offer you a below market price for your property. Given the choice, I would much rather have cash values inside my life insurance policies (or in an investment side fund) that I can access at a moment's notice than have equity tied up in a property, that can only be accessed once the bank approves me or someone wants to purchase my property. Once again, a coordinated approach can offer additional safety features and greater access to the capital during life's challenging times.

Prepayment Strategies

Initially, when we consider only the interest cost, it looks as if you'd be better off to prepay. This is the comparison that most people look at and is often only part of the discussion that gets any mention. It is true that you do save interest by prepaying, but you're also losing interest as well, not to mention the tax deductions. When you factor in the time value of money, you see a different picture. It makes sense to consider the time value of money in mortgage decisions as well.

If you prepay your mortgage, you do save interest. Once you park your money in your home, you no longer earn interest on that money. Your house may appreciate, but it appreciates at the same rate for a person who has paid in cash, as one who has completely financed their purchase. Any money you put in your house by prepaying is basically earning zero growth. In addition, you must consider tax deductions. Many are deferring taxes in other places and paying more than required in their mortgage. Those tax savings have an opportunity cost associated with them, and it can add up to a great deal of money. Prepaying early with expensive dollars rather than paying over the life of your loan with inflated dollars can cost you money, too.

Many strategies have been employed in an effort to help consumers shorten their mortgage durations. Two of the most common include bi-weekly programs or extra mortgage payments? These programs are designed to create a thirteenth payment each year. By taking a 52-week year and dividing it into 26 bi-weekly periods, the bank has essentially found a way to get you to send them more of your money each year. Proponents of the plan argue that it is a strategy designed to help knock 5 to 7 years off of the life of your 30-year mortgage loan. Under further examination we see that the concept makes sense, but we are missing an essential component. We are not earning any interest on our extra payments!

Consider the following: We have a monthly mortgage payment of about $2,000 on a $330,000 mortgage at 6 percent interest. If we send this extra sum to the bank, we will essentially mail them an extra $2,000 per year or about $60,000 over the life of the loan. It is this extra $60,000 that allows us to knock off a few years of interest on the back end of the loan. To me, this is like investing in a 30-year CD at the bank that pays 0 percent rate of return. You wouldn't invest in that type of a contract, so why do it with your mortgage?

Strategy 1: Send the bank extra payments.

# of Years	Annual Savings	Rate of Return	Total Account Value
30	$2,000	0%	$60,000 Principal Reduction

Strategy 2: Invest your extra payments into a well-diversified long-term portfolio.

# of Years	Annual Savings	Rate of Return	Total Account Value Side Fund
10	$2,000	8%	$31,290
15	$2,000	8%	$46,698
20	$2,000	8%	$98,845
30	$2,000	8%	$244,691

Now consider the potential economic advantage that we can create if we invest that same extra annual mortgage payment into a side fund. In this hypothetical example, our $2,000 payments growing at 7 percent interest would grow to be worth over $200,000 in 30 years. By managing the process on our own, we are able to keep more wealth in our control and possibly pay off our home even sooner (if we still want to). You also have those dollars available to you and your family in the event of an emergency or for an opportunity. Your planner now has many years to convince you not to pay it off, once you get to the point where you have the money to pay off the loan.

Prepaid Mortgage Principal

You forfeit opportunity each time you prepay principal. If mortgage interest rates are low, you may benefit more by investing the money and maintaining more control over your money. Understanding this issue may lead you to stop prepayments so as to allow you to place that money in a more suitable account where you can derive additional benefits.

Home Equity Review

Remember our lesson on down payment math. Once the money is in your house, you may lose the use of the money. In the event of a disability, you may not have access to your equity because the bank may not take the risk to refinance you without being able to work. What if interest rates climb and your money is tied up in your home? You would have to borrow from the bank at higher interest rates. Locking in for 30 years, especially at a low interest rate gives you the opportunity to benefit from increases in the market interest rate. You could also lose your equity due to a lawsuit. Even if you can get to your money, it most often will cost you to access it through legal fees and closing costs.

Home Equity to Eliminate Debt?

Mortgages are different than most other types of consumer debt, such as credit cards or personal loans. The interest you spend on your mortgages is usually tax deductible. Since the interest you pay on credit cards, automotive financing, and other loans may not be deductible, your mortgage may offer you some distinct advantages on accomplishing some tax relief.

It can spread your debt payments over a much longer period of time, which could minimize your monthly obligations. If you use your mortgage interest to pay off nondeductible debt; remember that once the debt is paid, you must save the payments you would have otherwise made to the original debt. Not doing this means that you will spend your future income by extending the payments on these consumer loans for a much longer period of time. This strategy may also provide you with the funds necessary to pay other debts at a potentially lower interest rate because your debt is secured by the value of your home or property versus non-secured debt. Owing to the fact that current tax law allows you to deduct the interest and decreases on your mortgage interest. Therefore, you may be able to transform a nondeductible debt payment on an automotive loan, credit card, or other consumer finance loan into a deductible mortgage loan, perhaps cutting it by approximately 30 percent!

Remember, the key is to always be an honest banker with yourself. You should take the savings differential (new payments versus. old payments) each month and apply that to a systematic savings program to retire that debt as quickly as possible. That way you can maximize the tax deductions legally allowable to you under current tax law. Use them to either build wealth or eliminate debt as quickly as possible.

Real Estate versus Retirement Savings Plans

Compared with tax advantage retirement plans, real estate may prove to be a suitable alternative for retirement funds, with different types of risk.

Example: A person is contributing $12,000 to a pre-tax retirement savings plan. How many uses does he get from his money? Only one use! He can't even access the money without paying the taxes and incurring a penalty for early withdrawal if he is less than 59½ years old. Earnings from the plan have to stay inside the plan until retirement. If he used the same $12,000 to purchase real estate, the owner can potentially derive some additional benefits. These benefits include tax benefits and potential access to equity for other investment opportunities or emergencies.

If he purchases a rental property, he can use the rental income for other things, such as purchasing a municipal bond portfolio, maximizing his insurance coverage, funding his Roth IRA, or contributing to a side fund for purchasing more real estate in the future.

We are not saying that your 401(k) is a bad place to save. It's just a generic answer to a problem that requires a multiple product solution. If you are contributing more that your employer's match, you may want to consider directing your other potential contributions (above the employer match level), into another account (maybe a real estate strategy). This is one example of a coordinated approach that can create multiple uses for your money. Otherwise, you may end up putting more eggs in the same basket.

Some additional benefits include not having mandatory lock-out periods. You can access values before age 59½ and you don't need to liquidate by age 70½. Your heirs will potentially get a step-up in basis at the time of your death, as compared to a fully taxable event when they inherit your retirement funds. Let's not forget that you actually get to use the property! Would you rather gather the family in your shore house or around the kitchen table to stare at your 401(k) statements?

Mortgage Protection Insurance

Creditors and banks are careful to secure themselves by making us purchase property and hazard insurance. Why should the borrower not equally protect his own family's interest in the mortgage as the debtor? Both parties are equally important in this arrangement, and both have personal estates to protect against depletion through loss. Property insurance protects the lender and his dependents against loss to his estate, while life and disability insurance do exactly the same thing for borrowers.

It is strange that publications on insurance give so much emphasis to the protections of the creditors through fire, marine, and other forms of property insurance, and yet so little mention is made to the protection of the debtor's interest in his mortgage obligation with life insurance. At the time of the borrower's death, it is certainly to his family's advantage to have the mortgage also die. Have the life insurance proceeds promptly liquidate the outstanding mortgage balance in full. This leaves the family or business entirely clear of any indebtedness. This is the best way to hedge your mortgage. Ideally, this should be accomplished by owning a permanent life insurance policy that will also build cash values.

Private Mortgage Insurance

Private mortgage insurance (PMI) is the insurance designed to protect lender or an investor against a potential loss if the borrower stops making mortgage payments. PMI should not be confused with mortgage life insurance. Mortgage life insurance is designed to protect the homeowner or mortgage by paying off the mortgage if the homeowner dies. Sometimes, there will be a disability provision, as well. Private mortgage insurance protects lenders against loss if a borrower defaults on their loan. It may also assist the buyer by allowing him to put down as little as a 3 to 5 percent down payment on the purchase of the property in lieu of the traditional 20 percent, which is usually required by lenders.

This may help certain borrowers achieve the goal of home ownership sooner and limit the amount of time required to save up for their down payments. It is typically required when the Loan to Value Ratio (LTV) exceeds 80 percent. The advantages of having private mortgage insurance include the ability for people to purchase a house sooner because they do not have to save up and accumulate the typical 20 percent down payment.

It may therefore increase their ability to purchase a home or generate greater buying power. With most PMI plans, you are eligible to cancel the insurance in the future, once the following conditions are met: (1) Once your balance is less than 80 percent of the home value, you may cancel your PMI; (2) Each lender has its own criteria, though most require some sort of an appraised evaluation of the property in order to determine that you have indeed satisfied the 20 percent equity criteria. A disadvantage of private mortgage insurance is that it adds to the monthly payment expense of a mortgage or to the ownership of real estate. It protects the lenders interest, but it does not protect the homeowner, and typically the lender selects the provider of the insurance.

You rarely have the opportunity to comparison shop for the private mortgage insurance, although you do have the ability to choose which bank you borrow from. PMI is also based on the entire loan amount, but only allows you to borrow up to 20 percent more than before. For example, if you buy a house for $100,000 and buy PMI to obtain 100 percent financing, you would be able to borrow $20,000 more. However, the PMI amount will be based on the $100,000, not on the $20,000 of additional capital that you borrowed. Under current law, PMI premiums are not tax deductible.

Home Equity versus Cash Values

Real Estate versus Insurance

We find it interesting that many people seem to like that they can put extra money into their house with additional principal payments. We wonder if they understand that their home equity has a 0 percent rate of return. Home equity builds independent of the property value itself, which appreciates or depreciates exactly the same, weather the home is financed or not. Many people are voluntarily adding money to their mortgages every month in an effort to pay down the debt faster.

Meanwhile, if we ask them to put money into an insurance policy that builds cash value, they look at us like we're crazy, even though it has a rate of return. Every company has a different rate of return, but something is still more than 0 percent rate of return versus overfunding your mortgage. Many insurance companies offer very competitive guaranteed cash value returns. I believe every house should be paid off, but it should be paid off on your terms, and paid off with your money when you choose to spend them, not simply when the mortgage commitment ends.

Investment Properties

Rental properties can also be a great strategy. There are plenty of books on the market if you're interested in real estate. Our goal is to help you understand that as an investment, real estate has been an attractive alternative for many people. It certainly has risks, but that risk can be minimized. There are also unique advantages to investing in real estate.

Real Estate can offer multiple uses for your money. A well-performing rental property may provide you with additional cash flow. You can redirect your potential rental profits to cover shortfalls in other savings areas such as educational savings plans or other accumulation goals. You may even want to purchase permanent life insurance, so that you can create a death benefit that will actually pay out.

Real estate can offer more tax advantages than any other investment. Real estate has tax benefits for the mortgage interest payments, depreciation, insurance, and maintenance costs. It offers tax-deferred growth, tax-free gains, and a stepped-up cost basis at death, along with other potential tax advantages.

Summary

Mortgages are an emotionally-charged subject. Mortgage strategies can mean different things to different people. Do not do the following: It is never recommended that your money that you were contemplating putting into your home, especially when the earnings from an investment would be required to make the mortgage payment.

Cash flow is the issue. While having the mortgage loan would possibly provide tax savings and the money invested in a place other than your home could possibly have a greater return than if left in the home; the decision to take advantage of those possibilities should not require the earnings from the invested money to make your mortgage payment. Additional unsuitable clients include those who simply take the standard deduction and have no plans to itemize these deductions. They would not benefit from the tax concepts. Individuals who have insufficient cash-flow, and for those that the math makes sense, but would not feel comfortable having a mortgage payment because of emotional concerns.

Your home and rental property belong in your financial game plan. Without these assets, your overall financial plan will be weaker. If you follow the pyramid planning outline, add permanent life insurance to the mix and a portfolio of tax-free municipal bonds to supplement your retirement savings plan, you may begin to build a very versatile program. Our strategies are designed to be suitable for the following types of people:

➤ Clients with current interest rates that are higher than the rates on new mortgage loans that are presently available.

➤ Clients who currently have nondeductible debt payments and access to home equity.

➤ Clients who are currently purchasing a new home or who are considering selling a home.

➤ Clients with 15-year mortgages, who would prefer to be in control of their money and who want to maximize their tax deductions. This is owing to the fact that there are more tax savings in the first

15 years of a 30-year mortgage than there are in the entire duration of the 15-year mortgage.

> Clients who are currently approaching the later years of a 30-year mortgage or who wish to maintain control of their money and want to increase their tax deductions by refinancing.

Through refinancing, tax deductions may be reduced in an amortizing loan as the interest expense reduces. Refinancing allows you to stretch the present balance over 30 years that in turn increases the interest deductions and lowers the payment in many instances. There are also clients who are currently contributing to a qualified pension plan in an effort to defer taxes but who would want to consider reducing their tax burden while financing their home. Some clients may also wish to reduce taxes when prepaying their principal balance on their present mortgage.

Prepaying your principal over time may reduce the interest owed and the potential tax deductions available. Writing one large check when you have the money to pay off the loan would maximize your access to any available tax advantages along the way. Clients with large qualified pension plans may wish to consider taking advantage of the exclusion from the sale of their primary residence, when considering a distribution from their retirement plans.

If they have sufficient qualified money to make the mortgage payments, this may free up the proceeds from the sale of their home that would come to the client as a tax-free gain. The money coming out of the pension plan would then be taxed at ordinary income but the money that's going to make payments on their new house could be deductible. This would allow the client to do some estate planning with the money that would have been in their home and potentially subject to an estate tax. On the contrary, it's never recommended that a client would invest money that they were going to put into their home.

Chapter Highlights

➢ Down payments explored. How much is the right amount down? Understand why paying cash may not be the best option.

➢ Understand how to use different financing strategies to minimize your wealth transfers.

➢ Do you understand mortgage spreads and how banks make money?

➢ 15- versus 30-year mortgage rates explored. Understand the difference between the two programs.

➢ Review your home equity programs for opportunities to use your home equity to turn non-deductible debt into deductible debt.

CHAPTER 15
COLLEGE FUNDING

The Challenge

How can you manage to send your kids to the college of their choice without raiding your retirement nest egg or heading to the poor house?

The current costs:

Public School: About $8,000 per year.

Private School: About $15,000 per year.

Savings Goal

In order to have college fully funded by the time your child starts college, you would need to either deposit about $110,000 the day your child is born, or save approximately $1,035 per month for the first 18 years of your child's life. The investment would need to grow at a rate of return of 8 percent *every year* (not very likely), and the stock market could not correct itself. At a 6 percent rate of return, you would need to contribute $1,250 each month to reach this goal. Very few families are able to save enough money to reach this goal in time.

Cost of College

The cost of attendance includes things like tuition, fees, books, general living expenses such as rent or dorm costs, transportation, and personal expenses a student could be expected to incur during the academic year.

For many Americans, providing a college education for their children is an important family goal. It may represent the most important family financial decision you will make. Unfortunately, many families are making it all wrong. Funding a college education can be one of the largest expenses that you are likely to face. Next, your home may be your largest financial challenge. Where you save and how you go about funding it can make a dramatic difference in the final costs.

We want our children to have the best possible education. There are many different options to consider. Many are designed to simply accumulate funds over time for a particular need. They also give you only one use, which can lead to many lost opportunities and costs.

Paying for an education has never been an easy task. Over the past several years, it has become even more of a challenge as college costs rise faster than the general inflation level. Very few families seem to be able to save enough to fully fund four or more years of higher education.

What Will it Cost?

As mentioned earlier, in order to have college fully funded by the time your child starts college, you would need to either deposit about $110,000 the day your child is born, or save approximately $1,035 per month for the first 18 years of your child's life.

The investment would need to grow at a rate of return of 8 percent *every year* (not very likely). In order for you to hit your goal, the stock market could not correct itself. At a 6 percent rate of return, you would need to contribute $1,250 per month to reach this goal.

Never Too Early . . . or Late

When it comes to college savings, getting an early start helps. However, it's never too late to begin saving for your educational objectives. Starting early can make a meaningful difference, by potentially reducing the amount that you or your child may need to borrow (and transfer wealth) to pay for school.

Ways to Pay

The providers of financial aid assume that parents have the primary responsibility for their child's higher education. The aid is generally considered a supplement, not a replacement. How much you can afford to pay determines whether your child will qualify for financial aid, including federal loans. Your child may be eligible for the difference of what a college costs and the amount that you have been determined to be responsible for.

Factors that determine eligibility for it include income, family assets including savings and investments, the number of other persons in the family also paying for tuition, and family expenses, both ordinary and unusual. There are several factors that influence what you will get. These include the financial resources of the college or university (understand that different universities may actually award a different financial packages). Ironically, since the amount your responsible for is typically fixed, you may end up receiving a larger grant package from a college that has a higher price tag.

Financial Aid

The financial aid process varies widely from institution to institution. Many families are of the opinion that they will not qualify for financial aid simply because they are not living at the poverty level. Nothing could be further from the truth. Many institutions rely on a formula to determine a typical family's estimated financial contribution. This is the amount of money that they feel would be appropriate for that family to cover in terms of the overall economic burden of paying for the college education. It is interesting to note that sometimes you can actually receive a better package from an institution that has a higher sticker price. Therefore, when selecting a college, it is critical that you understand all of the moving parts.

Don't eliminate a university or a college based on the fact that the annual tuition cost is a higher listed figure. Remember, it is quite possible that you could apply to one school that costs $30,000 a year and they will calculate your estimated family contribution at one number, and at a $20,000 a year school that may actually end up calculating your estimated family contribution at a higher figure than the more expensive college. In the end, the only thing you care about is your family's estimated financial contribution. If the university wants to bear the difference, why not have your child attend a school of their choice.

As mentioned previously, our parents were able to send us to Ivy League schools. Owing to a combination of athletic and academic scholarships, my family was able to minimize the costs of sending us to these institutions. Of course, we helped by taking on student loans and doing our part with work-study and other programs to help offset the economic burden to our family. However, it is very interesting to note that in the years when two children were in college at the same time, our parents actually ended up paying substantially less per child for college than they did when only one child was in college at a given time. These are all factors that need to be considered in an effort to develop a comprehensive financial funding strategy for college and other secondary education goals. Your ultimate goal should be to select the right planner who has the knowledge, expertise, resources, and contacts to help you develop a game plan.

Start developing a strategy early. Many families wait until junior or senior year of high school to begin to inquire about financial aid, grants, loans, and scholarships. By this time it is usually too late. In the world of financial aid, the early bird gets the worm. Start to plan several years out. Most aid is based on family contribution based formulas. Therefore, the needier you appear on paper, the more aid you are likely to receive. Many families actually do receive aid.

For many students, some type of financial aid in the forms of grants, loans, scholarships, and work-study programs will be needed to make the dream, a reality. Financial aid is available. The federal government through the Department of Education provides billions of dollars a year in student aid through various programs. Private organizations and foundations, state governments, as well as schools and universities themselves are also additional sources of financial aid and funding.

Applying for Financial Aid

The vast majority of financial aid is awarded through a standardized process that in general, proceeds as follows: pre-application for federal student aid (FAFSA). The student and his or her family complete the free application for federal student aid. This is a single form used to apply for all types of federal aid. It is also used to apply for state financial aid at many public and private colleges.

The FAFSA collects information such as family size, number of family members in college, as well as financial data such as income, benefits, and net assets. The government calculates the amount a family is expected to contribute toward a student's education referred to as the expected family contribution (EFC).

Eligible needs-based financial aid is determined by taking the college's calculated cost of attendance and subtracting the EFT. The difference, if any, is the amount the student may receive on a need-based form of financial aid including grants, loans, and scholarships.

Financial Aid Packages

Once the need-based eligibility is determined, the college financial aid office will attempt to provide for that need with a combination or package of financial aid funds that may include grants, loans, scholarships, and work-study programs. The amount and type of financial aid will vary widely between colleges.

Factors include the needs of other students relative to yours, and any special interest in your child, which may include a particular academic, athletic, or performing arts talent. If you are turned down for aid, you can appeal the decision especially if your financial situation has changed since you applied. You may also be able to show that the numbers alone do not provide an accurate picture of your personal situation.

Grants

In some cases, a financial aid package may not cover all of the costs, leaving a gap that a student and his or her family must cover from other sources. Federal financial aid is the largest source of financial aid provided to college students in the United States and is from programs funded or administered by the federal government. Much of this support comes in the form of student loans. A major element in student aid includes a Federal Pell Grant. Pell Grants are designed to assist very low income undergraduate students and award them based on expected family contribution. Only families with very low EFCs are awarded Pell Grants.

Pell Grants do not have to be repaid. Federal supplemental educational opportunity grants are awarded to undergraduate students with exceptional financial need. Federal Perkins loans are federal low interest loans. They are awarded based on need and on the availability of funds. No interest accrues while the student is attending the school at least half time. Repayment begins nine months after the student ceases to attend at least half time.

Federal Work-Study Programs

The federal work-study program provides federally funded employment for qualified students in both on-campus and off-campus positions. The amount a student can earn is limited to the amount of the award.

In addition to the financial aid programs provided through the federal government, there is also a wide range of aid available through other organizations, these include state programs. Many states and their governments offer their own financial aid programs. These may include need-based grants as well as work-study programs, loan forgiveness programs, and merit-based scholarships. Some of these are career specific.

Scholarships

Scholarships can be based on either academic or athletic ability. Some schools also have their own student loan programs to replace or supplement federal loan programs.

Military Aid

The armed forces also have a number of available programs to enable prospective, active duty, and former service personnel to attend college. Reserve Officer Training Corps (ROTC) and Navy Reserve Officer Training Corps (NROTC) scholarships are available at a number of schools. Current active duty personnel can also apply for tuition assistance through their education officer. Various GI Bills, Naval, and Army college funds are additional sources of financial aid . . . not to mention the Military Academies.

In the end, much of what will be required will be up to you. No matter what career choices our kids make, we want them to have all of the opportunities that a strong educational foundation can provide. Take advantage of every possible program available. This allows you to maintain the greatest amount of wealth-building potential possible.

Make sure that your plan will work under all circumstances. Your family's educational funding program should be protected even if you become disabled or die prematurely. Take steps to insulate your savings from financial market declines as well. What if interest rates change or you are involved in an accident or a lawsuit? Most people's plans don't provide for these contingencies.

What should you do? Begin the college planning process early in your children's lives. You should avoid using only predesigned products for college funding that tie up your money and keep it locked in, generating only one use. The best plans use a combination of financial products and strategies, not only one product acting alone.

College funding comes from a coordinated financial plan. These areas include real estate and mortgage strategies, home equity loans or lines of credit, 529 education savings plans, UGMA accounts, U.S. savings bonds, government bonds, laddered CDs, stocks, mutual funds, and cash. If your child is under the age of 10, permanent life insurance can also serve as an effective component in a college funding strategy when combined with your other assets.

Chapter Highlights

➤ Fully understand the cost of education and the different potential ways to funding it.
➤ Use a coordinated approach to pay for your educational needs.
➤ Focus on a layered approach to save over a single product solution.

CHAPTER 16
RETIREMENT STRATEGIES

Figure 16.1   Turn your enemies into slaves!

Retirement Strategies Examined

➢ How much will I need?

➢ Where will it come from?

➢ How much should I save?

Retirement planning begins with a dream and a vision. The most important step to take is to dream a little bit and think about how you would like to envision your ideal retirement. Do you want to continue to live in your current home or will you relocate? Perhaps you'll move to a warmer climate down south or out west? What types of activities will you be involved in when you retire? Do you plan on traveling? Would you like to see the world? Do you want to get engaged in activities such as golf, tennis, boating, or perhaps other active engagements?

Once your vision is clear, you can begin to calculate the cost of funding your dreams, in both current dollars (and future dollars). In doing so, you can at least provide yourself with the conceptual framework necessary to understand why it's important to save for your dreams, and more importantly why it's important to save today for a retirement that may be many years off. Having that definite purpose burned and ingrained deep in your mind will help you maintain the discipline necessary to stay on course with your retirement savings strategies.

Remember, you don't need to have a perfect picture in your mind, but it's helpful to have a broad understanding of the type of retirement you want to live. Most people skip this task and instead focus only on accumulating a specific dollar amount by a certain point in time. I guess they hope that the magic number will be enough. By doing it that way, you don't necessarily have an understanding of whether you've saved enough for the type of retirement lifestyle you want to achieve or not. When these people are asked if they're going to be okay in retirement, many just shrug their shoulders.

Today, you are probably used to going to work each week and earning a paycheck. We call this *Man at Work*. Eventually, the program is designed to help you move to a position where your capital will provide income for you. We call this *Capital at Work*. The key point here is that ultimately, you want your money to work as hard as you do.

In order to accomplish this task, it is imperative that you begin a disciplined savings strategy and focus on a program that will increase the chances of growing your capital at regular and predictable rates over a period of time. By the time you reach retirement, your capital should be in a position to begin paying you back.

Where are you anticipating getting your money sources at retirement?

The following sources may be considered: Social Security, pensions, sale of a business, private investments (stocks, bonds, and mutual funds), life insurance cash values, investment dividends, family-limited partnerships, reverse mortgages, rental income, and so on. There are many avenues to derive retirement income. Most financial planners only consider a few of these possible sources. People seem happy to tie up their retirement money in plans for many years. This approach can cause problems in other aspects of their financial lives. Make sure that your plans are working together to create additional benefits.

Not everyone follows the same path. When I first joined the financial services business, I was living at home in an effort to try to save as much money as possible, so that I could begin building my own wealth. When I first graduated from school, I did not have a large list of clientele. As a way to generate additional income, I decided to take a job as a personal trainer at a local gym franchise. This gym franchise was only about a year old at the time.

The owner had been a retired electrician who took it upon himself to rollover his retirement plan assets from his existing employer sponsored retirement plan. He distributed a substantial portion of his retirement assets and diversified his investments, including the purchase of a gym franchise. By purchasing the gym franchise, he was able to buy a business with cash flow. The business was able generate a substantial income for himself that was much higher than the income that he could have derived by taking his retirement plan and investing into the traditional fixed income investments such as CDs, savings bonds, or other income generating assets.

The gym was able to provide him with not only a salary, but also a business that he could sell in the future and that provided additional jobs for his family. His sons and daughters actively worked in the business and were able to derive second incomes through their employment at the gym. These second incomes allowed them to purchase homes and fund retirement plans at substantially higher levels than what they would have been able to do on their own.

This work experience was one of the defining moments in my life, and it allowed me to experience the positive effects of circulating capital firsthand. There were certainly risks involved for the gym owner, but he made calculated business decisions and chose to buy into a well-established franchise that offered him a clear game plan for success. To this day, nearly 15 years later, he and his family own that gym and continue to derive an income. They have also seen substantial appreciation in their business investment. To us, this is one of the great stories about chasing the American Dream. We see these stories all around us.

Retirement Income Strategies

It is impossible to predict with any accuracy the variability of investment returns and their impact on your retirement portfolio. The best way you can try to minimize volatility is by diversifying your portfolio across various asset classes and developing multiple streams of income to use throughout retirement. Staggering the targeted timelines for use of your different assets can give you the ability to tap into certain areas while others may be down. Coordinated planning can allow underperforming assets a chance to heal.

The worst thing you can do is to continue to pull income or diminish the capital base of a poorly performing asset class. Even with diversification there's no guarantee that your portfolio can sustain you throughout retirement once you begin taking income. The best strategy is to have multiple streams of revenue working in concert with one another in order to accomplish your goals.

Some of those sources may include a business, diversified real estate portfolio with rental incomes, government programs such as Social Security, a pension if available from your employer, privately qualified planned savings such as a 401(k) or other deferred compensation programs, and other personal supplemental investment programs, as well as the cash values of your permanent life insurance policy.

Remember, you have financial institutions, government, and corporations as partners to contend with for life. Financial institutions want their commission's fees and charges. Governments want taxes, and corporations want your money in the form of inflation and products to spend on.

Sequence of Returns

We must also consider the sequence of returns and how they can impact your retirement plan. Most people would be very pleased if they could earn 10 percent on their investments in retirement. Many of the investment industry materials are misleading because they assume smooth rates of returns. As we know, markets do not just go straight up each year. They bounce up and down each year.

Occasionally the movements are severe. One of the biggest misconceptions by investors and financial professionals alike is that average returns and arithmetic returns are the same thing. They are not! For example, the market could sometimes average 0 percent, and you could still lose money. Consider the following example. You invest $100,000 in the stock market, and the market goes down by 10 percent in year one. At the end of that year, your account value is worth $90,000. Year two, the market increases by 10 percent. This would give an average rate of return of zero over the two years, however, your $90,000, which represents a much smaller capital base has grown by 10 percent, leaving you with an account value of $99,000. Although the market averaged 0 percent or a flat rate of return over that two-year period, you lose money!

The same thing is true over longer periods of time. While the market may average 8 to 10 percent over long time frames, we know that the market rarely performs in a predictable fashion, and it almost never performs in an annualized sequential predictable upward rate of return.

Therefore, any proposal, illustration or financial plan based upon the straight line average rate of return is flawed at best. Consider the following example.

Imagine for example that you have retired at the end of 1999, after one of the most prolific investment decades of the century. Most of us remember that time that Allen Greenspan referred to the market's never ending games as "irrational exuberance," only to be followed up quickly by the tech bubble burst. Had you retired in 1999 with $1 million you would have seen a steep decline in the year 2000 through 2004. 2005, 2006, and 2007 saw the return of market gains, only to have the rug ripped out again in 2008 from a market crash. While the market may average strong returns overtime, the reality of financial investing is a somewhat different picture.

In the next scenario, we can see how this type of strategy played out in real life. This individual has amassed $500,000 in their retirement savings plan, and their financial advisor has run all the typical reports suggesting that it is time to retire, and the advisor actually believes that his client will succeed if he sticks to a conservative investment allocation with just the right balance between stocks and bonds.

The advisor believes that the market will average 10 percent over the long haul; he feels it's appropriate to have his client roll his money into a balanced investment allocation. With a market average rate of return of 10 percent he suggests that the client will be able to make his required distribution of $30,000 per year, and still have the capital account grow due to the surplus in interest gains. His software shows the account will grow at a rate of 10 percent per year ($50,000) and the client will draw down 30,000 per year to supplement his income. Given the coordinates, the advisor tells the client that he will never fail. Let's take a look and see what actually happened.

In retirement, it's also often the sequence of returns that will cause an investment to succeed or fail. Investment losses early in retirement and may jeopardize the sustainability of a portfolio and its ability to generate income that will last a lifetime. This is owing to depleting the capital base in the early years and taking out withdrawals that are too great to bear from the remaining principal. One way to minimize that risk is by diversifying your asset classes accordingly. Take a look at the following chart.

Average versus Actual Returns (also covered earlier).

10 percent returns? Sign me up! . . . Not so Fast.

Most people would jump at the chance to earn 10 percent average annual returns in retirement. But, averages can be misleading, especially for retirement portfolios used to generate income. In retirement, it's often the steep rate of return that will cause investment success or failure. Investment losses in early retirement may jeopardize the sustainability of a portfolio and its ability to generate meaningful income that will last a lifetime. Additionally, losses near the end of your time horizon can cause you to lose large amounts of wealth at a time in your life when you cannot afford to replace it.

The example below illustrates two hypothetical retirement portfolios, assuming the following:

Initial portfolio values: $500,000 for each portfolio.
Portfolio I: S&P 500 calendar year returns from 1969 to 1994.
Portfolio II: Simply reverses the order of the S&P 500 returns.
$30,000 annual withdrawals. Withdrawals increase 3 percent per year to account for cost of living inflation increases.
Average Annual Return: 10.1 percent on each portfolio
Portfolio I, Total Income: $1,156,591
Portfolio II Total Income: $1,156,591
Ending Account Balance Portfolio I: $19,369
Ending Account Balance Portfolio II: $2,555,498

10 Percent Average Returns

Portfolio 1				Portfolio 2			
Year	Investment Return	Withdrawal	Account Balance	Year	Investment Return	Withdrawal	Account Balance
1	-8.40%	$30,000	$427,900	1	1.30%	$30,000	$476,600
2	4.00%	$30,900	$414,030	2	10.10%	$30,900	$493,646
3	14.30%	$31,827	$441,410	3	7.60%	$31,827	$499,385
4	19.00%	$32,782	$492,275	4	30.40%	$32,782	$618,417
5	-14.80%	$33,765	$385,752	5	-3.10%	$33,765	$565,419
6	-26.50%	$34,778	$248,942	6	31.50%	$34,778	$708,917
7	37.30%	$35,822	$305,976	7	16.80%	$35,822	$792,335
8	23.70%	$36,896	$341,596	8	5.20%	$36,896	$796,799
9	-7.30%	$38,003	$278,793	9	18.60%	$38,003	$906,602
10	6.60%	$39,143	$257,966	10	32.00%	$39,143	$1,157,844
11	18.60%	$40,317	$265,631	11	6.10%	$40,317	$1,188,270
12	32.10%	$41,527	$309,451	12	22.40%	$41,527	$1,412,559
13	-4.90%	$42,773	$251,484	13	21.10%	$42,773	$1,667,978
14	21.10%	$44,056	$260,516	14	-4.90%	$44,056	$1,542,024
15	22.40%	$45,378	$273,416	15	32.10%	$45,378	$1,992,099
16	6.10%	$46,739	$243,383	16	18.60%	$46,739	$2,315,890
17	32.00%	$48,141	$273,197	17	6.60%	$48,141	$2,419,903
18	18.60%	$49,585	$274,290	18	-7.30%	$49,585	$2,194,633
19	5.20%	$51,073	$237,535	19	23.70%	$51,073	$2,663,688
20	16.80%	$52,605	$224,883	20	37.30%	$52,605	$3,604,638
21	31.50%	$54,183	$241,605	21	-26.50%	$54,183	$2,597,028
22	-3.10%	$55,809	$178,282	22	-14.80%	$55,809	$2,157,378
23	30.40%	$57,483	$174,997	23	19.00%	$57,483	$2,508,718
24	7.60%	$59,208	$129,107	24	14.30%	$59,208	$2,808,257
25	10.10%	$60,984	$81,111	25	4.00%	$60,984	$2,859,042
26	1.30%	$62,813	$19,369	26	-8.40%	$62,813	$2,555,498

Figure 16.1   10 Percent Returns

The hypothetical example is for illustrative purposes, and is not representative of any particular financial product. Past performance is no guarantee of future results.

No one can predict the variability in investment returns and their impact on a retirement portfolio. It seems like a birth year or retirement lottery. What will the sequence of returns be during your retirement? At best, you can try to minimize volatility by diversifying your portfolio across various asset classes. Even with diversification, there's no guarantee that your portfolio can sustain you to retirement once you begin taking income. To combat this risk, we suggest a layered approach to retirement savings, including assets that offer guaranteed returns and income sources . . . to balance out your variable asset life-cycles.

Today, many people are finding that the traditional means of funding a comfortable retirement can no longer be relied on. The caps that are placed on qualified retirement plans, the minimum income replacement percentage of Social Security, and the dwindling number of employer provided pension plans, meaning that a much greater portion of your retirement savings must come from other sources. Where will your retirement income come from? What makes this even more of a challenge is the fact that the more you earn, the more you will need to save.

The more income you make, the lower the percentage of pre-retirement income will be replaced by Social Security becomes. The income benefit decreases proportionately as your income level rises. This means that you will have to save the difference yourself! To see the estimated Social Security retirement income benefit for yourself, use the Social Security quick calculator, at www.ssa.gov.

Individuals with the necessary risk tolerance of long-term investments can take advantage of the upside potential of equity investments to accumulate assets for retirement. However, equity markets may be subject to periods of volatility. This raises the question, what would happen if you retire at a time when the stock market and bond prices are both declining (or it may happen a few years into retirement). What effect will this have on your retirement accounts and what can you do to minimize impact on your retirement income streams?

Taking the income from an equity based retirement account during a period of negative returns can have a significant adverse effect on the future value of the account. This may ultimately impact the amount of income you have available during retirement, as well as the amount of legacy be left to your family.

It's important to include a conservative element in your retirement income strategy now that will give you the future financial flexibility to more effectively manage your retirement income during changing and challenging economic conditions. This is different from having a well diversified asset allocation (or diversification), we are talking about assets that would be held separately and used for this specific purpose. Do you have assets earmarked specifically for the down years in the financial markets? If not, where will your income come from during these negative market performance years? How will your investment portfolio be able to heal?

In order to implement this type of strategy, you would need an alternate source of income that's not significantly impacted by short-term market volatility. Some options might include certificates of deposit, and other conservative savings vehicles. These conservative assets may offer lower overall investment returns over the long run when compared with equities. However, they represent a stable source of income that is essential to your retirement income distribution strategy. If an insurance needs analysis indicates that you should consider the purchase of additional life insurance, and death benefit protection, a whole life insurance policy with a limited premium payment could provide the pre-retirement income protection that you may need (from policy cash values), along with the accumulation of cash values that will build up inside the contract to be used to provide supplemental retirement income during your retirement.

Annuity features may include tax deferral, professionally managed investment choices, death benefits, and living benefits. Some of these features are referred to as riders, which are available at an additional fee. Product guarantees are based on the claim's paying abilities of the issuing company and don't extend to the variable component of the contract if applicable. Annuity payouts offer income that you cannot outlive and can be an excellent way to create retirement income for the following reasons.

They eliminate the risk of outliving your assets. They offer a guaranteed stream of payments for life, or over a specific period of time. Annuity payments are guaranteed for as long as you live, if you select a life annuity option. For this reason, they can be a compelling alternative to systematic withdrawals from a portfolio that can't guarantee lifetime income. You must recognize that these guarantees are based on the claims paying ability of the issuing company and it is important for you to select a carrier with strong financials.

Whole life insurance offers a guaranteed policy cash value along with the potential for additional cash values from policy dividends. The policy cash values can provide a stable source of income that is not impacted by short-term market volatility. Whole life insurance can provide tax-deferred accumulation of policy cash values and tax-free retirement income with partial surrenders up to the policy cost basis. In addition, the income tax-free policy death benefit can protect your income during your working years and ultimately assure your family legacy. These advantages make whole life insurance a good choice for individuals who want to benefit from the protection, cash accumulation, and tax advantages the product offers.

Distributions in most policies, including cash dividends and partial or full surrenders are not subject to taxation up to the amount paid into the policy or your cost basis. Access to cash values through borrowing or partial surrenders will usually reduce the policy's cash value and ultimate death benefit. Be careful, they can increase the chance the policy will lapse and may result in a tax liability if the policy terminates before the death of the insured. For these purposes, you should work carefully with your personal CFO or insurance professional to determine whether these strategies make sense for you. A supplemental retirement income strategy might be right for you if you recognize the importance of including your fixed income component into your coordinated retirement income portfolio.

If you have a protection need that life insurance can meet, if you want to assure legacy to your family by providing an income tax-free ultimate death benefit, a life insurance product that includes cash values that you can access for supplemental retirement income. This may appeal to you as part of a diversified, comprehensive financial strategy. Whole life insurance offers guaranteed policy cash values and the potential for additional cash value growth through policy dividends. The policy cash values can provide a stable source of income that is not impacted by short-term market volatility.

As you can see from the 10 Percent Average Returns Table, it is imperative that most of the average rate of return financial planning tools be used as a guideline only for your wealth accumulation planning goals. It also becomes critical for you to have a layered strategy toward accumulating and building wealth. One of the products that may help you get there is life insurance. We will explore this product in great detail at a future point. However, it is important to consider its impact on your plan.

Places to Save

Think back to our study of the 100 men. Only four retired with over $50,000 per year of incomes. The elimination of the traditional defined benefit plan has made recreating a retirement paycheck even more difficult. How and where you save for the future, will impact your ability to achieve financial independence during retirement.

Exploration of the Qualified Plans and 401(k)s

Qualified retirement plans have become one of our favorite ways to save, especially for retirement. Qualified plans, specifically the 401(k) plan, have become household terms. Without them, many people wouldn't save anything at all for retirement. People usually enroll because it's easy to do. It can be payroll deducted by your employer right out of your paycheck. The forced savings is very convenient way to save. Most times you don't even feel the pain and many plans offer a wide range of investment choices.

Qualified plans were originally designed to serve as a place to save as a supplement for our retirement income needs. Today, with the elimination of many fixed pension plans, retirement savings plans have become the primary retirement income savings vehicle for many. They can be a great place to start, but many people are relying solely on these to solve their retirement dilemmas. Additionally, there are a few myths surrounding the retirement plan products that need some further examination.

Considerations and Potential Pitfalls

Pre-tax retirement plans are one good vehicle for saving; however, they should not get all of your retirement dollars. There must be balance in your retirement planning assets in order for your retirement to be secure and safe.

There are advantages and disadvantages to every financial product or plan. Be careful not to overuse any one source of retirement fund and make sure to truly understand the consequences of such an action. Your golden years should be happy and fruitful, a time to enjoy life after all your years of labor. Pre-tax retirement savings plans are still the financial products that are most misunderstood by both financial advisors and the general public.

Professional Advice?

Does your plan offer an advice feature? You may not have an advisor to help you manage the money in your pre-tax retirement plan. The task of management is up to you and most people do not have the time or the knowledge to manage their money successfully. Make sure to work with a professional to design a well diversified asset allocation strategy.

What if you pull out the money at a different age than initially anticipated? You may need other liquid dollars in case the age of distribution is moved. Where will tax rates be in the future? You may also need other tax deductions to offset the income from the retirement account. You also need life insurance to protect these assets from estate and income taxes if you die with money in the plan. Putting all your eggs in one basket is never a good idea.

Tax Considerations

We don't pay taxes on the annual gains in our accounts. By deferring the tax each year, you are keeping more of your money rather than paying taxes each and every year. People feel good knowing that the growth of their account is compounding without a current tax. Qualified plans defer the tax and the calculation of the taxes due. If taxes are higher in the future, you lose. If they are lower (and your overall tax bracket is lower), you win. Where do you think taxes are headed?

People believe that they are saving taxes when they participate in a pre-tax retirement savings program through their employer or in a personal plan. This is not entirely accurate. The misunderstanding lies in the phrase *tax savings* rather than the more accurate term *tax deferral*. Pretax retirement savings plans do not save taxes, they only defer them to the date of distribution from the plan. There is no income tax savings in any year that you deposit money into a pretax retirement savings plan.

Lower Taxes in the Future?

This may not be true. This approach may or may not be to your advantage. If you manage to save enough money for retirement, which you should, then there is a good chance the amount of tax deferral will be significant and can put you into the higher income tax brackets when you start to take money out of the plan.

Many individuals may find themselves in a higher tax bracket for one of the two following reasons: the accumulation of money in their account can produce a large retirement income; or when added to other income sources. The tax law can change and it's possible that the rate will be higher when they retire. They may also end up in a higher bracket anyway because they no longer have any deductions, such as home mortgage interest, business deductions or dependents.

Why would anyone want their retirement income to be lower, just to be in a low bracket? I don't understand that mindset. You should probably aim to recreate a retirement income close to your current income in order to maintain the same lifestyle. We should aim to be in the same or higher tax bracket at retirement. Many planners say you'll probably be able to retire with two-thirds of your income and then default to a lower tax bracket. If you're working with a planner whose goal is to help you retire with two-thirds of your current income, do yourself a favor and fire him. Too many people are preparing for financial failure by shooting for a lower tax bracket. Telling you to retire with less money so you pay fewer taxes is not a great idea. Do you really think that taxation is going to be lower in the future? Why would you want to work for one standard of living and then retire with a pay cut to a lower standard of living?

Ordinary Tax versus Capital Gains Tax

The capital gains rate may be lower at the time of distribution but consumers forfeit that tax benefit when they join a pre-tax or post-tax retirement savings plan. Additionally, there are no tax write-offs for market losses.

The Employer Match

Getting a match from an employer is a good thing and certainly adds to the value of the pretax retirement savings plan. This additional contribution can help to make up for a lot of financial sins. In some cases, it may be in your best interest to contribute all that you can to your qualified plan, even amounts above the company match. However, since the only benefit above the match is a tax deferral, there are many other products that can give you additional benefits beyond only tax deferral.

How should they be funded? Generally speaking, it makes sense for you to consider contributing up to your employer's company match level. After that you should seriously compare any additional contributions to other investment options that may offer more access, different investment options, or additional tax benefits. Taxes will probably not be going away in the future. All of the demographic data suggests that there will be fewer workers and more retirees. This trend, coupled with an increase in government spending and social programs, creates the likelihood for potential future tax increases.

History of Taxes

It would be a different story if the government could guarantee that you'd be taxed at the same tax level (or less) that you were when you put the money into the 401(k). What if tax levels jump to 35 percent or higher from your current 25 percent? This looks like a 10 percent increase in taxes, but it's about a 30 percent increase in tax levels. Planners often recommend maximizing these plans without a second thought. This approach can create other issues.

The decision to contribute to a retirement savings plan is an individual one. Some people might be better off never investing in a retirement savings plan depending on their own individual circumstances while others will benefit greatly. This decision should not be generalized. The decision should be carefully weighed.

Retirement savings plans cannot be tapped into until at least normal retirement age (minimum age 59½). What happens if you need money before then? Lots of events in life occur from age 22 to 59. What then? There are penalties for early withdrawal, limited investment choices, no continuation in the event of death of disability, and there is tax uncertainty. You may able to build up a large tax-deferred nest egg, but remember the nest egg is not completely yours. In general, the government owns a huge piece of that nest egg.

Annuities[*]

I want a financial do-over! Visit any playground across the country and you will hear children shouting for do-overs. Wouldn't it be great if we could get the same do-over in life as the children on the school yard? Some financial products can allow us to do just that.

---

[*] Please see the financial disclaimer on page 348 for more information.

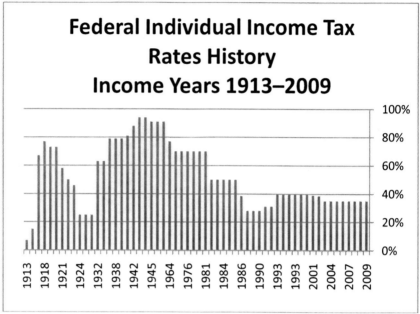

Federal Individual Income Tax Rates History Income Years 1913–2009

Figure 16.2   Which way are taxes headed next?

If you want to guarantee a stream of income during your retirement years, you may want to look at annuities. They come in two varieties: fixed and variable. Here I want to focus on variable annuities. Much has been written about variable annuities, both positive and negative. You should understand what they do and what they're designed for. Variable annuities are not necessarily a bad investment; however, they do carry risk as their performance is directly linked to the market. You see, with a variable annuity, you can choose to invest into a number of professionally managed sub-accounts. The value of these sub-accounts varies daily with the market so you can benefit from market growth, but may also experience a loss of value in down markets. Variable annuities are generally a long-term investment vehicle designed to provide income payments for life. They offer valuable features including tax deferral, a death benefit, and other living benefits which may or may not be beneficial to you. These are complicated investment products and are not suitable for all. You must speak with your investment advisor and review the product prospectus before investing.

Fixed annuities provide steady stream of income which is not linked to the market such as a variable annuity. These safer investments protect you from loss; however, you will miss out on any opportunities for growth owing to changes in the market.

All annuities can provide income payments, which is an excellent way to create retirement income for some of the following reasons.

✓ They can potentially eliminate the risk of outliving your assets if you choose to annuitize your program.

✓ It can provide you with guaranteed payment for life or for a specific period of time.

✓ They can offer you fixed payments that provide a steady income; or the possibility of variable payments that may offer income growth potential as a hedge against future inflation risk.

These annuity payments are generally guaranteed for as long as you live under the life annuity option and may be payable for beyond your life expectancy if a joint annuity option is selected. For this reason, it can be a compelling alternative to systematic withdrawals from a portfolio that can't necessarily guarantee a lifetime income, owing to potential market fluctuation.

Practical Application: Retirement Do-Over?

Retirement Insurance? The primary fear among many retirees is running out of money. A coordinated plan of life insurance, investments, and annuity strategies can help your plan come to life in many different ways. We have seen through the course of our discussion that life insurance is more than simply death insurance. Now, we want to show you how using life insurance can help you maximize the use of your retirement assets.

There are two types of people in retirement: those who have a recapitalization provision and those who don't. One of the greatest fears for Americans is the fear of outliving their assets. If this happens, they have one of two choices. They can either reenter the work force at an advanced age, or they will be forced to live on the charity of others, which may include their family members, children, the state, or the federal government. None of these options have ideal outcomes.

Therefore, most people take precautions to make sure that they do not run out of money. One of the greatest challenges that face Americans is to determine the appropriate time to retire. It is a difficult question that we are often asked by our pre-retirement clients. Different financial planners will calculate retirement distribution needs and ideal circumstances in different ways.

In an effort to simplify the discussion, let's take a look at two scenarios. Scenario one is an overview with a client who has saved most of his or her money in their traditional qualified retirement plan, and who has built up equity in their primary residence. At retirement, this person will likely meet with a financial professional to determine what level of distribution (or pay down) from the account is suitable. Some clients will choose to only live off the interest on their accounts, leaving the principal intact for their surviving spouse or as a potential estate for their children or their beneficiaries.

Let's assume they have accumulated $1 million. They can earn 5 percent a year and would generate $50,000 of pre-tax interest for them to help offset their living needs. If the account continues to earn $50,000 annually, a $1 million account will remain constant in value, and they will have an annual surplus of $50,000 that adds to any guaranteed income or pension streams that they're entitled to during retirement. This is how many people fund their retirement.

The challenge occurs when either the market correct itself significantly and their capital base is depleted, or as inflation eats away at the purchasing power of their money. In both scenarios, it's likely that they will need to supplement their annual income needs by either raiding the principal base or assuming more risk in their underlying portfolio in an effort to generate a rate of return that annually outpaces the impact of the erosion of their buying power owing to inflation.

Since they have no other assets, recapture strategies, or provisions in place, these clients will typically spend very conservatively and limit their activities in retirement. They are hoping to mitigate the risk of a financial market correction.

Next, if we take a look at scenario two, we will see that they also have accumulated $1 million in retirement assets and home equity values. This client has followed our segmented, integrated retirement planning strategies and knows that with a tiered approach to income, they can weather the financial storms. Instead of having the bulk of their assets in one or two accounts, they have diversified wisely and have purchased combinations of IRAs, 401(k)s, tax-free Roth IRAs, annuities that are designed to guarantee some portions of their principal, along with permanent life insurance.

Here, the key factor is that they have layered their income strategies, and have been smart enough to purchase permanent life insurance. The former client has no life insurance. His term insurance expired many years ago. He bought term insurance and invested the difference. As a result, he and his spouse will not have a shot to replenish their capital base upon the death of either spouse.

The second client knows that since he was smart enough to purchase permanent life insurance for he and his spouse, there will be an ultimate gain for the surviving spouse, which will occur at the death of the first spouse. As a result, they can spend their assets more aggressively.

At the death of the first spouse, they know that their capital base will be replenished by the death benefit of the permanent policy for the surviving spouse. By doing this, they have created several advantages over other strategies. The first is the recapitalization feature that permanent life insurance assures for the surviving spouse. The second is that they also accumulate cash values in the policy on a very favorable basis.

It is likely that the cash values will be equal to or greater than the internal rate of return on many of their other fixed income asset classes. Additionally, the cash values can be accessed on a tax favored basis from policy loans. In any given year, where the portfolio may be depleted by a market correction, they can choose to leave the capital fully invested and instead opt to pay distributions or interest from the cash value accumulation for their life policies. By using this type of strategy, it may allow their equity portfolio to heal itself over the natural course of market cycles. The more cash value they have, the longer their equities have to heal.

In a down market, the former client (with all of his eggs in one basket), will be forced to continue his downward spiral by making additional distributions from his already depleted equity accounts. This is not an ideal position to be in during retirement. As you can see, having life insurance during retirement is the best strategy possible for either spouse. If both spouses happen to live longer than anticipated and deplete the remaining capital base comprised of their retirement assets, they can choose to use the accumulated cash values in those permanent policies to supplement retirement in later ages.

Additionally, they may want to consider a reverse annuity mortgage, knowing full well that the reverse mortgage will likely be paid off by the life insurance proceeds of the policy. As soon as the first spouse passes away, the capital will be available to either repay the reverse annuity mortgage or to provide additional capital to the family to sustain them at that time . . . until the second death. There will also be a second death benefit paid to their heirs at this time.

Real Estate As a Retirement Supplement?

Almost all of us have heard of a 401(k), which is nothing more than a line of code in the Internal Revenue Service (IRS) tax law. This part of the code says that we can defer income on a current basis and have it taxed in the future. Qualified and 401(k) plans have been around for only a few decades, while mortgage interest deductions have been around much longer. In fact, for many years prior to the invention of qualified plans, people relied heavily on real estate to supplement their retirement income.

Consider the following: a 401(k) contribution provides you with a tax deferral and a tax calculation. However, you will likely be locked out of access to that money until you hit age 59½. You will face mandatory liquidation schedules beginning at age 70½ under current tax law. You will have limited access to your capital while it's deferred, and you will be giving up control over the assets. In fact, the only tangible benefit that you are driving is tax deferral. A second possible benefit may be a company match on a small portion of your personal contribution.

Our goal is to maximize access to capital and maximize the use our clients have on their money. What if we were to consider purchasing some real estate with some of our retirement savings? If we obtained a mortgage, we could use a potential mortgage interest deduction today, as opposed to deferring the tax. Would you prefer a real tax break today, or the promise of a future tax calculation in the future?

Secondly, we would gain greater access to our capital. We could sell or potentially refinance the property at any time in the future (based on market conditions). This would increase our potential liquidity and access to our own capital. We would no longer be subject to lockout periods until age 59½ or mandatory liquidation schedules beginning at age 70½. Our capital and assets would be our business. Upon our death, our heirs would also receive a step up in basis on the cost of the property relative to the date of our death. This is in contrast to being taxed on the full amount (at ordinary income schedules), which is the case with the qualified plan distributions upon death. More importantly, our heirs could gain multiple benefits of utilizing the property, which include: vacation use, holidays, memories, photographs, videos, and decades upon decades of use and enjoyment. I don't know too many families that would prefer to gather around the table, take out their 401(k) statements, and gaze at them with amazement instead of hitting the shore house for a weekend.

Throughout my career, almost every client I've sat with has, at some point, dreamed about owning additional property, either as an investment property or a second home for vacations. This usually ranks among their top four or five priorities financially. Unfortunately, most people usually accumulate most of their net worth in two very liquid places. They build their net worth in either their 401(k) retirement plans or in the home equity of their primary residence. The only way to get the capital out of these two areas is either to retire, sell the property, or refinance. Any of those strategies open you up to potential tax implications and leave you at the mercy of financial markets, and the decisions of others.

We also know from previous discussions that they're relatively illiquid investments that require a certain set of circumstances to occur before the capital can be accessed. This is why we urge people to build wealth in multiple places. Again, one of our favorite places to help you build wealth is by using the magic of the cash values in dividend-paying permanent life insurance policies. These policies provide a relatively safe and secure place to invest in the long run. Many insurance companies can provide historical dividend schedules that date back to well over 100 years. Many also provide guaranteed cash values similar to rates of return on CDs and other guaranteed investments. By using these cash values to help build your wealth, you not only guarantee yourself a rate of return, you also give yourself the opportunity to pick up those additional benefits.

Finally, should you pass away before you realize your dream, you're guaranteeing success through the use of the ultimate death benefits. No matter what, your plan will come to fruition, as your family or others that you've loved and cared for over your lifetime will actually realize the benefits when that death benefit becomes payable to them. We see over and over again that life insurance is truly the only product that guarantees that what you intend to happen—actually will happen. While this is certainly not the only place to build wealth beyond your qualified plans and personal residence, it should rank high among the priorities of places where you would put additional capital to save for your future goals.

Real Estate and Retirement

If you plan on purchasing real estate around the time you retire, you will often be in a better position to borrow while you're still employed. We can't tell you how many clients have come to us right after they retired looking for a mortgage for their retirement dream home. Many of these executives were earning well over $200,000 per year for the last decade of their careers, and now find themselves in a position where they have substantially less income available to qualify for a loan.

It makes it very difficult to qualify for a mortgage when you're only guaranteed a steady income source is Social Security and a small pension. Many lenders want to see income sources that are likely to continue for at least three years. Some lenders may also discount distributions from your own private 401(k) or retirement plan assets. These accounts can be volatile in their performance and may not provide a stable base of income. How ironic, since we have been taught to believe that 401(k)s and retirement plans will often provide the bulk of our retirement incomes. The same banks that sell these instruments to the public won't put enough stock in them to use them as real income. Those who have defined benefit plans usually find it a little bit easier as long as they're not trying to borrow large amounts of capital. Therefore, if you are considering purchasing a retirement home, it may be wise to begin that purchase transaction well in advance of your actual retirement.

If wishes were fishes, great things would happen all around us. Every once in a while, the fishes and loaves fail to multiply effectively and we're forced to create a new game plan. You will need to design strategies to work around both finite and fluid timelines. Design an exit strategy for your retirement savings plans to avoid being taxed when you need money the most. Remember, our portfolios don't always perform exactly as we imaged. Prepare for the worst and expect the best.

Required Minimum Distributions

There are many seniors who have reached the age of 70½ and must begin taking required minimum distributions from their qualified plans to avoid a 50 percent penalty. Many of these individuals have sufficient assets and would prefer not to touch their pension and retirement money but are forced to because of government regulations.

This is a large source of capital to potentially redirect to any number of investment alternatives.

Design a plan that puts all of these pieces together. Remember, you have to be just as savvy in the spending of your assets as you were in saving and accumulating wealth to avoid these unnecessary transfers. As you begin your planning, you will probably want to liquidate your least valuable assets first. Many seniors are concerned about running out of money. You have the option to withdraw interest only, principal and interest, or draw down your assets. You should carefully weigh the impact of each method.

Chapter Highlights

➤ Know where you stand financially. Are you going to be ready for retirement? Make sure that your review your targets regularly.

➤ Your retirement income will likely come from several different sources. Avoid putting all of your eggs in only one basket or one product, such as a 401(k).

➤ If possible, use a layered approach to your retirement income planning strategies. Try to coordinate different financial products for different purposes (income, growth, inflation hedge, and so on.). This can allow you to better survive market corrections in retirement.

CHAPTER 17
ESTATE AND LEGACY STRATEGIES

"We make a living by what we get.
We make a life by what we give."
—Sir Winston Churchill

Estate planning is the process of arranging ownership and the use of assets in a manner that helps meet lifetime financial objectives. It also helps provide for survivors needs, and the disposition of property at the time of death. A well-implemented estate plan can help to create and conserve assets during life, provide an orderly distribution of assets that meets the estate owner's objectives and intentions, provides peace of mind and family harmony, assures that cash is available to pay unavoidable taxes and costs, and minimizes the death taxes and estate settlement costs attributable to the estate.

Planning for Your Heirs and Your Legacy

Part of the financial planning process should typically include a strategy designed to protect your assets for your family or your heirs. Be prepared. The tax collector, courts, federal government, and your state government may each want a piece of the pie. There are many different ways to protect what you own after you die. A will can be relatively simple. Some trusts may be a bit more complex. With much at stake, it generally pays to consult an attorney or a qualified professional preparing any documents that may affect your estate. It is also crucial that you coordinate these strategies with your personal CFO to make sure that your assets are titled properly and coordinated with your will and trust documents respectively.

What is estate planning? If you have substantial wealth, it makes sense to have a comprehensive plan involving gifting strategies, trusts, and a will, along with other coordinated planning strategies. The more assets you have, the more estate planning can potential preserve for your heirs. Proper estate planning may save tens of thousands or even hundreds of thousands of dollars. Estate planning generally requires long-term strategies and professional coordination. Most of these documents are not static, but will need to be updated and changed as your assets, goals, and your estate evolve over time.

The rich get richer because they focus on keeping their wealth within their family and on building the legacy that they have dreamed about. What will your legacy be? How will the world speak your name in years to come? Will the world remember you when you're gone, and what will your legacy look like?

Everyone can benefit from estate planning and legacy planning. You don't need to be rich to have a legacy plan. Unfortunately, even those who achieve great success in life financially may not leave the legacy that they've always wanted. Recent studies have also shown that a very small percentage of family businesses will successfully survive two generations.

Roughly one half of all family businesses do not survive even to the second generation. This has more to do with legacy planning and multigenerational business strategy issues than the general health of that business. Fewer still, will survive the third generation. This means that you can spend every waking moment of your life building your business with very little chance of your grandchildren being able to enjoy your business legacy. Take time, energy, and effort to focus on designing legacy planning and succession strategies.

As you work with financial professionals to create a proper estate plan, some items you may want to examine include: updated wills, review various forms of property ownership, beneficiary designations of insurance contracts and retirement plans, impact of federal gift tax and federal estate taxation, a proper estate evaluation, review of marital deductions, use of trusts, review of your durable power of attorney, and consider Medicaid planning.

Estate planning is often one of the most overlooked aspects of planning. It will require creative thought and insight to coordinate your estate plan with your financial plan so that they are not working independently, but in an integrated and coordinated fashion. Many times, the process can be as simple as having your attorney updates your will, or the creation of an irrevocable insurance trust.

Taxes

Estate taxes will also likely impact your legacy strategy if you have managed to accumulate any significant wealth. You'll want to work with a qualified professional or team of professionals including accountants, attorneys, and other insurance and investment professionals to create a coordinated and integrated game plan to design a proper legacy strategy for your heirs. Estate taxes can occur both at the federal and the state level.

Estate planning is not just for extremely wealthy individuals. When a person passes away, there are typical problems which if not planned for properly, create a burden on those who are left behind. These burdens can be felt by both the family and the business. Proper estate planning can eliminate or reduce some of these problems. Review your will and trust documents to ensure these meet your goals, and work within current tax laws for both your federal and local state laws.

Some of the financial burdens include estate settlement costs. These are primarily consisting of probate fees and death taxes. Probate fees are generally paid by the executor of the estate, court, or attorney who handles probate. Death taxes may include estate taxes that may be subject at both state and federal death tax schedules. At higher levels these taxes can consume as much as 50 percent of your estate!

No matter how much wealth you accumulate or how large your estate, taxation can also consume a large portion of your wealth at the time of your demise. You should work with a team to review your legal and tax programs from your individual tax and legal advisors. These individuals are experts in their particular fields and your personal CFO should help you develop an estate plan along with these specialists to best meet your personal and business goals.

Liquidity Issues

If an estate's assets are not properly arranged, there may not be enough liquid assets to pay estate settlement costs. There could also be cash flow issues if there is not enough income to care for loved ones who are left behind, such as your spouse, business partner, and underage children. Assets may be subject to probate delays and expenses as you try to transfer assets. Avoid having to sell assets in a hurry to raise short-term capital. This is a common problem with estates that are tied largely to the value of a business or real estate holdings. A well designed life insurance plan can step forward to meet these financial demands in your time of need.

Assets transferred to minors may be held in cumbersome guardianship accounts until they reach age 18 or even 21 in certain states, before they are distributed outright to the children. This type of structure may not be in line with your goals for your family. Care of minors also becomes an issue. Parents can nominate the guardian for their minor children in their will. Many times this is overlooked or not updated accordingly. Have you reviewed your guardianship arrangements? If so, do the guardians know that they have been named? If the wrong person is chosen to manage the assets left for minors, the assets may end up being lost or unnecessarily reduced, therefore, proper coordination of the assets is essential.

In some instances, an estate plan involves more complex and sophisticated planning techniques, such as complete gifting strategies, limited partnerships, Limited Liability Companies (LLCs), evaluation discounts, charitable remainder trusts, or Grantor Retained Annuity Trusts (GRATs). As income tax laws are constantly changing, it's important to work with a team of professionals that will keep you abreast of how these changes can affect your personal estate plans. Your charitable giving can say more about who you are and the legacy you want to leave. What type of legacy do you want to leave behind?

Final Wishes: Insurance Protection

Do you have the right amount and type of insurance for life insurance and disability needs, and are they coordinated with your other assets and legal documents?

As you review your estate and legacy planning strategies, it is important to also revisit your beneficiary designations on your life insurance policies and qualified plans periodically. All too often, policyholders select their beneficiaries at the time of issue of a particular policy or contract, but many do not take the time to review their beneficiary designation as their situations change. Perhaps you have added another child to the family, divorced, or remarried. Have your plans been updated accordingly, or will you unintentionally end up disinheriting a family member or an entity (charity) that you care about. The same is true for your qualified retirement plan beneficiaries. Take the time to review beneficiary arrangements and make sure that these plans are also complete and up-to-date with respect to your stated intentions. These elections may have a substantial impact on your ability to transfer wealth effectively to your children and grandchildren and they may impact the legacy that you leave behind. Take time to review these designations at least annually.

A quick word on life insurance. When the inevitable day comes and you leave this world, we hope that someone will benefit from your legacy. Usually this includes your immediate family members. I have met with thousands of people in my career, many of whom have little or no life insurance, some who had adequate amounts, and others that were insured to their maximum capacity. Unfortunately, very few of these individuals left any specific instructions outlining the specific use of these proceeds (beyond their deaths). Few of these people left any specific instructions detailing exactly what these proceeds were designed to accomplish, and why they purchased these policies. It's great for your heirs to receive this important protection, and it's also important for them to know how you intended them to use these provisions.

When I pass away, I am confident that my family will have the appropriate level of resources to continue to live their current standard of living. However, I don't want them to simply receive a large check. I hope that they will understand that I viewed them as a valuable piece of financial property throughout my life. I want them to understand that I used the cash values for business purposes, financial emergencies, and even educational expenses at different points in my life. I want them to understand how much I valued having these policies. I want them to understand that paying for these policies was a sacrifice at times, but it was also a top priority for our family business. These policies provided me with the peace of mind that came with knowing that I would be able to honor my promises to my family in sickness, health, and even death.

Most of us can agree that providing insurance and other financial security for our family is not an inexpensive proposition. Step one is selecting the appropriate level of insurance death benefits to leave to your beneficiaries. Step two (which is as important or potentially more important), is leaving specific instructions as to what the dollars should be used for. This can be done in several ways:

1. This can be achieved informally, by detailing a specific outline designating your final wishes. This can be as simple as writing a letter or drafting instructions for your heirs. While these instructions would not be legally binding, at least they will offer some guidance from you detailing your wishes and your intent for these proceeds. Some of these uses may include income replacement, or using a portion of the proceeds to pay off the mortgage. Perhaps you want them to invest the proceeds conservatively in a side fund that can be used to create interest income, which can then be used to pay for the mortgage and other recurring expenses. Another use may include, apportioning some of the assets to pay for education of your children, spouse, or other heirs. Other uses may include contributing to charities, religious contributions, gifts to higher educational institutions, and other philanthropic wishes.

2. Another option(s) is to exercise some control from the grave by actually implementing a more formal plan. This will typically include creating a trust and appointing a trustee or trustees to make sure that your wishes are carried out according to your plans (this will cost extra).

Wills, Trusts, and Documents

Estate planning occurs at many different levels, although most of us associate estate planning with the rich and ultra-rich. They may include asset projection modeling, gifting strategies, ownership issues, and charitable planning. These are central to just about everyone's wealth management needs. Your will and supporting documents may be the most important documents you ever sign. Are there other trust instruments that you should review or use? Some if these include special needs trusts, irrevocable trusts, generation skipping trusts, living trusts, and so on.

Do You Have a Will?

Wills and trusts are an important component of your risk management and estate planning game plan. A will may be one of the most important documents that you will ever put your signature to. More than half of Americans do not have a current, valid will. Without a will, courts may end up deciding who's entitled to your assets, as well as who maintains custody of your minor children. Is this the legacy that you want to leave behind?

There are many varieties of wills and trusts to fit the needs of every individual, only a qualified attorney should draft these documents. There are many to choose from. A basic will is a basic or simple will, generally giving everything outright to a surviving spouse, children, or other heirs. Sometimes, this is referred to as an "I love you will." In addition to a basic valid will, a trust may be necessary to guarantee that what you want to actually happen with your assets upon your demise.

What Is a Will?

The first step in estate and legacy planning is simply to create a will, which is nothing more than a legal document that transfers what you own to others. These people are called your beneficiaries, and the transfer occurs when you die. It also names the people who you want to carry out your wishes. These people are called executors. You should make a will as soon as you have sizable assets, or when you get married. Certainly by the time you have children, a will should be complete and up-to-date. A will can also clarify your wishes and may save your heirs additional legal and court fees. It can also be helpful in naming guardians to take care of your children after you pass on.

Inheritance taxes are typically paid by your heirs, those who inherit your assets. The tax is based on their share of the inheritance and their relationship to you. If your assets exceed the federal estate tax threshold, which changes frequently, then an estate tax may also be levied on your assets. Generally speaking, the larger the estate . . . the greater the tax rate. These inheritance taxes can sometimes exceed 50 percent of the value of the asset.

Legal and Court Fees

If you die without a will some assets will be forced into the probate process. Additionally, if someone contests the will or makes a claim against your estate, it will need to be disputed. If this happens, your heirs can expect court costs and additional legal fees in addition to the potential for long delays in settling the estate in a timely fashion.

Making a Will

More than half of Americans die without a will. If you are in this group and have no relatives, your assets go to the state where you live. The legal term is *escheated.* Which is how your friends and relatives may feel! If you don't have a will, you will die intestate. The law of your state then determines what happens to your estate and your minor children. This process, called *administration*, is governed by the probate court and is notoriously slow, often expensive, and subject to some surprising state laws. For example, in some states, if you're remarried and have children only from your first marriage, your spouse could get your entire estate, and your children may receive nothing! If you are unmarried and childless, your estate will be divided among relatives, friends, partners, and so on. Charities and entities that you care about may not share in any of your assets.

Overview of Wills

Your signature and those of two witnesses make the will authentic. Witnesses do not have to know what the will says but they must watch you sign it and you must watch them witness it. Handwritten wills, called *holographs,* are legal in about half of our states but most wills are typed and follow a standard format. If your estate is large, hire a professional. Don't be a cheapskate!

There are many reasons to update and change your will. Your will is really a work in progress throughout your life, and you can expect to have to update it from time to time. The birth of a child, the death of a beneficiary, a divorce or a new marriage, a substantial increase in your personal wealth, or a change in tax laws can all be reasons to update your will. Major changes require a new will that clearly states that it supersedes the previous version. Minor changes are usually handled with a codicil or a written amendment that you sign and date with witnesses.

Leaving People Out

You can disinherit anybody except your spouse, and in some community property states, you can even do that! If you want to disinherit some or all of your children, you should do so specifically. This way it is much harder to contest. Other people may simply be omitted, or you might want to leave them $1 to make your point more clear.

Timing is also an issue. You may want to require that a certain beneficiary must survive you by a specific length of time, often 45 days, in order to inherit. This provision may save double taxes and potential court costs if the beneficiary should die shortly after you do, perhaps in a common accident. It also allows you to determine who gets your property next. Timing can also be critical when married couples die at the same time. A simultaneous death clause in your will may pass your property directly to your surviving heirs.

Living Wills

A living will expresses your wishes about being kept alive if you're terminally ill or seriously injured. Do you really need a professional to draft your will? The more complex your situation or the more assets you have, the more it makes sense to consult a lawyer who specializes in wills or estate planning. Attorneys frequently charge by the hour, so you can save money by providing detailed records and making key decisions before your meeting.

Wills you prepare yourself using a standard format are valid if you have all the necessary information and are properly signed and witnessed. Requirements do vary from state to state, so it's important to know the laws where you live. You may also consider having your lawyer review any will you write yourself.

Trusts

Trusts are legal entities. They function similar to corporation. They allow you to set up places to shelter income and assets for your heirs. Trusts may allow you to provide for minors and others who are unable to manage their finances. They can help you potentially save on taxes, control the assets that you leave to your heirs and specify how the assets in the trusts can be utilized or spent. Your estate is comprised of any assets that you own in your name including your life insurance policies and retirement plan assets. It also includes half of what you own jointly with your spouse (which may include your home or joint accounts). Your share of anything you own in common or just property you own with business partners will also be included. Assets that are held in trusts and custodial accounts in which you are the trustee or the custodian may also be included, and everything that you own jointly with any individual other than your spouse will also be included.

Review and Updates

It is critical that you review and periodically update your estate plan and its documents from time to time. What you want to happen may not happen. To no fault of your own, some of the moving parts may become misaligned over time. This is why it's critical to have your advisors work on periodic what-if scenarios and hypothetical testing.

An example might include having your advisors, your personal CFO, and your legal team, coordinate to run a hypothetical probate example. Many people are shocked when they find that they have spent thousands of dollars in drafting legal documents designed to dictate the disposition of their assets properly . . . only to find out that their accounts were not titled properly (to coordinate with the documents). I can't tell you how many times I have seen people spend thousands of dollars and many hours working with their estate planning professionals to draft the proper documents, only to have the plan unintentionally thwarted by an officer at a local bank or an investment broker who decides that it is better to have the assets owned differently. Therefore, it's critical that you work closely with your personal CFO to make sure that your estate plan is complete and up-to-date, and that your documents and accounts are also coordinated properly. Even your will is a living document that needs to be updated and changed from time to time. It is a work in process that will be used for different purposes at various stages throughout your life.

Beneficiary Claim Instructions and Checklist

In the event of a death claim in your family, call your personal CFO as soon as possible. Here are a few helpful ideas.

✓ Retrieve the deceased's will and request that your attorney begin taking steps to begin the probate process.

✓ If the deceased had a safe deposit box in his or her own name ask your attorney to advise you about the proper way to retrieve its contents since laws may differ from state to state.

✓ Review your important papers and documents including insurance policies, business agreements, income tax forms, bank books, military records, membership cards, and so on. Some of these may entitle you to benefits of which you are not aware. Request ten to twelve certified copies of the death certificate so that you'll be able to file insurance and Social Security claims and re-title joint assets.

✓ Contact the deceased's employer to discuss any final or deferred compensation to which you may be entitled, as well as life insurance, pension, and profit sharing plan benefits, and if appropriate accident insurance with the employee benefits or human resources office.

✓ It may be helpful to write down any union, professional, or fraternal organizations, alumni associations, and other groups to where the deceased may have belonged. Membership might also entitle you to death benefits usually through group life insurance policies.

✓ Gather the necessary paperwork for outstanding debts and promissory notes. Check with these lenders to see if any debts carried an insurance rider that would pay the debt in-full.

✓ Retrieve the deceased's will and request that your attorney begin taking steps to begin the probate process.

✓ If the deceased had a safe deposit box in his or her own name ask your attorney to advise you about the proper way to retrieve its contents since laws may differ from state to state.

✓ Review your important papers and documents including insurance policies, business agreements, income tax forms, bank books, military records, membership cards, and so on. Some of these may entitle you to benefits of which you are not aware. Request ten to twelve certified copies of the death certificate so that you'll be able to file insurance and Social Security claims and re-title joint assets.

✓ Contact the deceased's employer to discuss any final or deferred compensation to which you may be entitled, as well as life insurance, pension, and profit sharing plan benefits, and if appropriate accident insurance with the employee benefits or human resources office.

✓ It may be helpful to write down any union, professional, or fraternal organizations, alumni associations, and other groups to where the deceased may have belonged. Membership might also entitle you to death benefits usually through group life insurance policies.

✓ Gather the necessary paperwork for outstanding debts and promissory notes. Check with these lenders to see if any debts carried an insurance rider that would pay the debt in-full.

✓ If the deceased was a veteran notify the Veteran Administration to apply for benefits.

Where Are Your Important Documents and Records?

You should take steps to identify the location of important documents so that your loved ones or heirs maybe able to find them easily. This includes documents that maybe held in your home, safe deposit boxes, business office, or other locations.

Location of Documents	Home	Business	Other
Your Will (original)			
Will (copy)			
Spouses Will (original)			
Spouse Will (copy)			
Power of Attorney			

Location of Documents	Home	Business	Other
Living Will			
Burial Instructions			
Cemetery Plot Deeds			
Safe Deposit Boxes			
Safe Combinations			
Trust Agreements			
Life Insurance (personally owned)			
Life Insurance (group)			
Disability Insurance			
Casualty/Homeowners Insurance			
Partnership Agreements			
List of Checking and Savings Accounts			
Bank Statements			
List of Credit Cards			
Health Insurance			
Certificates of Deposit			
Checking Accounts			
Passbook Savings Accounts			
Investment/Brokerage Accounts			
Stock Certificates			
Mutual Fund Accounts			
Bonds			
Retirement Accounts			

(continued)

(*continued*)

Location of Documents	Home	Business	Other
Individual Retirement Accounts			
401(k) Accounts			
Annuity Contracts			
Stock Option Plans			
Income Tax Returns			
Gift Tax Returns			
Real Estate			
Title(s)/Deed(s)			
Rental Property Records			
Notes / Private Loan Agreements			
Mortgage Documents			
Offsite (possessions)			
Automobile Records			
Boat Ownership Records			
Birth Certificates			
Passports			
Citizenship Papers			
Adoption Papers			
Military Discharge Papers			
Marriage Certificates			
Children's Birth Certificates			
Divorce or Separation Documents			
Names/Addresses of Friends and Relatives			

Have you reviewed the beneficiaries of your insurance policies? Has your family unit changed in size or make up? This is one of the areas that can go untended for many years for most clients and by most agents. This should be a part of your annual review process with your personal CFO.

Chapter Highlights

➢ Do you have documents in place?
➢ When was the last time you updated your will or guardianship arrangements?
➢ Where are your documents stored?
➢ How are they tracked?
➢ How often are they updated?
➢ Who reviews them? How often? (We recommend annually by a professional.)

CHAPTER 18
TIME FOR ACTION

"The superior man is modest in his speech, but exceeds in his actions."

—Confucius

Figure 18.1   Are you ready to take charge of your money?

What Can You Do Now?

Our parents taught us that if you're not part of the solution, then by default you must be part of the problem. The challenge is that most people lack any significant amount of ambition. Today many people stand by waiting for someone else to fix the problems of society, the economy, protection, policing, and national and local political problems.

By default, this need for someone else to fix their problems creates a difficult political environment. A political environment (bordering on socialism) where unfortunately the benevolent few in government are outnumbered by the greedy and materialistic population of world government in a position of power and prestige. Today, we see a continued cycle of excessive worldwide government spending designed to stimulate growth. This strategy seems to enrich the same participants of the corrupt government gravy train over and over again.

The solution: If you're not ready to take charge of your life and take action, you are wasting your time reading this book. The solution is simple promote change from within. You must get in the game and start running. In case you missed it, the starting gun went off years ago and you need to get off your rear end and do something now.

The key to empowering yourself to take action and create a long-term plan. Your long-term plan should be to amass as much wealth, as quickly as possible, and by any means necessary, as long as those include methods that are legal, moral, and ethical. Anything outside of that realm will likely leave you in violation of the law and ultimately, incarcerated by the jailer. Much like the game Monopoly, you will find yourself going directly to jail and you will not pass go. You will not collect two hundred dollars.

You must also operate within the confines of the tax code. The code is designed to prevent you from rising from your current position as a worker, to the ruling class. Once you get to the ruling class, it will be up to you if you become the world's first benevolent dictator or to help the new ruling class change its ways and become more benevolent leaders.

Take Action

Your first step is to get a financial physical from a well-qualified financial professional. Take the time to take a snapshot of your financial affairs, relative to where you want to be in the future. See if you can identify areas where you are simply transferring your wealth. Find the money, do something productive with it, and eliminate every unnecessary transfer of wealth and expense that you don't have to pay. Stop paying attention to the pennies, by cutting coupons, while dollar bills are flying out the window.

You have a choice, you can continue to live in fear, or you can dare to attempt to live the life that you always dreamed it could be . . . and maybe to become the person that you've always wanted to be. This exercise should also help you define your picture of success in advance.

Know Where You Stand Financially

Take a financial checkup exam. Where are you today, relative to where you want to be in the future? Most people have no idea whether they're going to succeed financially or fall short of their long-term goals. Most of the planning that's done is either needs-based or finite in nature. They're linear plans that use spreadsheets, which are not three dimensional and do not take into account all of the moving parts in your life. They simply illustrate a concept in a vacuum and assume that everything will play out exactly as shown—with a small disclaimer at the bottom that says sometimes things don't go this way.

Focus on your wants and the maximum value that you can achieve and then work backward. How much do you need to put in to have a good chance of having all that you want to have? As opposed to "What's the minimum that I have to put in?"

Mindset and Vision

It's always important to keep an open mind. When we stop growing, we stop learning and start moving in the wrong direction. We turn off or tune out the ability to receive information and ideas because we believe we already know everything there is to know about a particular topic. When this happens, many great ideas and opportunities are lost.

How to Get Started

The most important words that come to our minds are desire and commitment. Without it, it will be very difficult to accomplish a task. You must have a commitment to get out of financial prison and debt, and it must be fueled by a burning desire and passion to be financially healthy. This may require a change in your priorities. Recognize that controlling your finances as they relate to the banking system is one of the most important things that can be done in your financial world.

We recommend that you find a financial professional that is thoroughly familiar with this type of planning. In this case, such a professional would be thoroughly familiar with the questions that would help you find out just how you're spending your money and also show you ways to redirect that cash flow to your own accounts.

Above all, it requires patience and dedication. You must stick to the task at hand. It's going to take years to get started and it needs to be a long-term, if not a lifetime commitment. This is much like developing a physical conditioning program. First step is to evaluate your current condition, work with a coach or a trainer and design a program of both exercise and diet that you stick to regularly. As you make progress, your coach will make changes and adjustments to your overall plan in an effort to improve your ultimate result. This planning strategy works. Millions of people can attest to the fact that this program works both financially and physically.

Questions you should ask yourself are: How committed are you to achieving your goals? Do you have a definite plan for accumulating riches? What are you afraid of? Focus can help you overcome your fears. Once you consider the cost of achieving your goals, you must be determined to pay the price. It will be easier once it is time to actually *pay the price*. If you have already decided that the price of success is worth paying, you can move forward without hesitation. Most people are interested in success, but they are committed to living in a *safety zone*. They are not willing to pay the price. The following exercise can help you decide what's important in your life.

Write your answers out and then take a minute to circle those that you are truly committed to accomplishing. What will it take to accomplish each goal? How much time will be required? What will the financial cost be? Create a written budget for each and develop a savings and funding strategy for each goal. Are you ready to pay the price for success?

Summary

Your goal should be to build a sound financial plan using various interconnected, coordinated, and integrated components. The obstacles of your success include taxation, other expenses, bills, wealth transfers, the possibility of running out of time, procrastination, and your lack of discipline. It is time to stop pointing fingers and start taking responsibility for our actions, both individually and collectively.

Practical Exercise
What do you want out of life?
Take a minute and list a few goals.

What do you want to become?

1.

2.

3.

4.

5.

What do you want to acquire?

1.

2.

3.

4.

5.

What do you want to accomplish?

1.

2.

3.

4.

5.

A Call to Action

Figure 18.2   Build a winning team!

Are you ready to take responsibility for your actions? Are you ready to change your future and create a new future to fulfill your destiny? It's time to stop complaining and stop blaming others for what you've done or chosen not to do. There is no bailout plan for you—no life preserver and no do-over! You only get one shot at life. You need to step up and take action. If you don't, you will automatically choose a plan based on pure luck, and may likely end up on the road to financial ruin. Let's let the others help you build wealth.

Step 1: No Excuses!

Build the right habits and create a new mindset. Eliminate waste, recapture your money, and put it to work for you! This requires a conscious commitment on your part to take responsibility for your life . . . no excuses! It's going to take you at least 30 days of modeling this behavior before you begin to think this way.

Step 2: Create Your Environment

The next step is to not tolerate excuses from others around you. In your personal, family, or your professional life, you should work hard not to accept excuses, point fingers, or blame anyone in your life. If they're in your life, try to help them fix it or get them out of your life quickly. Surround yourself only with positive people.

The enemies of your ability to build wealth may be deeply grounded in your personal concept of money and the belief systems that you have come to hold dear that may have been taught to you in your current environment including your family. There's no reason to worry about the future. Worry is a futile, emotional state and it becomes a self-fulfilling prophecy when all you think about is negativity; it's bound to follow you and seep into your life in every way imaginable. If you don't take action . . . the things that you were afraid of will most likely become your reality.

I work with people who have the desire to improve their lives, a commitment to make it better, and who have the sense of urgency to take action. I am only willing to work with people who are serious about their money, who are friendly, and who are in a position to make definitive decisions. Even if the decision is no, you're not going to move forward. That's fine. I want to teach you how to control your environment. I want people who are willing to do whatever it takes to succeed as long as it's legal, moral, and ethical.

Whiners Need Not Apply

Avoid whiners at all costs. These people typically have minimal drive, and lead a subpar quality of life. They lack any long-term vision, tend to shy away from challenges, are resentful of others, and are bitter toward the world and the success of others. Their dialogues are filled with words like can't, won't, not worth it, and I'll try. One of the most important lessons that our parents and the military drilled into us, is as follows "I'll try means I'll fail." You need to decide that you're going to succeed . . . then make it happen.

Also, try to avoid the happy campers or those moving to the middle of America. This is not defined in terms of your income or social status, but rather your emotional state. These are the people that carry a motto like: "I can do better and should do better, but at least I'm not doing as bad as . . ."

They lead a seesaw existence in life filled with ups and downs, but ultimately find themselves on the downswing of the seesaw. They look at what *is* versus what *could be*, they also lack vision, they're constantly saying remember when, they're in a comfort zone, and their perception of failure is negative.

They're generally, conservative risk takers or non-risk takers by nature. We want to work with people that have an end-game focus on their mind. Who understand that failure is a part of success, and while we hate failure bitterly, it is a necessary part of our learning process.

Partner with people who understand that life and the pursuit of money is a journey, not a destination. They must understand that setbacks are natural and a normal part of the wealth building process. Seek to minimize that risk through proper risk management and coordination, while creating efficiency within your plans. We want people who embrace change, who are persistent and steadfast in their beliefs, and who believe that the plan will work over time. In short, we want to work with people who say "I want to get better than I am." People who are constantly striving to improve themselves, their standard of living, and their quality of life. Surround yourself with people who say, "He did it. Why can't that be me?" and not "If I can do it . . ." but "How can I do it?" Our strategies are designed to show you exactly that. You can succeed where others fail.

I explained earlier, during our discussion on the history of money that most people do not understand the laws of money, science of money, or how it actually behaves. Many people believe they can create their own plan by simply using some mathematical calculators they find online or shown to them by their insurance or financial professionals.

Time to Step on *the Scale*

Judging your health by how your jeans fit, as opposed to a regular weigh in and an annual physical performed by a medical professional is not a substitute for a proper assessment of your health. The same is true of your finances.

It is time to take a look at your complete financial picture. Time to take your head out of the sand and assess the moving parts separately and collectively. Not going to the doctor (therefore preventing your doctor from being able to tell that you are sick) is not the same thing as being healthy!

Rules to Live By

Be debt free. Save definite amounts, and build an integrated plan sequentially. Make sure that as you begin to save and grow wealth on your financial model, the anchor of financial debt cannot weigh down your disciplined savings strategies. It doesn't do you any good to fill your left pocket if someone comes along and siphons the money out of your right pocket. If not, we're back to driving down the high-way with one foot on the gas and one on the brakes. You shouldn't have any nondeductible debt in your model at all, so work hard to eliminate your debt, even if it means that you have to work multiple jobs. Do your best to become debt-free. Good luck and we hope to see you on the road to wealth.

Figure 18.3   Carve a new future for yourself!

Chapter Highlights

➢ Commit to making financial changes in your life now. Are you willing to pay the price for success?

➢ Implement a regular savings and investment program. Start small and build up your savings amounts (target of 15 to 20 percent pre-tax savings levels).

➢ Know where you stand financially. Implement your emergency fund, coordinate your insurance programs, and know if you will be able to retire.

➢ Identify opportunities where you may be transferring wealth and then take steps to eliminate them and recover those dollars for your own use.

APPENDIX A

SAMPLE CASE: PUTTING IT ALL TOGETHER

The following clients are age 40. We are measuring a 25-year planning timeline. We will assume an inflation rate of 4 percent.

The opportunity cost rate of return for these decisions will be specified separately by product line.

Financial Inventory

Here is a quick summary of our hypothetical client's financial situation.

This client is doing all he can to maximize his savings and retirement programs. He is attempting to protect his family with proper insurance products, and he looks through the following options.

1. Our first category is *term life insurance*. This client has a premium of $500 per year going into his plan, that purchases a $500,000 at a 30-year term life product.

2. Additionally, this client is adding $12,500 to his 401(k) plan annually. The account currently has an 8 percent rate of return, and the company matches the first $5,000 dollar for dollar. (His total annual contributions are $17,500.) He currently has $50,000 in the plan.

3. They also have a *nonqualified brokerage* account with a nationally recognized money manager that has $100,000 in an account that currently returning an 8 percent rate of return (but market performance has been volatile). Additional contributions of $200 per month are being invested. The account does not seem to be growing very much.

4. They have a *tax-deferred annuity* that has $50,000 in the account growing at 8 percent. They are not contributing additional dollars to either the annuity account.

5. They own a *personal residence* that is valued at $500,000, and have a current mortgage obligation of $300,000. The mortgage is a 30-year fixed rate mortgage currently at 6.5 percent interest rate. The house is scheduled to be paid off in 27 years under the current scenario. They are also making extra mortgage payments in an effort to pay off the mortgage sooner.

This client has no other assets.

6. Other expenses include premiums that total about $2,500 for auto coverage, $800 for homeowner's insurance, and $600 for the umbrella policy.
7. Debts: The client owes $15,000 on a credit card carrying an interest rate of 9 percent and an auto loan of $25,000 at a rate of 7 percent.
8. The client receives an annual *tax refund check* in the amount of about $4,000.

Planning Issues to Consider

➤ *Term life insurance* will become worthless in 30 years and builds no cash value. Life insurance needs may extend past 30 years.
➤ A 401(k) retirement plan offers a deferral of the tax and the tax calculation.
➤ In a *brokerage account*, we have additional potential problems. We have potential *compound tax issues* that must be addressed.
➤ In the *annuity category*, there are deferred taxes.
➤ Our next asset classification is *real estate*. The client owns their primary residence valued at $500,000. He has a mortgage obligation of $300,000. The problem is that although they have a great rate at 6.5 percent, they have a 15-year amortizing mortgage. The problem here is that they lose liquidity and access to their principal payments. They are also making $300 in extra mortgage payments in an effort to pay off the mortgage sooner.

Potential Alternate Strategies

Insurance Cost Recoveries

Many clients have insurance issues because they have the wrong coverage in place or pay for it the wrong way. The first thing we need to determine is whether they have the appropriate coverage in place.

Luckily, this client has other assets. It may make sense for them to consider increasing their deductibles, which would only impact them in the event of a claim, and in the case their auto insurance claim that was specifically their fault. If the client has a claim, paying the difference will not be fun, but they can cover it from other assets. Hopefully, they will not have a claim every year.

In this hypothetical example, if the client were to raise her deductibles from $250 up to $1,500, on each of the two cars in the household, they may save about $250 per vehicle or $500 per year. Now they have a choice. It can go back into their cash flow to improve their lifestyle, or they may choose to save it somewhere. If they choose to save it, we hope they get a rate of return. On a hypothetical basis, if they were to earn 5 percent over 30 years, that money would grow to roughly $30,000. If you divide that by 30 years, it could generate the equivalent of about $1,200 a year. That will have the effect of helping to offset their auto insurance premiums.

If instead, they could earn 8 percent over a long period of time with a properly diversified balanced investment approach, that money would grow to $47,000 over the same time period and if you divide it over the years, they've recovered roughly $1,900 per year. By adopting the strategy, it's very possible that they could recover everything that they've paid into their auto insurance. If they earn higher rates of return that might require more risk, it's possible that they could recover all their money plus some interest. The client should consider reviewing all of their property insurance policies: auto insurance, homeowner's cost, and umbrella policy costs to look for potential savings.

Term Insurance

The same principle could apply to their term life insurance. This client is paying $500 for term insurance. We're going to assume that if they didn't buy the insurance, and we're not suggesting that they do, and they saved that $500 a year now represents an additional $500 at a 6 percent rate of return. That money would grow to $42,000. At 8 percent, it would grow to over $61,000. That's the true cost of term insurance. It's not simply $500 for 20 years. That would only be $20,000. The total cost includes the $500 premium for 20 years compounding at interest that could grow to over $61,000. The trick is how to find money to convert the temporary term insurance into permanent life insurance that offers many additional benefits beyond a permanent death benefit.

These are potential areas where we may be able to help him free up and find some money. *Potential long-term savings recoveries from insurance strategies: $100,000+.*

Compound Taxes

The next area is compound taxes. By looking at our compound tax table, we can see how this client's compound taxes are affected over time. Based on a $100,000 account earning 8 percent, he receives a Tax Form 1099 for $8,000 at the end of the first year. If he's reinvesting dividends and capital gains within his brokerage account that means he needs to pay this tax out of his cash flow. That's not a strong position to be in because ultimately, it's costing him goods and services that he could otherwise purchase.

Each year the problem gets better. Next year he has $108,000 earning 8 percent. Instead of paying the tax on not only $8,000, he's going to pay tax on a larger number. One solution may be to flatten the taxes out by sending the tax directly to the IRS from the $8,000 gain. At a 30 percent tax bracket between state and federal taxes. That means $0.30 of every dollar is going to be sent to the government for the privilege of living in this country.

On interest of $8,000 multiplied by 0.70, they're left with $5,600 that they can redirect to other tax advantaged areas. The other $2,400 has been confiscated for tax purposes. They now have some choices. Where can they put that $5,600 if they want it to continue to grow? We'd want to put it into places where it may have some additional tax advantages. One option may be to consider a variable annuity, a fixed annuity, or some type of tax-deferred product. This will delay the tax problem with a tax deferral, but may not fix it.

We can also consider a Roth IRA, if qualified, where it may accumulate tax-free. We can explore the 529 plans where it may grow potentially tax-free if used for a qualified higher educational expense. We can also reinvest the proceeds in municipal bonds that may provide a taxable equivalent yield that is greater than their other investments.

Much will depend on their income tax bracket and whether they're subject to alternative minimum tax or not. The client could also explore the possibility of real estate based investments, which may offer other different advantages, especially if there's a mortgage involved. He can also explore one of my favorites—permanent life insurance. By using permanent life insurance, it not only will create a cash value accumulation growth that could be equal to or greater than what they're doing currently, but it also provides a second benefit, a death benefit. When making a final decision, we must always consider the after-tax results for this client (net of all expenses . . . including opportunity costs).

Deferred Taxes

Another area to focus on would be the annuity. As annuity grows, so does the tax, just like a 401(k). If the client tells us he has $100,000 in his 401(k), we usually tease them a little bit and say "Your statement says $100,000, but how much do you really have in there?" They look at us a little puzzled and say "Well, I have 100,000." We'll have to tell them, no they don't. You probably have about $60,000 or $70,000 in there. The IRS has $30,000 to $40,000 in there with you, because we need to account for the future tax due, which you haven't paid yet. This can create a false sense of security.

401(k) Retirement Plan Review

This client is aggressively saving for his future retirement goals. His employer matches only the first $5,000 of contributions. Since the employer does not match above this level, any contribution above this threshold only achieves one benefit (tax deferral). As we have seen, this may not end up being all it's cracked up to be. Are there better places to apply with the other $7,500? It may be a better decision to pay the taxes and eliminate some consumer debt (a guaranteed elimination of a high interest cost), to convert his expensive term insurance into wealth building permanent life insurance, or to purchase a tax favored asset such as municipal bonds. *Cash Flow Recovery: $7,500.*

The same applies to *annuities*. The $50,000 annuity has an assumed 8 percent compound rate of return. The account would grow to about $342,500 assuming a straight-line 8 percent hypothetical rate of return, which we know is never guaranteed—these are hypothetical numbers only for illustrative purposes. Therefore, the client would grow their account to approximately $342,500.

When you pull the money out, whether in part or whole, it will be subject to taxes. Some will be subject to ordinary income taxes depending on where the tax code stands in the future on the gains of that contract. Again, if taxes rise in the future relative to where they are today, this will have been a bad financial mistake. If the taxes are lower in the future than they are today, the client wins, at least in theory.

Any gain above your cost basis (initial deposit) is going to be taxed similarly. Our first strategy is our systematic liquidation strategy. Here we'll be taking a portion of the asset and liquidate it to pay the taxes due annually. We can then use the remaining capital to reinvest in a tax favored environment.

In this scenario, much like the compound tax strategy, the client would pay the tax on a portion of their investment. Let's assume they draw down at 10 percent because most carriers allow a 10 percent free withdrawal. If we draw down the account principal at 10 percent per year, $5,000 of the $50,000 would be distributed annually. Again, about 30 percent would be confiscated for taxes—they'll be left with about $3,500 to reinvest somewhere in their model. *Potential Cash Flow recovery: $3,500.*

We have at least five options. Here are a few ideas:

1. We can purchase dividend paying permanent life insurance.
2. We fund our Roth IRAs (if we qualify).
3. Use 529 College Savings Accounts.
4. Municipal Bonds.
5. Real Estate and a handful of other tax advantage vehicles.

Our goal is to increase the net output of their plan, along with increased liquidity features as we compare the net result of the annuity values versus the residual annuity values plus the new tax-favored investment account values. What is the total of that new combined output? Typically, there's an advantage especially when we go further down the exponential curve.

Mortgage Strategies: 15 Years versus 30 Years

Our final strategy, centers on an emotionally charged subject . . . their mortgage. It's interesting that they have a 15-year fixed rate mortgage, with a principal and interest payment of $2,491 per month. They pay $2,491 each month for the privilege of living in that home and borrowing the bank's money. After 15 years, they'll own it outright. If you ever take a look at an amortization schedule, you may be surprised to see how very little of that $2,491 goes toward reducing the principal in the early years.

What if they consider a 30-year mortgage, with a 30-year fixed rate payment plan? This program would result in a new rate of 6 percent and a monthly payment of $1,798.

Since the client was already used to paying close to $2,500 per month, he should be able to save the difference between his current payment and the new lower payment amount. Remember, payment is usually more important than rate. This is true in most scenarios.

In order to calculate the potential benefit of a 30-year mortgage, we're going to have to subtract the original mortgage principal and interest payment of $2,491, and we'll have to subtract the new monthly payment of $1,789. That leaves us with a savings of $693 a month. Now, if we multiply the $693 a month times 12, we'd come up with $8,312. To simplify our math for this example, we'll just round down to $8,300. If $8,300 is annually invested at a compound rate of return for 30 years, it will grow to $696,800, at a hypothetical rate of return of 6 percent. At 8 percent, it grows to over a $1 million in the same time frame.

We know that the market rarely returns 8 percent in any single year, but many advisors tell us that over the long term, there's a good chance that with a balanced portfolio, they can generate average returns of approximately 8 percent. What if you were able to achieve a second or third use on the dollar? It's quite possible that you can achieve a compound rate of return greater than 8 percent.

If somehow you could get the rate of return up to 10 percent, either through getting second or third uses of the dollar or through absorbing and taking on a little bit more risk in the equation, that cash would grow, your side fund could potentially grow to more than $1.5 million, and you would've picked up all the tax deductions.

What about year 15? His old loan would have been done by then. What if he wants to stop paying his mortgage then? In 15 years, the side fund would grow to about $205,000 at 6 percent, $243,000 at 8 percent, and $290,000 at 10 percent. In most cases, he would be able to terminate the loan agreement and pay off the mortgage with the side fund, if he chooses. The best 15-year mortgage plan is usually a 30-year mortgage combined with a savings plan designed to pay off the note in year 15.

Remember, our client was on schedule to pay off his previous mortgage in 15 years. Then he was planning on saving aggressively for retirement. If he begins saving his full 15-year mortgage payment in year 16, once the mortgage is paid off, his money would grow to only $61,460 in 15 years at 6 percent. At 8 percent, the position improves to $73,000; and at 10 percent his savings would grow to $87,000. This is owing to a shortened duration for accumulation (only 15 years). In reality, few ever save this much once the home is paid for.

Your side fund accumulations also provide you with a much stronger liquidity position in the event that you lose their job, become sick, hurt, disabled, or cannot work.

Don't forget his retirement game plan. He has been aggressively saving into his 401(k) plan at work. This money has not been taxed yet. They will be taxed in the future when he begins his distributions. Without his mortgage interest deduction, he may end up paying more taxes on these distributions than necessary. Given the choice and the control available, which position would you rather be in?

Mortgage Strategy Potential Savings: Several Hundred Thousand Dollars

Debt Elimination

Line of Credit? If he establishes an equity line of credit, he could use it to pay off his car note and/or reduce credit card balances. He's paying 9 percent interest on the credit card and 7 percent on the car loan. By using the equity line of credit, he could lower the interest rate to about 5 percent. The new monthly payment on the credit card would go from $150 to about $75 per month. The car payment would be reduced from $350 to $250 per month. The interest on these loans would then be tax deductible and he could save another $100 per year in tax savings. *Potential Savings: $150 to 200 per month.*

Tax Refund

Owing to how he elects to pay his taxes, he is providing the government with a $4,000 interest free loan each year. By changing his withholding elections, he can potentially earn interest on these dollars throughout the year . . . or retire his consumer debt more aggressively (a guaranteed rate of return). It may even be enough to make your car payments. This frees up dollars for use in other areas to improve your cash flow or save for the future. Call the human resources department and have them adjust your tax exemptions so you won't continue to overpay on your taxes. *Potential Cash Flow Recovery: $333 per month.*

These strategies are based on a simple laboratory experiment that uses assumed rates of return, assumed interest rates, and assumed inflation rates. They are by no means designed to serve as a concrete financial plan, but rather to serve as a game plan or a roadmap for you on the road to wealth. We hope that you are beginning to understand how different pieces can work together to create additional benefits, how taxes impact you, and what you can do to minimize the impact of wealth depleting forces over the long run. When you take a look at product implementation, you should consider the overall costs (both short- and long-term) and what cost recovery mechanisms are available.

Sample Case 2

These clients have combined incomes of $150,000 (husband $100,000, wife $50,000).

Goals include retirement planning, tax savings, college funding, and cash flow improvement.

What they have for:

Retirement: They are maxing out their contributions to their 401(k) plans (employer matches first 5 percent of income dollar for dollar). They have saved $500,000 for retirement planning goals.

Short-term emergency account: $2,000 (clients do not have adequate liquid cash reserves).

Life Insurance: 30-year term life of $500,000 on the husband only (term will expire worthless plus lost opportunity costs).

Disability and Long Term Care Insurance: None (big risk potential).

College Savings Accounts: $80,000 in a 529 account.

Clients are not able to currently make ends meet each month. They run a monthly short fall of about $900 per month. This is causing their credit card balance to rise.

Strategies

Clients may be over contributing to their retirement savings plan such as a 401(k). It is causing a cash-flow crunch. By lowering their contribution from $20,000 to $7,500 they will still achieve the maximum employer match and increase their cash flow by $12,500 annually. This is the classic example of one area of their plan hurting another. If they have the other $12,500 at year end they can still opt to contribute the additional amounts.

Debt is killing them: see their info below.

In Figure A.1, we have traded bad (non-deductible debt) for good (deductible mortgage debt). They are using a cash-out refinance strategy to pay off their debts. They have now eliminated their non-deductible debt and created positive cash flow. The net result is a savings of $3,139 per month (or $37,668 per year). Even if they save this amount in an account that does not earn interest, they would have an additional $226,000 over 6 years. This side fund can pay off the original 15-year mortgage ahead of schedule.

Between just these two strategies we see a completely different annual cash flow position change. Their cash flow has improved by $37,668 (debt move) + $12,500 (401(k) change). Total cash flow change $50,168. The clients can now work with their personal CFO to see if they should.

➤ Add to their 401(k) Plan

➤ Build their Short-Term Emergency Fund

➤ Add to their College Funding Savings

➤ Purchase Disability Insurance

➤ Purchase Long-Term Care Insurance

➤ Convert their Term Life to Permanent Life Insurance

➤ Improve their Cash Flow

➤ Purchase Real Estate

Clearly, we are not done, but these two simple changes make a big difference. None of these strategies involve any additional out-of-pocket outlay. They are simply using their existing assets more effectively. Coordination is the key.

Debt Snapshot

Type of Debt	Term (months)	Rate	Amount Owed	Old Payment	New Payment on Higher Mortgage	New 30-Year Mortgage Rate
Mortgage 1	180	6.5%	$90,000	$1,600	$1,011	5.5%
Mortgage 2	360	9%	$25,000	$500	$0	
Home Equity Line	Interest only	5%	$0	$0	$0	
Auto 1	60	5%	$25,000	$600	$0	
Auto 2	60	6%	$0		$0	
Credit Card	Open	14%	$38,000	$1,050	$0	
Totals			$178,000	$4,150	$1,011	

Figure A.1   Debt Snapshot

APPENDIX B
EXAMPLE DETAIL SPREADSHEETS

Year #	Annual Savings	Cumulative Amount Saved	Opportunity Rate of Return	Cumulative Opportunity Cost	Cumulative Account Value
1	500	$500	8.00%	$0	$500
2	500	$1,000	8.00%	$40	$1,040
3	500	$1,500	8.00%	$123	$1,623
4	500	$2,000	8.00%	$253	$2,253
5	500	$2,500	8.00%	$433	$2,933
6	500	$3,000	8.00%	$668	$3,668
7	500	$3,500	8.00%	$961	$4,461
8	500	$4,000	8.00%	$1,318	$5,318
9	500	$4,500	8.00%	$1,744	$6,244
10	500	$5,000	8.00%	$2,243	$7,243
11	500	$5,500	8.00%	$2,823	$8,323
12	500	$6,000	8.00%	$3,489	$9,489
13	500	$6,500	8.00%	$4,248	$10,748
14	500	$7,000	8.00%	$5,107	$12,107
15	500	$7,500	8.00%	$6,076	$13,576
16	500	$8,000	8.00%	$7,162	$15,162

(continued)

(*continued*)

Year #	Annual Savings	Cumulative Amount Saved	Opportunity Rate of Return	Cumulative Opportunity Cost	Cumulative Account Value
17	500	$8,500	8.00%	$8,375	$16,875
18	500	$9,000	8.00%	$9,725	$18,725
19	500	$9,500	8.00%	$11,223	$20,723
20	500	$10,000	8.00%	$12,881	$22,881
21	500	$10,500	8.00%	$14,711	$25,211
22	500	$11,000	8.00%	$16,728	$27,728
23	500	$11,500	8.00%	$18,947	$30,447
24	500	$12,000	8.00%	$21,382	$33,382
25	500	$12,500	8.00%	$24,053	$36,553
26	500	$13,000	8.00%	$26,977	$39,977
27	500	$13,500	8.00%	$30,175	$43,675
28	500	$14,000	8.00%	$33,669	$47,669
29	500	$14,500	8.00%	$37,483	$51,983
30	500	$15,000	8.00%	$41,642	$56,642

Figure B.1   Auto Insurance Example

Year #	Annual Expense	Cumulative Expense	Opportunity Rate of Return	Cumulative Opportunity Cost	Cumulative Total Cost	Net Value of Term Insurance Death Benefit
1	$1,000	$1,000	8.00%	$0	$1,000	$300,000
2	$1,000	$2,000	8.00%	$80	$2,080	$297,920
3	$1,000	$3,000	8.00%	$246	$3,246	$296,754
4	$1,000	$4,000	8.00%	$506	$4,506	$295,494
5	$1,000	$5,000	8.00%	$867	$5,867	$294,133
6	$1,000	$6,000	8.00%	$1,336	$7,336	$292,664
7	$1,000	$7,000	8.00%	$1,923	$8,923	$291,077
8	$1,000	$8,000	8.00%	$2,637	$10,637	$289,363
9	$1,000	$9,000	8.00%	$3,488	$12,488	$287,512
10	$1,000	$10,000	8.00%	$4,487	$14,487	$285,513

Year #	Annual Expense	Cumulative Expense	Opportunity Rate of Return	Cumulative Opportunity Cost	Cumulative Total Cost	Net Value of Term Insurance Death Benefit
11	$1,000	$11,000	8.00%	$5,645	$16,645	$283,355
12	$1,000	$12,000	8.00%	$6,977	$18,977	$281,023
13	$1,000	$13,000	8.00%	$8,495	$21,495	$278,505
14	$1,000	$14,000	8.00%	$10,215	$24,215	$275,785
15	$1,000	$15,000	8.00%	$12,152	$27,152	$272,848
16	$1,000	$16,000	8.00%	$14,324	$30,324	$269,676
17	$1,000	$17,000	8.00%	$16,750	$33,750	$266,250
18	$1,000	$18,000	8.00%	$19,450	$37,450	$262,550
19	$1,000	$19,000	8.00%	$22,446	$41,446	$258,554
20	$1,000	$20,000	8.00%	$25,762	$45,762	$254,238
21	$0	$20,000	8.00%	$29,423	$49,423	$0
22	$0	$20,000	8.00%	$33,377	$53,377	$0
23	$0	$20,000	8.00%	$37,647	$57,647	$0
24	$0	$20,000	8.00%	$42,259	$62,259	$0
25	$0	$20,000	8.00%	$47,239	$67,239	$0
26	$0	$20,000	8.00%	$52,618	$72,618	$0
27	$0	$20,000	8.00%	$58,428	$78,428	$0
28	$0	$20,000	8.00%	$64,702	$84,702	$0
29	$0	$20,000	8.00%	$71,478	$91,478	$0
30	$0	$20,000	8.00%	$78,797	$98,797	$0
31	$0	$20,000	8.00%	$86,700	$106,700	$0
32	$0	$20,000	8.00%	$95,236	$115,236	$0
33	$0	$20,000	8.00%	$104,455	$124,455	$0
34	$0	$20,000	8.00%	$114,412	$134,412	$0
35	$0	$20,000	8.00%	$125,165	$145,165	$0

Figure B.2   Term Life Insurance Premium Example

Age	Year #	Annual Savings	Cumulative Amount Saved	Opportunity Rate of Return	Cumulative Opportunity Cost	Cumulative Account Value
25	1	$200	$200	8.00%	$0	$200
26	2	$200	$400	8.00%	$16	$416
27	3	$200	$600	8.00%	$49	$649
28	4	$200	$800	8.00%	$101	$901
29	5	$200	$1,000	8.00%	$173	$1,173
30	6	$200	$1,200	8.00%	$267	$1,467
31	7	$200	$1,400	8.00%	$385	$1,785
32	8	$200	$1,600	8.00%	$527	$2,127
33	9	$200	$1,800	8.00%	$698	$2,498
34	10	$200	$2,000	8.00%	$897	$2,897
35	11	$200	$2,200	8.00%	$1,129	$3,329
36	12	$200	$2,400	8.00%	$1,395	$3,795
37	13	$200	$2,600	8.00%	$1,699	$4,299
38	14	$200	$2,800	8.00%	$2,043	$4,843
39	15	$200	$3,000	8.00%	$2,430	$5,430
40	16	$200	$3,200	8.00%	$2,865	$6,065
41	17	$200	$3,400	8.00%	$3,350	$6,750
42	18	$200	$3,600	8.00%	$3,890	$7,490
43	19	$200	$3,800	8.00%	$4,489	$8,289
44	20	$200	$4,000	8.00%	$5,152	$9,152
45	21	$200	$4,200	8.00%	$5,885	$10,085
46	22	$200	$4,400	8.00%	$6,691	$11,091
47	23	$200	$4,600	8.00%	$7,579	$12,179
48	24	$200	$4,800	8.00%	$8,553	$13,353
49	25	$200	$5,000	8.00%	$9,621	$14,621
50	26	$200	$5,200	8.00%	$10,791	$15,991
51	27	$200	$5,400	8.00%	$12,070	$17,470
52	28	$200	$5,600	8.00%	13,468	$19,068
53	29	$200	$5,800	8.00%	14,993	$20,793

Age	Year #	Annual Savings	Cumulative Amount Saved	Opportunity Rate of Return	Cumulative Opportunity Cost	Cumulative Account Value
54	30	$200	$6,000	8.00%	16,657	$22,657
55	31	$200	$6,200	8.00%	18,469	$24,669
56	32	$200	$6,400	8.00%	20,443	$26,843
57	33	$200	$6,600	8.00%	22,590	$29,190
58	34	$200	$6,800	8.00%	24,925	$31,725
59	35	$200	$7,000	8.00%	27,463	$34,463
60	36	$200	$7,200	8.00%	30,220	$37,420
61	37		$7,200	8.00%	33,214	$40,414
62	38		$7,200	8.00%	36,447	$43,647
63	39		$7,200	8.00%	39,939	$47,139
64	40		$7,200	8.00%	43,710	$50,910
65	41		$7,200	8.00%	47,783	$54,983
66	42		$7,200	8.00%	52,182	$59,382
67	43		$7,200	8.00%	56,932	$64,132
68	44		$7,200	8.00%	62,063	$69,263
69	45		$7,200	8.00%	67,604	$74,804
70	46		$7,200	8.00%	73,588	$80,788

Figure B.3   Tax Refund Example

Age	Year #	Annual Expense	Cumulative Amount Saved	Opportunity Rate of Return	Cumulative Opportunity Cost	Cumulative Account Value
22	1	$2,200	$2,200	6.00%	$0	$2,200
23	2	$2,200	$4,400	6.00%	$132	$4,532
24	3	$2,200	$6,600	6.00%	$404	$7,004
25	4	$2,200	$8,800	6.00%	$824	$9,624
26	5	$2,200	$11,000	6.00%	$1,402	$12,402

(continued)

(continued)

Age	Year #	Annual Expense	Cumulative Amount Saved	Opportunity Rate of Return	Cumulative Opportunity Cost	Cumulative Account Value
27	6	$2,200	$13,200	6.00%	$2,146	$15,346
28	7	$2,200	$15,400	6.00%	$3,066	$18,466
29	8	$2,200	$17,600	6.00%	$4,174	$21,774
30	9	$2,200	$19,800	6.00%	$5,481	$25,281
31	10	$2,200	$22,000	6.00%	$6,998	$28,998
32	11	$2,200	$24,200	6.00%	$8,738	$32,938
33	12	$2,200	$26,400	6.00%	$10,714	$37,114
34	13	$2,200	$28,600	6.00%	$12,941	$41,541
35	14	$2,200	$30,800	6.00%	$15,433	$46,233
36	15	$2,200	$33,000	6.00%	$18,207	$51,207
37	16	$2,200	$35,200	6.00%	$21,280	$56,480
38	17	$2,200	$37,400	6.00%	$24,668	$62,068
39	18	$2,200	$39,600	6.00%	$28,392	$67,992
40	19	$2,200	$41,800	6.00%	$32,472	$74,272
41	20	$2,200	$44,000	6.00%	$36,928	$80,928
42	21	$2,200	$46,200	6.00%	$41,784	$87,984
43	22	$2,200	$48,400	6.00%	$47,063	$95,463
44	23	$2,200	$50,600	6.00%	$52,791	$103,391
45	24	$2,200	$52,800	6.00%	$58,994	$111,794
46	25	$2,200	$55,000	6.00%	$65,702	$120,702
47	26	$2,200	$57,200	6.00%	$72,944	$130,144
48	27	$2,200	$59,400	6.00%	$80,753	$140,153
49	28	$2,200	$61,600	6.00%	$89,162	$150,762
50	29	$2,200	$63,800	6.00%	$98,208	$162,008
51	30	$2,200	$66,000	6.00%	$107,928	$173,928
52	31	$2,200	$68,200	6.00%	$118,364	$186,564
53	32	$2,200	$70,400	6.00%	$129,558	$199,958
54	33	$2,200	$72,600	6.00%	$141,555	$214,155
55	34	$2,200	$74,800	6.00%	$154,404	$229,204
56	35	$2,200	$77,000	6.00%	$168,157	$245,157

Age	Year #	Annual Expense	Cumulative Amount Saved	Opportunity Rate of Return	Cumulative Opportunity Cost	Cumulative Account Value
57	36	$2,200	$79,200	6.00%	$182,866	$262,066
58	37	$2,200	$81,400	6.00%	$198,590	$279,990
59	38	$2,200	$83,600	6.00%	$215,389	$298,989
60	39	$2,200	$85,800	6.00%	$233,329	$319,129
61	40	$2,200	$88,000	6.00%	$252,476	$340,476
62	41	$2,200	$90,200	6.00%	$272,905	$363,105
63	42	$2,200	$92,400	6.00%	$294,691	$387,091
64	43	$2,200	$94,600	6.00%	$317,917	$412,517
65	44	$2,200	$96,800	6.00%	$342,668	$439,468

Figure B.4   Smoking Example

Age	Year #	Annual Savings	Cumulative Amount Saved	Opportunity Rate of Return	Cumulative Opportunity Cost	Cumulative Account Value
22	1	$2,000	$2,000	6.00%	$0	$2,000
23	2	$2,000	$4,000	6.00%	$120	$4,120
24	3	$2,000	$6,000	6.00%	$367	$6,367
25	4	$2,000	$8,000	6.00%	$749	$8,749
26	5	$2,000	$10,000	6.00%	$1,274	$11,274
27	6	$2,000	$12,000	6.00%	$1,951	$13,951
28	7	$2,000	$14,000	6.00%	$2,788	$16,788
29	8	$2,000	$16,000	6.00%	$3,795	$19,795
30	9	$2,000	$18,000	6.00%	$4,983	$22,983
31	10	$2,000	$20,000	6.00%	$6,362	$26,362
32	11	$2,000	$22,000	6.00%	$7,943	$29,943
33	12	$2,000	$24,000	6.00%	$9,740	$33,740
34	13	$2,000	$26,000	6.00%	$11,764	$37,764
35	14	$2,000	$28,000	6.00%	$14,030	$42,030
36	15	$2,000	$30,000	6.00%	$16,552	$46,552

(continued)

(continued)

Age	Year #	Annual Savings	Cumulative Amount Saved	Opportunity Rate of Return	Cumulative Opportunity Cost	Cumulative Account Value
37	16	$2,000	$32,000	6.00%	$19,345	$51,345
38	17	$2,000	$34,000	6.00%	$22,426	$56,426
39	18	$2,000	$36,000	6.00%	$25,811	$61,811
40	19	$2,000	$38,000	6.00%	$29,520	$67,520
41	20	$2,000	$40,000	6.00%	$33,571	$73,571
42	21	$2,000	$42,000	6.00%	$37,985	$79,985
43	22	$2,000	$44,000	6.00%	$42,785	$86,785
44	23	$2,000	$46,000	6.00%	$47,992	$93,992
45	24	$2,000	$48,000	6.00%	$53,631	$101,631
46	25	$2,000	$50,000	6.00%	$59,729	$109,729
47	26	$2,000	$52,000	6.00%	$66,313	$118,313
48	27	$2,000	$54,000	6.00%	$73,412	$127,412
49	28	$2,000	$56,000	6.00%	$81,056	$137,056
50	29	$2,000	$58,000	6.00%	$89,280	$147,280
51	30	$2,000	$60,000	6.00%	$98,116	$158,116
52	31	$2,000	$62,000	6.00%	$107,603	$169,603
53	32	$2,000	$64,000	6.00%	$117,780	$181,780
54	33	$2,000	$66,000	6.00%	$128,686	$194,686
55	34	$2,000	$68,000	6.00%	$140,368	$208,368
56	35	$2,000	$70,000	6.00%	$152,870	$222,870
57	36	$2,000	$72,000	6.00%	$166,242	$238,242
58	37	$2,000	$74,000	6.00%	$180,536	$254,536
59	38	$2,000	$76,000	6.00%	$195,808	$271,808
60	39	$2,000	$78,000	6.00%	$212,117	$290,117
61	40	$2,000	$80,000	6.00%	$229,524	$309,524
62	41	$2,000	$82,000	6.00%	$248,095	$330,095
63	42	$2,000	$84,000	6.00%	$267,901	$351,901
64	43	$2,000	$86,000	6.00%	$289,015	$375,015
65	44	$2,000	$88,000	6.00%	$311,516	$399,516

Figure B.5   Consumer Spending Example

ACKNOWLEDGMENTS

I would like to thank my clients for believing in me and for adding purpose to my life. I thank my many mentors that I have had (and who I will continue to learn from) throughout my career. Our industry is filled with tremendous individuals who are a credit to their profession and this country. I am proud to have worked with them, trained them, and learned from them.

To my family, thank you for your understanding and encouragement while I focused on the completion of this project. It took me longer than expected to finish. May we make up for this lost time by building hundreds of new memories together.

I also would like to thank a few people for helping me succeed so far in my life and for providing me with the inspiration to put these words on paper. I'd like to start with my parents, who taught me the necessary lessons in life and who gave me something more valuable than money alone, for money can be taken away as history has shown. They gave me knowledge and taught me to respect others and respect myself. They taught me to be a part of the solution, to step up and take action when others don't, to be optimistic in all aspects of life, and to be able to laugh at myself, (which has become quite a pastime in my family). They taught me to be humble, and to expect nothing but the best for myself and those around me. For these reasons and many others they are my heroes.

I'd like to thank my wife, Barbara, who has not only stood by my side, but has served as my inspiration since the day I met her. She's one of the few people in my life, who constantly teaches me things on a daily basis. She has taught me more things than she will ever know. She is a constant optimist and believes in the inherent good in people. Barbara keeps me grounded when I tend to stray from that belief. She has given me the gift of love, companionship, friendship, and the joy that comes with being a father and her husband. She enhances my life in every way possible. I am lucky to have her as my soul-mate.

My son Christian provides me with daily inspiration to lead by example. He is our sanctuary at the end of a long day. I love to watch him learn and grow. He reminds us of what is truly important in life. I am proud to be his father. He is my greatest accomplishment and I hope I can live up to his expectations as a father and as a role-model. My favorite parts of the day are seeing him wake up, and walking into the house to see him and my wife.

I would like to thank my brother, who has taught me that there is no limit to the human drive for success in every aspect of life; he truly combines the theory of the total in his intellectual achievements as a Harvard graduate, his gregarious quest for life as a human being. His Harvard educated brain and his perspective contributed greatly to this finished work. Thank You Brad!

I'd like to thank my sister, who looks for the kindness and good in every person she meets, and who has taught me to look for the good in everyone who comes into our lives. She is a graduate of Cornell University and is a fashion industry insider in New York City. Her background and insight has helped me better understand the marketing habits of corporate America. Kelly, you are a superstar!

I thank my father-in-law for teaching me that there are such things as benevolent dictators; men who take the stewardship provisions of other men more seriously than they take the stewardship of their own provisions. As a union leader, he fought to create strong, fair, and even-handed contracts for the men in his union, which still stands today as one of the strongest labor unions in New York City. Thank you to my mother-in-law, for the gifts and talents that she has bestowed on me. Her kindness and generosity are unmatched.

I also want to thank Chris Wolfe for being my business partner. Your knowledge and analysis on case design is unmatched. Your organizational skills and personality have added greatly to our practice. You have taught me more than you may ever know. I look forward to many years together of working hard to improve our client's lives.

I thank the any athletic and business coaches that have touched my life and taught me lessons throughout my learning years and development, and the United States military for teaching me to strive to something greater than personal wants and desires, for teaching me organization, the value of proper command and control mechanisms, communications, the chain of command, and the relentless pursuit of perfection.

A book is only unique in the expression of ideas, which rarely, if ever, claim just one originator. When we collaborate to solve problems there is no limit to what we can accomplish. Ideas are the result of countless interactions with people who influence the path one takes. I wish to express sincere gratitude for the wonderful people who have helped and inspired me. I am especially grateful for the many teachers and mentors in my life. Thank you for sharing ideas and brainstorming during our careers. Each of you has impacted me and helped me to grow as a person and as a professional.

Thank you to Lauren Freestone (freelauren@hotmail.com), who copyedited, proofread, and composed this book. I appreciate all of your work.

Special thanks to: Robert Burns, Mike Brogan, Christopher Wolfe, Joseph Grogan, Vincent Maetta, Christopher Furrule, Jason Mellor, Anthony Canderozzi, Joseph Sylvestri, Joe Naselli Sr., Jim Meehan, Joe Naselli, Jr., Fran Naselli, Jim Burns, Bernie Audet, Jimmy Cleary, John Mazzola, Ron Van Dina, Bill Valone Sr., Bill Valone Jr., Greg Napolitano, Jack Napolitano, Sean Barry, Joe Jordan, Dan Lilley, Eric Arenas, Nick Ballas, Robert Azzolini, Michael Cole, Robert Favata, Tracy Hussey, Peter Osborn, Ray Austin, David Tao, Greg Shephaer, David Weingartner, James McTigue, Kinney Lynch, Rod Labat, Thomas Johnson, Tony Siciliano, Patty Trombley-Ball, Tom Brinton, Catherine Cackoeski, Sherry Messinger, Robin Velez, Mike Bobertz, Holt Mc Gee, Nick Oglesby, Matt Barnes, Bryan Gillespie, Mark Kellogg, Thom Grogan, Janette Ortiz, Arlene Reddington, Victor Goldman, Brendan Kenney, Thomas Carolyn, Thomas Barbaccia, Craig Thompson, Joel Zalvin, Ron Van Dina, Jeff Wine, Ed Barrett, Corrado Gugliotta, David Porter, Michael Yoken, Terry McMahon, Michael Trabucco, John Natoli, Greg Straka, Scott Schuebel, Todd Patterson, Brendon Naughton, John Maddrill, Bryan Gaskamp, Paul Karlitz, J. Schuler Griffin, Tim Powers, Roman Matusz, Gavin Chambers, Gregory Cohn, Brian Lee, Paul Bullara, Chris Cuccia, George Koroghilian, Ed Youmell, Brian Cooper, Robert Fakhimi, Andrew Moore, Pete Novak, John McCloskey, Scott Rich, Howard Cowan, Ron Lee, Richard Nolan, Winston Wei, John Limongelli, Joseph Limongelli, Steven Ferrara, Jack Howley, Anthony Mazzei, Howard Elias, Paul Blanco, Chris Ceponis, Marc Colby, Glenn Noland, Reggie Rabjohns, Dan Ceschin, Mike Amine, Jerry Corless, Richard Marooney, Shawn Will, Steve Levy, Dom Nappi, Duane Bartlett, Jesse Daniels, Dave Kroll, Steve Matthews, Dennis Quinn,

David Labricciosa, Trent Fetters, Bob Hagenberg, Bob Kaplan, Roman McDonald, Ed Vrablik, Peter NeJad, Kevin Kynoch, Brian Graime, Jay Fox, Joe Jordan, Greg Napolitano, Ken Heiser, Russell Bert, David Boretz, Michael Rizzuto, Joseph Rizzuto Jr., Mike Vaccaro, Bruce Gluck, Sean Barry, Matt Doherty, Justin Lieberman, Evan Kutner, Dylan Levy, Diane Brunner, Michael D'Altrui, Warren Beyer, Mary Ann McMahon, Laura Riley, Jeff Joyner, Gary Garland, Sam Lowy, Shane Dommin, Michael Connohan, Katie Beherns, Tom Mazza, Chuck Fullerm Frank Simone, Bryan Gilrane, Josh Jones, Andrew Gonzales, Julian Yson, Gary Pannuzzo, Mike Leotsakos, Matt Doherty, Father Kevin Downey, Krista Mendes, Adele Kircher, Tom Schroll, Barbara Exposito, Eileen MacDougall, Jenn Carlin, Martin Picinic, James Del Masto, John Mendes, Sean Donlan, Don Burnaford, Todd Burnaford, Norman Chevlin, Ed Curbelo, Suzanne Donlan, John Duffy, Matthew Elo, Bob Gasperini, Steve Gochman, Frank Gordon, Christopher Gravatt, Delores Gravatt, Bill Herlan, Andy Horn, Judi Hurley, Paul Jetter, Tara Krampert, Charles Labmert, Charles Levinsohn, Matt Mallette, Jeff Shapiro, David Shaw, Roy Silver, Mark Trust, Michael Vaccaro, Chris Venuto, Mike Webb, Jim Wheelock, Mary Whittaker, Tom Wieczerak, John Wieckowski, Joel McKenzie, Frank Di Gesu, Marti Cook, John Pratt, Eileen MacDonald.

ABOUT THE AUTHOR

 Keith has been studying, practicing, and teaching personal finance and economic lessons for over 15 years. He has worked with corporations, business owners, corporate executives, accountants, attorneys, professional athletes, entertainers, labor unions, municipalities, and nonprofit organizations to develop and coordinate their financial strategies. By using the information in this book, you will put yourself in a position to better use, build, and protect your wealth in a more efficient and coordinated fashion.

Virtually anyone can benefit from using the strategies contained in this book. It takes the investment of time and a desire to gain knowledge about the secret science of money. From there, applying these lessons practically in your everyday life will help you take back control of your personal finances.

Coordinating and integrating your personal finances is the key to controlling an environment for your wealth to flourish. Using this approach can help you secure a more confident financial future for yourself, and create more opportunities for your future family legacy.

Keith is the president of the *Integrated Wealth Network*. He is a graduate of the *Wharton School of Business* at the University of Pennsylvania. He resides in New Jersey with his wife, Barbara, and their son, Christian. He is a frequent public speaker on matters of personal finance. Keith can be reached for speaking engagements or training seminars by e-mail at IvyWealthSecrets@gmail.com.

*Financial Disclaimers

This book is largely a reflection of the author's personal and professional experiences and contains a number of anecdotes to help illustrate his beliefs. Within this book are a number of hypothetical examples. These are used for illustrative purposes only and do not represent the performance of any specific product.

The author references certain products generally, including mutual funds, life insurance, and variable contracts, among others. It is important to note that variable products and mutual funds are sold by prospectus and are subject to market risk. Your principal value may decline. Like most annuity contracts, they contain exclusions, limitations, holding periods, surrender charges, and other terms for keeping it in force.

Before investing, carefully consider the investment objectives, risks, charges and expenses of the mutual fund and/or variable annuity as well as their investment options. This and other information is contained in the prospectus.

Pursuant to IRS Circular 230, the author and publisher are providing you with the following notification: the information contained in this book is not intended to (and cannot) be used by anyone to avoid IRS penalties. This book supports the promotion and marketing of life insurance and investment products and services. Prospectuses are available from your registered representative.

Neither the author nor the publisher provide legal or tax advice. Any discussion of taxes herein or related to this document is for general information purposes only and does not purport to be complete or cover every situation. Tax law is subject to interpretation and legislative change. Tax results and the appropriateness of any product for any specific taxpayer may vary depending on the facts and circumstances. You should consult with and rely on your own independent legal and tax advisers regarding your particular set of facts and circumstances.

Municipal fund securities are sold by offering statement, which is available from your registered representative. Please carefully consider investment objectives, risks, charges, and expenses before investing. For this and other information about municipal fund securities, please obtain an offering statement and read it carefully before you invest. Investment return and principal value will fluctuate with changes in market conditions such that shares may be worth more or less than original cost when redeemed. Diversification cannot eliminate the risk of investment losses.

Variable annuities are offered by prospectus only, which is available from your registered representative. You should carefully consider the product's features, risks, charges and expenses, and the investment objectives, risks and policies of the underlying portfolios, as well other information about the underlying funding choices. This and other information is available in the prospectus, which you should read carefully before investing. Product availability and features may vary by state.

Before deciding on a variable life insurance policy, you should carefully consider the investment objectives, risks, charges, and expenses of the policy and its investment options. The product prospectus and underlying fund prospectus contain this and other important information. To obtain a product prospectus, variable universal life insurance quote, or underlying fund prospectus, contact your investment professional. Read the prospectus carefully before making a purchase.

Advisors: Decorate Your Office in Style

To order custom framed reprints of the artwork
contained in this book please visit:
www.advisorpromotions.com

Visit advisor promotions online for all of your Wall Street themed gift needs.

 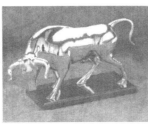 

Wall Street Gifts

- Statues
- Bookends
- Cufflinks
- Artwork
- Books
- Awards and Recognition
- Promotional Items
- Trade Show Give-Away Items
- Legal and Medical Themes

www.advisorpromotions.com

Additional Copies of this Book
Let this book promote your business.

Use it as an introduction to your unique value proposition as a financial professional. Help your clients and prospects view you in a new light . . . as their personal CFO.

Bulk ordering is available at discounted pricing. Additional quantities of this book can be purchased by calling: (888) 553-0068
Single Copy: $24.95
2-11copies: $19.95
Case Purchases: 12 books per case: $191.40 ($15.95 per book)
For shipping and insured U.S. delivery please add:$3.75 per copy.

Fax your order to us at (732) 831-6100
Advisor Promotions Order Form
CREDIT CARD PAYMENT AUTHORIZATION

VISA_____   MASTERCARD_____
            AMERICAN EXPRESS_____

NAME ON CARD:

_____

CARD NUMBER:

_____

V NUMBER (ON BACK OF CARD 3 OR 4 DIGITS) _____

EXPIRATION DATE: _____

ADDRESS: _____

CARD HOLDER ZIP CODE: _____

For immediate service, order by phone and charge to your credit card.
Call Toll-Free: (888) 553-0068
Orders may also be placed online at www.AdvisorPromotions.com.

CPSIA information can be obtained at www.ICGtesting.com
Printed in the USA
BVOW001221270313

316621BV00004B/8/P